# SAILING DIRECTIONS

## for the

## EAST and NORTH COASTS of IRELAND

First published (East Coast) 1930
Second Edition 1946
Third Edition (East and North Coasts) 1956
Fourth Edition 1965
Fifth Edition 1970
Sixth Edition 1979
Seventh Edition 1991
Eighth Edition 1995
Ninth Edition 1999
Tenth Edition 2002
Eleventh Edition 2008

© Irish Cruising Club Publications Ltd.

Irish Cruising Club Publications also publishes a companion volume *Sailing Directions for the South and West Coasts of Ireland*. Both volumes are available from booksellers and chandlers. The distributor for the island of Ireland is:

Argosy Books
Unit 11
Finglas Industrial Estate
Jamestown Road
Dublin 11

Telephone +353 (0)1 806 8466, fax +353 (0)1 806 8467, e-mail info@argosybooks.ie

In Great Britain both volumes may also be obtained from:

Imray, Laurie, Norie & Wilson Ltd
Wych House
The Broadway
St Ives
Huntingdon
Cambridgeshire PE17 4BT.

Telephone +44 (0)1480 462144, fax +44 (0)1480 496109, e-mail ilnw@imray.com.

Plans © Irish Cruising Club Publications Ltd. The plans contained in these Sailing Directions are not to be used for navigation. They are intended to assist the user to relate more readily to the text and should always be used with the latest up-to-date navigational charts.

Aerial photographs © Kevin Dwyer and other photographs © Geraldine Hennigan except where separately acknowledged.

ISBN Number 978 0 9558 199 1 9

Printed by Nicholson & Bass Ltd, Newtownabbey, Northern Ireland BT36 4FB

# SAILING DIRECTIONS

# for the

# EAST and NORTH COASTS of IRELAND

Information gathered by members of the Irish Cruising Club, supplemented
by the contributions of many others who sail, live and work around the coast of Ireland.

# Norman Kean

## Editor

with a foreword by Cormac P. McHenry
Commodore, ICC

*What joy to sail the crested sea and watch the waves beat white upon the Irish shore!*

Saint Columba, 563 AD

# Foreword

The introduction to the second edition of sailing directions for the east coast of Ireland, published in 1946, says that they were originally compiled in the year 1930 for the benefit of the members of the Irish Cruising Club. That first edition was published in Roneo form, and a hundred copies were ordered. The second edition was a small book in "Emergency Binding" and sold at 15/-. It covered the coast from Carnlough to Rosslare Harbour. Subsequently the coast north and west to Bloody Foreland was added, and finally the seventh edition included an extract of the description included in our companion volume for the coast as far west as Dunmore East.

Following editions included the latest information on the coast, its buoys and lighthouses, but this, the eleventh edition, has been totally rewritten by our Editor Norman Kean. Using the latest desktop publishing software, he has re-drawn all the chartlets to include much greater detail than was shown before and by his use of additional colour has made them clearer and much easier to use.

Another ICC member, Kevin Dwyer, re-flew the whole coast in September 2007, in one of the few periods of fine weather in that summer, and his stunning aerial photographs are taken to provide the maximum perspective for navigators. They give an overall picture and are invaluable for pre-cruise planning. Most of the surface photographs were taken by Geraldine Hennigan when she and Norman covered the coast, both by road and on board their ketch *Xanadu*, while preparing this edition.

Overall, this edition, building as it does on material accumulated by members of the Irish Cruising Club down the years since 1930 and incorporating the latest publishing technologies represents a substantial advance on previous editions and will be invaluable for any yachtsman cruising the east and north coasts of Ireland.

**Cormac P McHenry**

Commodore, Irish Cruising Club 2005-2008

*Front cover: Inishtrahull from the west; Rathlin and Fair Head on the horizon to the right, with the Scottish islands of Islay and Jura and the coast of Kintyre to the left*

*Fontispiece: Tory Island from the north, with Bloody Foreland across the Sound and the west coast of Donegal beyond*

*Harry Donegan*

*Wallace Clark*

# Preface

Sailing Directions for the East Coast of Ireland were first compiled in 1930 by Harry Donegan, a founder member of the Irish Cruising Club, and were revised in 1946 by his son, Harry Junior. Paul Campbell, Billy Mooney and Wallace Clark carried out a major revision in the 1950's, and the third edition, this time covering the East and North coasts, was published in 1956. Over the following 46 years the book went through a further seven editions, with new information provided by recreational sailors (ICC members and non-members alike), professional seafarers, Government agencies and many others. The ICC was a pioneer in the use of aerial photographs as an aid to navigation.

The present edition represents a thorough revision of the book. Every practicable port, harbour and anchorage was visited by sea in 2007, and much new survey work was carried out, particularly in the sandy estuaries. New information has been gathered on upgraded facilities, changes to navigational aids, and shoreside amenities. Some 30 additional anchorages and harbours are described, including most notably the port of Newry, now back in action after 34 years. The plans have been redrawn and clarified, explanatory captions have been added to the photographs, and new sea-level photographs have been provided, to illustrate transits and harbour approaches. The text has been substantially rewritten, and an effort has been made to impose greater uniformity of style and presentation, in the interests of clarity. Latitudes and longitudes have been provided for ports, anchorages and many of the dangers. The Appendices have been simplified and reduced in number. We recognise and try to reflect the fact that the typical cruising yacht is perhaps ten feet longer now than twenty years ago, but also that she has a reliable engine, VHF radio, GPS and often radar.

In the era of electronic navigation, the need for books of Sailing Directions is often questioned. To put to sea without satellite positioning, today, is verging on the irresponsible - the modern equivalent of going out without a compass. The navigator is no longer permitted to be uncertain of his or her position, for expectations have risen in parallel with capability. But the purpose of Sailing Directions, in conjunction with the charts (paper or electronic), is to enable a vessel to find her way from harbour to harbour in a safe and seamanlike manner; to inform the choice of harbours, routes and passage plans; to describe facilities and draw attention to features of interest; and to add to the satisfaction and enjoyment of a passage or a cruise well sailed. These basic needs have been unchanged for centuries, through every technological advance from Harrison's chronometer and the sextant to GPS, electronic charts and AIS. A good old-fashioned book is a handy thing, and a chartplotter makes pretty awkward bedtime reading.

A striking feature in recent years has been a change of policy on the part of several of the fishing ports. Harbours which once merely tolerated or simply discouraged yachts now offer a warm welcome, reflecting the realisation, usually frankly stated, that the fishing industry is in decline and that the harbour must look to the recreational market for its future.

Aerial photographs are by Kevin Dwyer, and sea-level photographs by Geraldine Hennigan, unless individually acknowledged.

# Contents

# Acknowledgements

Thanks are due to harbourmasters, marina managers and staff Phil Murphy, Aedan Jameson, James Heaney, John Barlow, Paal Jansen, Cian Gallagher, David Dignam, Carmel Smith, Raja Maitra, Rupert Jeffares, Larry Burke, Frank Allen, Noel Pepper, Brian McJury, Michael Young, Kenny Gibson, Fred Mullen, Matt Jenkins, Warnock Edmund, Andrew Jaggers, Kelly Robinson, Tom McKnight, John Morton, Richard McKay, Pat McKeegan, Ricky McArthur, Bill McCann, Aideen Corr, John McClenaghan and Nancy Doherty; to the staff of the UK Hydrographic Office in Taunton, especially Roger Millard, hydrographer responsible for the charts of Ireland; to Dermot Gray and Robert McCabe of Irish Lights, Carlingford Lough pilot Thomas Cunningham, William Todd of Todd Chart Services, Danny McCann of Foyle Ferries, Ian James of Laganside Development, Richard Bates of Belfast Port, Peter Conway of Warrenpoint Harbour Authority, Chris Morris of the Ocean Youth Trust and Martyn Todd of Down District Council; to Ed Wheeler, James Nixon, Connla Magennis, Alan Leonard, Leo Conway, Cliff Hilliard, Maeve Bell, Adrian Bell, John Petch, Joe Phelan, Graham Miller, Frank Jackson, Wally Carpenter and David Thompson. Robert South of the printers Nicholson & Bass provided much valuable advice on layout and design. Without the willing assistance, the skill and the knowledge of all these people, this edition could not have been produced.

Kevin Dwyer's beautiful aerial photographs have become a keynote feature of these Directions and an important aid to navigation. The present edition includes many spectacular new ones, including those opposite, and I extend, as always, our thanks to Kevin for his generosity, his skill and the many hours of hard work involved in taking these and preparing them for publication.

This edition features, for the first time, Geraldine Hennigan's photographs, taken while cruising the coast, and illustrating transit lines, dangers and harbour entrances. My thanks to Geraldine reflect not only her talents as a photographer but the endless patience and forbearance involved in being married to the Editor.

Norman Kean                                                                                    January 2008

*Dun Laoghaire Harbour and Marina*

*River Foyle and Londonderry*

# Important Information

**Please read this and the introduction which follows before using this book as an aid to navigation. The information which follows is essential to a proper understanding of the book and to the safety of your yacht and crew.**

**WARNING**

## Additions and Corrections

Additions and corrections are welcome and may be sent to the Editor at Burren, Kilbrittain, Co.Cork, phone +353 23 46891, e-mail sailxanadu@gmail.com. Amendments and updates are published on the Irish Cruising Club website, www.irishcruisingclub.com.

*Baily lighthouse, Howth, Co.Dublin*

# Introduction

This book is primarily aimed at the recreational sailor, with a vessel in the range 7 to 15 metres in length, having a draft of two metres or less, a reliable engine and an echosounder, probably GPS but not necessarily radar.

The coast described in the following pages is a cruising ground to stand comparison with any in the world. Its diverse harbours range from the major international ports of Dublin and Belfast and the bustling passenger and RoRo terminals of Rosslare and Larne to the remote and spectacular bays of Sheep Haven, the isolated islands of Tory and Rathlin, and the extraordinary and beautiful inland seas of Strangford Lough and Mulroy Bay.

and the towns of Wexford, Arklow, Wicklow, Drogheda, Dundalk, Larne and Coleraine are all locally important. Of the islands, only three have permanent populations – Rathlin and Tory, with about 130 residents on each, and Lambay, with just six. There are several others with seasonal or occasional residents, including Inishbofin and Copeland Island. The border between the Republic of Ireland and Northern Ireland runs through Carlingford Lough, to the south east, and Lough Foyle, to the north west. The border presents little in the way of bureaucratic restrictions, and for yachts from EU countries, usually none at all.

## TOWNS AND VILLAGES

Dublin (1,046,000) is the largest city on these coasts, and the greater Dublin area extends as far as Bray to the south and Skerries to the north. Belfast (276,000) is the capital of Northern Ireland, and its environs extend to Bangor on the south shore of Belfast Lough and Carrickfergus on the north. Londonderry, or Derry (110,000) is the second city of Ulster,

*The River Liffey in Dublin city centre*

## WEATHER

The famously capricious Irish weather is, in general, free of extremes. The climate is maritime, and is characterised by the passage of Atlantic depressions, with rapidly changing weather conditions. A typical depression produces lowering clouds and a rising southeast wind, followed by more-or-less continuous rain and a gradual veer to the south or southwest. The passage of the cold front is often quite sudden, with a clearance to showers and an abrupt veer in the wind to west or northwest. This may all happen within twelve hours and be followed by a day or two of moderating winds and sunshine as a ridge of high pressure passes, before the cycle begins again. But equally, an anticyclone can dominate for days or weeks at a time and the weather can be glorious, with cloudless skies, warm sunshine and limitless visibility. Statistically, summer winds blow from the west and southwest about 40% of the time. The mean daytime temperature is about 17°C in June, July and August, and Dublin gets about 70 mm of rain per month while Donegal gets 100 mm. Fog is rare in most places, averaging a day or less in a summer month, but is much more common along the North Channel coast between Larne and Rathlin Island. The one predictable feature of the weather is unpredictability, at least more than a few days ahead; but that said, it must be declared that weather forecasts, from both Irish and British Met services, are extremely accurate and reliable. The forecasts are regularly broadcast by the Coastguards on VHF and by local and national radio stations, and Irish and British forecasts are both transmitted on Navtex.

Severe storms are unusual in summer, but do happen, the infamous Fastnet Race storm of August 1979 being perhaps the best-known. The sea state in winds of force 9 and 10 can be awesome and dangerous, especially close to the salient points and in wind-over-tide conditions. On the north-west coast, a swell is rarely absent, and may become high and persistent if a deep depression passes within several hundred miles. The swell – particularly in combination with a tidal set – may raise steep and breaking seas in quite deep water; for example the Shamrock Pinnacle, north-west of Rathlin Island, has 15m of water but must be avoided in heavy weather.

*Seals on Ballykinler beach, Dundrum Bay, Co.Down; St John's Point beyond*

The seawater surface temperature offshore typically rises from 11°C in May to 15°C in September, and in the recesses of the longer inlets may reach 20°C or more in a warm summer.

Daylight hours are long in summer; at the solstice the sun rises over Belfast at 0445 and sets at 2210.

Weather forecast sources are listed in Appendix 2.

## TIDES

Tidal information based on the Admiralty Tide Tables and the Irish Coast Pilot is published with permission of the UK Hydrographic Office.

In most places on the east and north coasts the spring range is 3·0 to 4·5m, but there is an amphidromic point close to the east coast 25 miles north of Carnsore Point, and another close to Port Ellen on the Scottish island of Islay, 20 miles north-west of Rathlin Island. At these points there is no rise and fall of tide. The spring range at Arklow is only 0·6m, and at Rathlin 1·0m, because of the amphidromic points nearby. Close to these points there is also a rapid change in the tidal constant over short distances, and so these localities have some of the fastest tidal streams in Ireland; they are, as it were, the fulcrum of the tidal see-saw. When it is low water at Malin Head, it is almost high water in Belfast, and at low water in Kilmore Quay it is high water in Wicklow and Dublin. Between Carnsore Point and Dublin, and between Malin Head and Belfast Lough, the tidal stream is the first consideration in passage planning. The spring tide runs at 2·5 knots off Portavogie, 3 knots between Lough Foyle and Malin Head, 4 knots in Inishtrahull Sound and also close south of Wicklow Head and north of Larne, and 7 knots in Rathlin Sound. The tide floods into the Irish Sea simultaneously through St George's Channel and the North Channel, and the streams meet south of St John's Point, near Newcastle, Co. Down. Along the coast, moderate tidal streams prevail only between Howth and Strangford entrance, inshore between Portstewart and the Foyle, and west of Malin Head. Very fast streams are met in the narrow entrances of Carlingford Lough, Strangford Lough, Lough Foyle and Mulroy Bay. Strong to gale force winds opposed to strong tidal streams can raise steep and dangerous seas offshore, and an ebb tide against an onshore wind produces overfalls off the narrow entrances which can be hazardous to small craft. Many of the river entrances, particularly that of the Bann, require similar caution.

The tidal standard ports are Cobh (as far north as Wexford), Dublin North Wall (Courtown to Carlingford Lough), Belfast (Kilkeel to Coleraine) and Galway (from Lough Foyle westwards).

Details of tidal streams are given in Appendix 2 and throughout the text.

## NAVIGATIONAL AIDS

The coastal marks throughout Ireland are maintained by the Commissioners of Irish Lights, and harbour marks by harbour authorities, marina owners or the County or (in Northern Ireland) District or Borough councils. In some places privately- or locally-maintained marks exist, and these are described wherever they are considered reliable. IALA System A (red to port) is used in Ireland, and the standard of provision and maintenance is very high. The

5

4

MALIN HEAD

Tory I

Rathlin I

Mulroy
Bay

Greencastle

Portrush

FAIR HEAD

3

BLOODY FORELAND

Sheep
Haven

Lough
Swilly

Lough
Foyle

Coleraine

Ballycastle

Carrickfin

Londonderry

Glenarm

*ANTRIM*

*DONEGAL*

Larne

Carrickfergus

Belfast Lough

ROSSAN POINT

Bangor

**Belfast**

Portavogie

Strangford Lough

*DOWN* Ardglass

ERRIS HEAD

St John's Pt

Sligo

Newcastle

Warrenpoint

Kilkeel

Dundalk

Carlingford L

*LOUTH*

Clogher Hd

2

**IRELAND**

Drogheda

Lambay

SLYNE HEAD

Dublin

Howth

Dun Laoghaire

Kish
Bank

Galway

Bray

Codling Bank

*WICKLOW*

Wicklow

Arklow

Arklow
Bank

LOOP HEAD

Limerick

*WEXFORD*

Blackwater
Bank

1

Wexford

Waterford

Kilmore
Quay

Rosslare

Dunmore
East

CARNSORE POINT

VALENTIA

**Cork**

*Numbers indicate the area covered in each chapter*

principal lights are on Tuskar Rock, Wicklow Head, Kish Bank, Baily, Rockabill, St John's Point, Mew Island, Black Head, The Maidens, Altacarry Head (Rathlin Island), Inishtrahull and Tory Island; there is a light float off the South Rock, and there are LANBYs on the Arklow and Codling Banks. The conventional direction of lateral buoyage changes at Malin Head, but this has no practical implications on the north coast.

With conversion to solar energy, the power and the range of the major lights are being reduced (but not so as to concern the recreational sailor) and almost all the audible fog signals have been or are being discontinued. There is no prospect of lights being disestablished – if anything, quite the contrary – but the single surviving light float and the LANBYs may soon be replaced by less expensive aids. The most significant

*Irish Lights Vessel* Granuaile

recent advance has been the introduction of AIS (Automatic Identification Systems), for which transmitters are compulsory on large commercial vessels but are also being fitted to certain lighthouses and buoys. While AIS transmitters are, at the time of writing, rare on leisure craft, small AIS receivers are readily available and inexpensive. AIS transmitters on lighthouses and buoys are identified in the text.

Characteristics of lights and buoys are here described using the same standard abbreviations as in the Admiralty List of Lights. Arcs of visibility are expressed from seaward.

## CHARTS

Much of the coast of Ireland has not been surveyed since the mid-19th century, and many of the charts are still based, at least in part, on the old data. This includes Imray as well as Admiralty charts, and the chartplotter products directed at the leisure market. Satellite-derived positions are now more accurate than the charted data in many places, and the UK Hydrographic Office has issued a standard caution to the effect that reliance should not be placed upon satellite-derived positions in relation to several of the charts of the Irish coast *(see Appendix 1 for details)*. Professional-standard electronic charts (ECDIS or ENC) are compulsory on large high-speed ferries (and will ultimately be compulsory on all large commercial vessels), but cannot be prepared in the absence of survey data to current international standards.

This situation is being addressed urgently. Ireland has joined the International Hydrographic Organisation and there is to be an Irish Hydrographic Office, located in Drogheda (although Ireland has no plans to publish its own charts). The Irish Marine Institute has commenced a major survey project of the inshore waters, in collaboration with the UK's Maritime and Coastguard Agency, since the problem applies equally to Northern Ireland as well as the Republic.

All of this will take several years. In the meantime, the standard advice to the prudent navigator applies with full force in the waters around Ireland. Keep a good look out, maintain good traditional pilotage, and do not place undue reliance upon GPS when in close proximity to the coast or charted dangers. Bear in mind when using chartplotters that the data displayed is never any better than that on the paper charts, and that only a hairsbreadth fuse stands between the navigator and the loss of this vital information. Always carry the paper charts.

In certain places where the published charts are known to be seriously inaccurate, such as (at the time of writing) in Wexford Harbour and Trawbreaga Bay, these Directions point this out.

To landward, the Ordnance Survey maps are excellent and up-to-date, and provide detail not only for exploration ashore but landmark-

*Tau cross, Tory Island, Co.Donegal*

*Port of Larne, Co.Antrim*

spotting from seaward. On the smaller scale the 1:250,000 scale Holiday Map is recommended. For intimate details of the land, including the minor road network and locations of hundreds of antiquities, the 1:50,000 scale Discovery Series is excellent.

**PILOTAGE**

Visual transits are described where these are available and unambiguous, and most of them have been photographed, but in many places the Directions can only recommend giving a coast or a danger a berth of a specified distance. This is straightforward for those who are blessed with good distance judgement, but not everyone is, and apart from reminding golfers that a cable is a good 3-wood shot, the sensible course is to recommend full use of GPS and radar if available. Latitudes and longitudes are given for ports, anchorages, channels and some dangers to facilitate finding them on the charts. These are not necessarily intended to be used as waypoints. The quoted positions are usually in the approach to the charted feature in the sense in which the Directions are written, that is to say generally northwards and westwards; or in the case of a danger, on an appropriate clearing line.

The plans are intended to illustrate the text, and should not be used for navigation; that is to say that they do not necessarily show all the dangers, and that bearings, courses, clearing lines and positions should not be taken from them unless these are specified in figures. That is also why there are no latitude and longitude grids on the plans.

Depths and heights on the plans are in metres, and the plans are oriented north-south (true), with one exception (the plan of the Newry River). Depths are reduced to Lowest Astronomical Tide. Bearings quoted in the text and on the plans refer to true North. Magnetic variation in the region is approximately

*Dunluce Castle, Co.Antrim*

5°W (2007), decreasing 11' annually. These Directions run from south-east to north-west. To avoid needless repetition of descriptive material, they sometimes require the reader to skip to the next section or paragraph to find the approach to a harbour from the other direction, and the reader sailing from northwest to southeast will inevitably be flipping back and forward occasionally.

## ANCHORAGE, MOORING & BERTHING

On this coast, anchorage, where it is available, is free. Good ground tackle is essential, and that includes an ample scope of chain as opposed to all-rope or a nominal length of chain next to the anchor. In most places the holding ground is good. Weed and kelp may occasionally be a problem, and care must be taken to ensure that the anchor is well bedded in and not merely hooked in the weed. This involves going astern on the anchor, gently at first but then more and more forcefully until full astern, while keeping an eye on a transit on the beam. Lift and re-lay if not satisfied.

There are marinas at Kilmore Quay, Arklow, Dun Laoghaire, Poolbeg (Dublin) and Dublin city centre, Howth, Malahide, Carlingford, Ardglass, Portaferry (Strangford Lough), Donaghadee, Bangor, Carrickfergus, Glenarm, Ballycastle, Coleraine and Fahan (Lough Swilly), and more modest pontoon facilities at Quoile, Killyleagh, Island Taggart, Ringhaddy and Whiterock, in Strangford Lough; and at Rathlin, Portrush and Londonderry. Many of the harbours described have proposals for marina developments. Where these seem likely to be realised within the next few years, they are mentioned so that the intending visitor may check the latest information on the website, www.irishcruisingclub.com. Visitors' moorings are maintained in certain places by the County Councils and private businesses. The Council moorings are usually designed for 15 tonnes displacement and are equipped with large rigid yellow buoys which may or may not have pickup ropes attached. There may be a charge for the use of visitors' moorings; if so the details are often on a tag attached to the buoy. These Directions cannot give any assurances about the condition of these moorings, and visitors use them entirely at their own risk.

Piers and harbours may charge dues for visitors; when they do, a typical level is €10 or €15 / £7 or £10 per night. Marina charges are generally but not always higher than this.

In the following pages, when an anchorage is described as being sheltered (or not) from certain wind directions, the sense is always clockwise, so for example "W to NE" means

*Inishbofin, Co.Donegal*

"W through N to NE". A "mile" is the nautical mile of ten cables or 1,854 metres. Distances on land are specified in kilometres.

## PASSAGEMAKING

On most parts of this coast harbours and anchorages are closely spaced, but north of Rosslare there are no large and accessible harbours or sheltered anchorages until Arklow is reached. On this stretch, and also between Belfast Lough and Malin Head, the chief consideration is the tidal stream, whether coasting or crossing from England, Wales or Scotland. By getting the tides right it is possible to make good some remarkable distances – and conversely.

A table of distances around the coast is given in Appendix 3.

## SAILING ROUND IRELAND

Many each year prove to themselves that Ireland is indeed an island. The circumnavigation fits comfortably into a summer holiday, two weeks being a little tight, three giving more time to explore, and beyond that, the more the better. Clockwise or anticlockwise is a matter of

personal preference, as of course is the choice of which areas to explore and which to leave for next time. A major factor, naturally, is the weather. Bear in mind that on the west and north coasts, strong winds raise an enduring and often heavy swell, whereas on the south coast, and particularly on the east coast, light winds bring calm seas.

## RADIO COMMUNICATIONS AND SEARCH & RESCUE

The Irish Coastguard has its Marine Rescue Coordination Centre in Dublin, and Sub-Centres at Valentia Island and Malin Head. These three stations maintain constant listening watch on VHF. Valentia and Malin Head also listen on MF and are Navtex stations. There are also ten subsidiary transmitters, each with its own station name. The UK Maritime and Coastguard Agency has a Marine Rescue Co-ordination-Centre at Bangor harbour, which operates as Belfast Coastguard, with repeater transmitters around the coast of Northern Ireland. The Coastguard stations provide regular weather forecasts, navigational warnings and traffic lists, and coordinate search and rescue. The RNLI operates seamlessly throughout Ireland and has all-weather lifeboat stations at Kilmore Quay, Rosslare, Arklow, Wicklow, Dun Laoghaire, Howth, Clogher Head, Newcastle, Donaghadee, Larne, Portrush and Lough Swilly. Kilmore Quay, Wicklow, Clogher Head, Newcastle and Lough Swilly have 17-knot Tyne or Mersey lifeboats, and the others 25-knot Severns or Trents. Inshore lifeboats are stationed at Wexford, Courtown, Skerries, Kilkeel, Portaferry, Bangor and Red Bay. Airborne rescue is provided by Coastguard helicopters based at Shannon and Waterford, supported by the Irish Air Corps from Baldonnel near Dublin

*Dropping the pilot, Belfast Lough*

*Rathlin Island ferry*

and Finner, Co. Donegal, and by the Royal Air Force from Aldergrove near Belfast and bases in Kintyre, Anglesey and Cornwall.

Details of Coastguard Radio stations are given in Appendix 2.

## COMMERCIAL SHIPPING

The east coast of Ireland is busy with commercial shipping. There are Traffic Separation Schemes off the Tuskar Rock, in the approaches to Dublin and between Fair Head and the Mull of Kintyre, in which the usual International Rules apply. Dublin and Belfast are major international ports, while Rosslare, Dun Laoghaire, Dublin, Belfast and Larne have heavy passenger and RoRo traffic, including very large conventional and fast ferries on routes across the Irish Sea and further afield. Warrenpoint has busy container and RoRo terminals, and Londonderry and Drogheda also handle large tonnages of cargo. Smaller vessels use Wicklow, Dundalk, Greenore and Coleraine. Small car ferries cross the entrances to Strangford Lough and Lough Foyle, between Buncrana and Rathmullan in Lough Swilly and between Ballycastle and Rathlin Island, while a passenger ferry service operates from Magheraroarty and Bunbeg to Tory Island.

## FISHING

The fishing industry in Ireland and the UK is undergoing inexorable decline, but fishing is still important, and in fishing harbours yachts are rightly expected to accord priority to fishing vessels and their requirements. The major ports are Kilmore Quay, Howth, Kilkeel, Ardglass, Portavogie and Greencastle (Donegal) but many other places have significant fishing fleets.

The principal fishery close inshore is for shellfish – lobsters, crabs and prawns – and pot markers are met almost everywhere. These are usually orange plastic buoys, but dan buoys with black flags are also used. They generally mark the ends of a long string of pots on the bottom. It is normally safe to pass within a boat's length of a buoy, but beware of floating ropes, especially when two buoys are tied in tandem to cope with a fast tidal stream. Don't sail between them.

Sea angling is a thriving tourist business in many places; the boats often work to a regular

*Portavogie, Co.Down, one of Northern Ireland's principal fishing harbours*

*Rope culture of mussels, Mulroy Bay, Co.Donegal*

timetable and the skippers appreciate having their normal berths left available. In return, they are often the handiest source of wonderfully fresh fish.

Drift netting for salmon is prohibited in Ireland and the UK. Avoiding the nets used to be a major preoccupation of yachtsmen, but it may now be assumed that a buoy offshore marks shellfish pots.

Fish farming is carried out on the east Antrim coast and in Lough Swilly and Mulroy Bay. Fish farms are usually, but not always, marked by yellow buoys with flashing yellow lights. Parallel rows of buoys – often blue plastic barrels – usually indicate rope culture of mussels. There are shellfish beds in some places, with oysters and scallops cultivated, where anchoring and running aground are frowned upon. Mussel dredgers are active in Wexford Harbour, Carlingford Lough and Lough Foyle.

It is often convenient to raft up with fishing boats in harbour, but if doing this, a little courtesy and common sense are the key, as are good fenders and a willingness to keep antisocial hours. If in doubt, consult the harbourmasters for guidance. In many places, facilities for yachts

and fishing boats are well segregated anyway. It is worthy of note that several fishing harbours which once merely tolerated yachts now extend a warm welcome.

## DIVING
The north coast in particular is liberally strewn with wrecks, some ancient and many casualties of the great 20th-century wars. Several Spanish Armada galleons came to grief on the shores of Antrim and Donegal, and there are many wrecks around Rathlin Island. These are a magnet for divers, and diving boats, usually large rigid inflatables, are commonly seen. They display the blue and white International Code flag A, and should be given a wide berth. Unauthorised salvage of artefacts from wrecks more than 100 years old is illegal in the Republic of Ireland.

## OFFSHORE ENERGY INSTALLATIONS
At the time of writing there is a wind farm of seven turbines on the Arklow Bank, and projects are in hand to install wind turbines in Dundalk Bay and tidal generators in Strangford Narrows. International standards for marking such installations are under active consideration by the lighthouse authorities, but in the meantime they are marked conventionally. In close proximity to large wind farms, clutter may make radar screens unreadable.

## WILDLIFE
Whales and dolphins are common around Ireland, and the minke and pilot whale, the common Atlantic dolphin and the harbour porpoise are often seen. Bottlenose dolphins and fin whales are rarer, as are basking sharks. Jellyfish sometimes occur in huge numbers (and may even block engine cooling intakes) and at other times are nowhere to be seen – nobody

knows why. The harmless moon jelly is the commonest but the compass jellyfish and the stinging lion's mane are also seen. Sea anglers catch mackerel, pollack, whiting, ling, cod, haddock, dogfish, congers and small sharks. Grey and common seals are widespread.

Bird species include the various species of gulls and terns, gannets, kittiwakes, guillemots, razorbills, cormorants and shags, and the ubiquitous fulmar. Puffins nest on Rathlin Island and the Isle of Muck, off the Antrim coast. In the estuaries herons, oystercatchers and curlews abound, and waders arrive for the winter. Ireland is, in general, blessed in its freedom from aggressive and venomous creatures of all sizes, only partly thanks to Saint Patrick and his fine work on the snake population, now (as is well known) zero. There are few if any mosquitoes, even in a warm summer, and most of the coast is mercifully free of that scourge of Scotland, the midge.

PLACE NAMES
Names on this coast are derived from Irish Gaelic or Old Norse, and – particularly in the case of the former – the English transliterations are variable in spelling or usage. This may lead to confusion where the charted name differs in spelling from the local name – Carna versus Carne, Downies versus Downings, Carrickarade versus Carrickarede, Don O'Neill versus Dunnyneill. The very first place described in this book is a case in point; it is Kilmore Quay everywhere except on the OS maps and the charts, where it is simply Kilmore. This appears to be a uniquely Irish phenomenon, and

it dates back to the original Ordnance Survey of Ireland in the 1830's. It must be assumed that the authorities whom the surveyors of the time consulted – probably the landowners or clergymen – may occasionally have had individualistic opinions on the matter. Be that as it may, the Admiralty charts usually (but not always) follow the OS spelling. Where this is locally regarded as incorrect, the text uses the local name but refers to the charted name, for example "Carne (Carna on the chart)".

SUPPLIES
Availability of supplies of all kinds is detailed in the text. At the time of writing (2007) it remains legal in Ireland and the UK for leisure craft to use marked (rebated/agri/tractor) diesel, which is dyed green in the Republic of Ireland and red in the UK; but the European Commission has decreed that both countries must charge the extra tax. At the time of writing no decision has been made on how this is to be implemented, but an increase in price is inevitable. Tankers, and all marina and harbourside pumps, dispense marked diesel. In general, in the text, this is what is meant by "diesel". Petrol (gasoline) is generally available only at roadside filling stations, all of which sell taxed (road) diesel as well. Some of them also have a marked-diesel pump, and most of them sell bottled gas (propane or butane). Gas may pose problems of compatibility of fittings. The Irish standard fittings differ from the British ones, but either are easily bought. Camping Gaz, while expensive, can be obtained in many places. Outside the towns, the locations of banks and ATMs are mentioned in the text. ATMs in the Republic will supply euro, and those in Northern Ireland

*West Town, Tory Island*

sterling, against a card from almost anywhere in the world.

## PUBS AND RESTAURANTS

Ireland is legendary for the warmth of its welcome, and nowhere is this more marked than in its pubs, of which there are thousands. The pub is the local meeting-place where the best *craic* is often to be found. This Irish term, which derives from English but has developed to the point where it has no longer a direct English translation, describes the mix of conversation, banter, jokes, ribbing, argument and laughter that has made the Irish pub and its customers a worldwide success story; and this applies with equal force in both Northern Ireland and the Republic. It is in the pub that the curiosity of the island is seen in its highest form – "are you on holiday?" is not a straight question but an invitation to share your life story and your opinions, and in return to have the questioner reciprocate.

Equally, the quality of restaurants is outstanding. It would be a full-time job to stay current with the phone numbers, let alone the merits of individual establishments, so this book does not attempt it – the cruising sailor should carry an up-to-date tourist guide book as well and make full use of the tourist information facilities listed.

## WASTE DISPOSAL

Dumping of any waste overboard in Irish or British waters is forbidden by law. Waste disposal facilities in ports and harbours may be on the scanty side, and any opportunity to use a recycling facility should be seized. The law does not, however, require holding tanks for sewage on yachts, and in consequence there are very few pumpout stations. Most marinas and harbours prohibit the use of on-board heads while in port, and it is only common courtesy to use the facilities on shore.

## COMMUNICATIONS

Locations of public telephones are not listed, since mobile phones are almost universal. Mobile signal is available in most places up to five miles offshore, but there are still some blank spots both afloat and ashore. In emergency, it may be assumed that every house, shop and pub has a telephone anyway. The foregoing is not meant to suggest that the mobile phone is a satisfactory means of communicating distress at sea; there is no substitute for marine VHF. Wi-fi is rapidly becoming standard in marinas, although the user may have to subscribe to the provider; and Internet access is (formally or informally) available in most places.

## CUSTOMS AND IMMIGRATION

For most yachts arriving from other EU countries there is normally no requirement to report to Customs, and there are no passport formalities between the UK and Ireland. However the authorities are vigilant, their major preoccupations being drugs, firearms, illegal immigrants and the protection of Ireland's vital farming industry from illicit or diseased plants and animals. For an official statement of the requirements, see Appendix 6.

*Craic. The Pier Bar, Portsalon, Co.Donegal*

*Bray tunnel, Co.Wicklow, on the Dublin-Rosslare line*

## GETTING THERE

These parts of Ireland can be reached by road or rail from Dublin and Belfast or points north or south, and more directly by ferries from Scotland, England, Wales and France, or flights to the airports at Dublin, Waterford, Belfast, Carrickfin (Donegal) and Londonderry. Rosslare, Wexford, Arklow, Wicklow and the coastal towns around Dublin Bay have train connections with Dublin; Drogheda, Dundalk and Newry with both Dublin and Belfast; and Bangor, Carrickfergus, Larne, Portrush, Coleraine and Londonderry with Belfast. Bus services are widespread and comprehensive. Car rental is available in all the larger towns and at the ports and airports. Almost every mainland anchorage is reachable by road. To get to and around Ireland, as anywhere else, consult the Internet.

*Annalong, Co.Down*

# Chapter 1

## Kilmore Quay to Dublin Bay

*Kilmore Quay from the SSW*

The south-east corner of Ireland can be a surprisingly challenging place for a yacht. The coast near Carnsore Point is unimposing, but the strong tides, offshore rocks and lack of good landmarks make for tricky pilotage, and convenient and accessible harbours are few. The ferry port of Rosslare offers reasonable anchorage in its bay and the possibility of a temporary alongside berth, but Wexford harbour is difficult of access. The charming village of Kilmore Quay with its busy marina, a few miles west of Carnsore Point, is often the most convenient first port of call for a yacht arriving from south-west England or from France, whether she is bound north or west. North of Wexford, the coast is low and sandy, with offshore banks running parallel to the shore, and

the ports of Arklow and Wicklow are the only ones with good access south of Dublin Bay. Pilotage inside the banks is straightforward in any reasonable weather; they are well marked, and in the absence of strong onshore winds, there is little swell.

### Charts

The small-craft folio SC5621 covers the whole of this section in full detail. In terms of individual charts, AC1787 Carnsore Point to Wicklow Head and 1468 Arklow to the Skerries Islands cover almost the whole area of this chapter, with (on the small scale) 1410 St George's Channel, 2049 Old Head of Kinsale to Tuskar Rock or Imray's C57 analogously titled, or (on the large scale) AC2740 Saltee Islands, needed

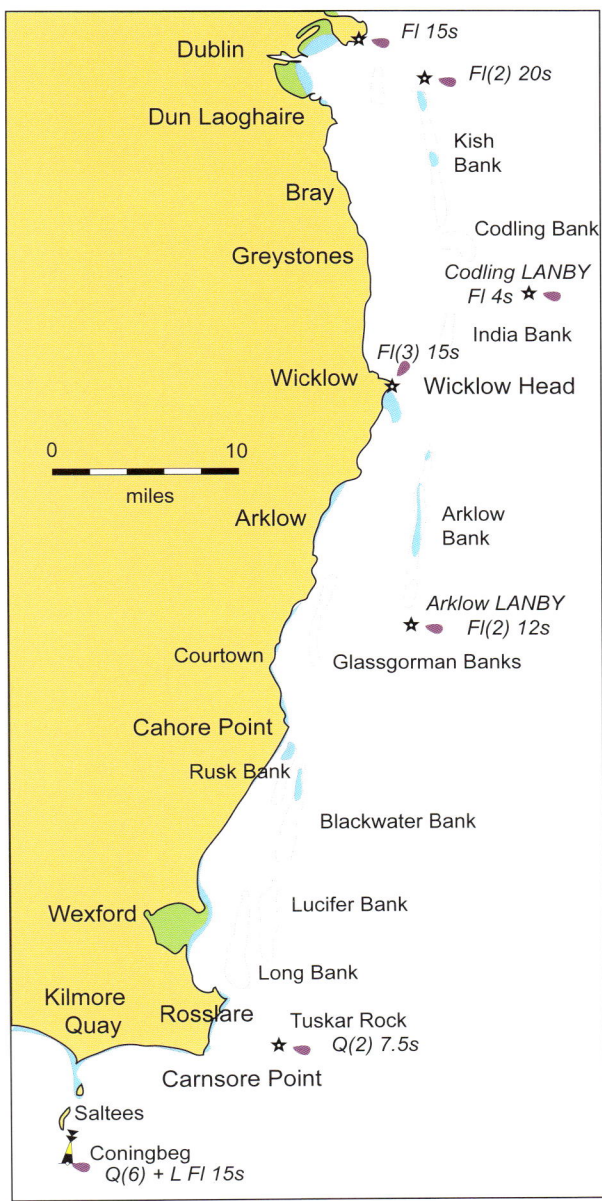

for coverage west to Kilmore Quay. AC2740 is essential if exploring the Saltees. AC1772 Rosslare Europort and Wexford is optional, and AC633 includes useful plans of Arklow and Wicklow harbours. AC1415 is useful for Dublin Bay, and AC1447 is optional if going up the Liffey. The Imray chart C61 has plans of Wexford, Arklow, Wicklow and Dublin Bay.

## KILMORE QUAY
52°10'N 6°35'·1W, *AC2049, 2740, SC5621.16, Imray C57 and Plan*

Kilmore Quay (Kilmore on the charts) is a busy fishing harbour but has a good marina and welcomes yachts. The approach to the harbour, through a channel dredged to 1·9m, has little room for error. In winds of F6 and above between SE and SW, or in a heavy swell, particularly near LW, Dunmore East, at the mouth of Waterford Harbour, 15M to the W, offers a safer option to the stranger. It is described in the companion volume *Sailing Directions for the South and West Coasts of Ireland*.

The Saltee Islands, S of Kilmore Quay, are surrounded by dangerous rocks, and this, combined with the low-lying and relatively featureless nature of the mainland coast here, makes for an area to be avoided in heavy weather or poor visibility.

### Tides
Streams run at up to 3 kn at springs through Saltee Sound, and can reach 4·5 kn over St Patrick's Bridge; elsewhere at 1·5 to 2·5 kn, turning E at −0110 Cobh and W at +0510 Cobh. Over St Patrick's bridge the E-going stream starts at −0250 Cobh. S of the Saltees the streams are rotatory clockwise. The N and E stream begins N at −0100 Cobh, reaches its greatest rate of 1·7 kn (springs) to the ENE at +0200 Cobh, and ends SE. The S and W stream begins S at +0530 Cobh, reaches 1·9 kn (springs) W by S at −0355 Cobh, and ends NW. Slack water lasts about an hour. There are ripples near and over all the shoals. In heavy weather there are overfalls S and E of the Saltees.

Constant (Great Saltee) +0014 Cobh, MHWS 3·8m, MHWN 2·9m.

### Dangers – approaches to Kilmore Quay, and the Saltees
**Coningbeg Rock** (dries 2·8m), 2·5M SSW of Great Saltee.
**Coningmore Rocks** (4m high), 1·5M NE of Coningbeg Rock and 1·5M S of Great Saltee
**Red Bank** (7·9m), 1.4M W of Coningmore Rocks, breaks in heavy weather
**The Brandies** (dry 0·9 and 2·5m), 1·5M SE of Great Saltee
**The Bore** (5.4m), 1·5M NE of the Brandies
**Long Bohur** (4m), and **Short Bohur** (7·3m), 1.5M E of Little Saltee and 1M N of the Bore
**Whitty Rock** (awash at LAT) and **Power's Rock** (0·3m) 3 cables NW of Great Saltee, and **Shoal Rock** (0·9m) 2 cables S of it.
**Sebber Bridge** (0·6m to 4m) boulder spit extending 7 cables N from Great Saltee
**Galgee Rock** (dries), 1 cable S of Little Saltee

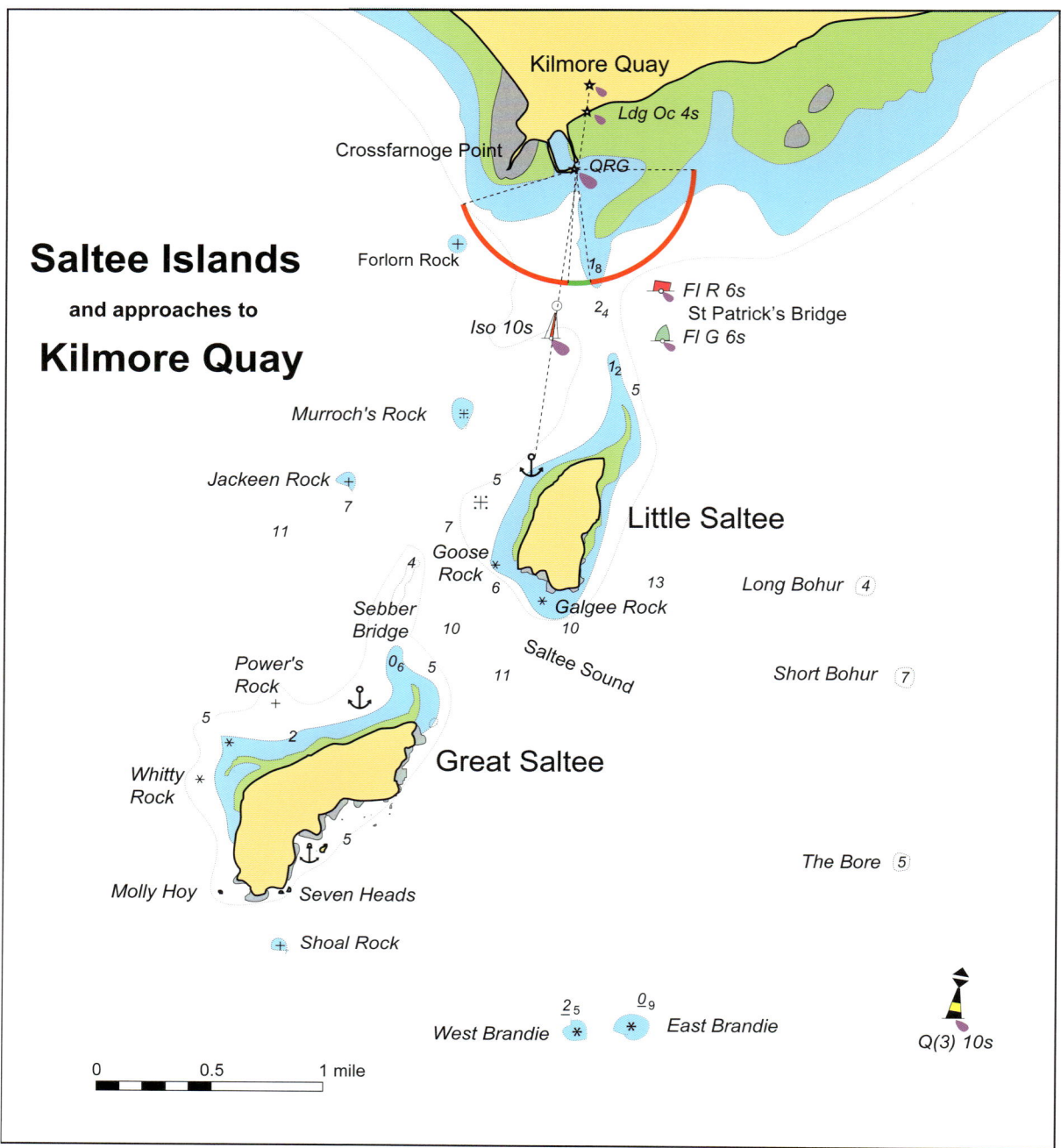

**Murroch's Rock** (awash at LAT), 5 cables NW of Little Saltee

**Unnamed rock** (awash at LAT), 3 cables W of Little Saltee

**Jackeen Rock** (1·5m) 8 cables W of Little Saltee

**Goose Rock** (dries 2·6m), 1 cable W of Little Saltee

**Forlorn Rock,** 1·5m, 4 cables SW of Crossfarnoge Point

**St Patrick's Bridge,** 52°09'·2N 6°34'·9W, gravel bar with 2·4m in mid-channel, between Little Saltee and the shore SE of Kilmore Quay.

**Lights and Marks**

**Coningbeg** buoy, S Card Q(6) + LFl 15s 9M, Racon (G), AIS, 9 cables S of Coningbeg Rock

**Red Bank** buoy, W Card VQ(9) 10s, AIS, 2.6M W of Coningmore Rock

**Bore Rocks** buoy, E Card Q(3) 10s, AIS, 8 cables SE of The Bore

**St Patrick's Bridge** buoys SHM, Fl G 6s, and PHM, Fl R 6s, both these marks about 3 cables to the E of the bar. Conventional buoyage direction N and E. On station 1st April to 12th Sept

**St Patrick's Bridge** fairway buoy, RWVS Iso 10s

*Approach to Kilmore Quay from the S; breakwater end and leading beacons centre R, church centre*

**Kilmore Quay** breakwater end, Q RG 7m 5M, R 269°–354°, G 354°–003°, R 003°–077° shows green over approach channel from S (including, further S, between Murroch's Rock and Little Saltee), red elsewhere

**Kilmore Quay** leading lights 008°, Oc 4s 6M, white with red stripe on grey concrete columns, front 3m, rear 6m.

**Offshore weather buoy**
**Buoy M5**, yellow, Fl(5) Y 20s, is moored 33M S of the Coningbeg Rock at 51°41'·4N 5°25'·5W

**Directions – Approaches to Kilmore Quay**
**From the W** the church building at Kilmore Quay provides the most prominent landmark, while the leading beacons are initially obscured by the pier. Give the shore at Crossfarnoge Point a berth of 5 cables to clear Forlorn Rock, then identify the fairway buoy, which is on the leading line for Kilmore Quay. Steer in on the line of the leading beacons 008° until the harbour entrance is abeam, then turn in. Be alert for traffic coming out as the entrance is only 20m wide. The dredged channel to Kilmore Quay is narrow and subject to strong cross tides; care must be taken to stay on the leading line. The charted transits on Ballyteige Castle are no longer of use since the castle is obscured from seaward by new buildings in Kilmore Quay village.

**From offshore to the S,** from a position close W of the Coningbeg buoy, a course of 350° leads 3 cables W of the Coningbeg Rock. If the rock can be clearly identified when abeam (it usually shows, or breaks) it is then safe to turn on to a course of 010°, which leads 5 cables E of Red Bank. and 4 cables W of Great Saltee. The safest approach to Kilmore Quay is to stay on this

course until clear well N of Little Saltee, leaving Jackeen Rock and Murroch's Rock to starboard. Then steer towards the fairway buoy W of St Patrick's Bridge until the leading beacons for Kilmore Quay are identified, then as above.

For directions for Saltee Sound and St Patrick's Bridge, see below.

**Marina**
The harbour, managed by Wexford County Council, has 4·4m alongside the E pier and 2.4m alongside the W pier, and contains a 60-berth

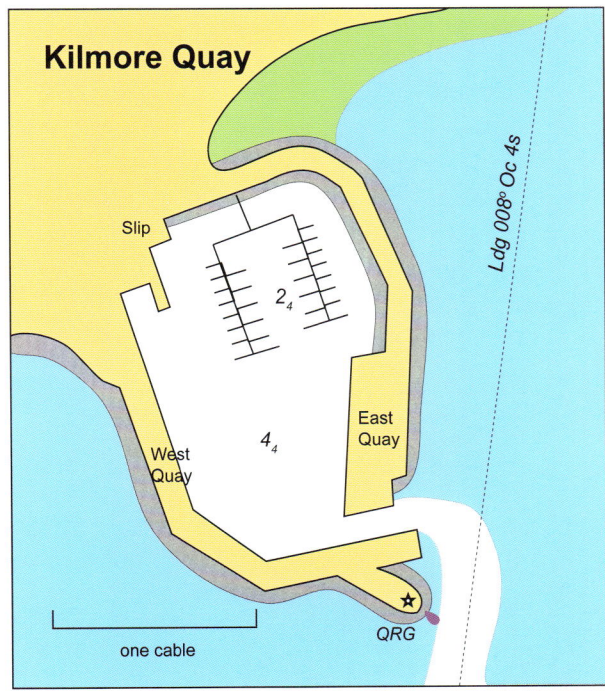

*Kilmore Quay entrance*

marina with least depth 2·4m. The marina is very busy in summer and it is advisable to make contact in advance; VHF Ch 16 and 9, phone 05391 29955, e-mail hmkilmore@eircom.net.

## Facilities

Water, pumpout and shore power on the pontoons; CCTV security. Diesel in cans; shops, pubs, restaurants, chandlery. Buses to Wexford. Bicycle hire. Taxis 087 912 2259. Repairs, Marindus Engineering 05391 29794. Doctor. RNLI all-weather lifeboat station.

## SALTEE ISLANDS

52°08'N 6°36'W, *AC2740, SC5621·16*

The islands are privately owned, and Little Saltee is farmed, although neither is permanently inhabited. The somewhat eccentric owners of Great Saltee request that when they are in residence (as indicated by the standard of the Prince of the Saltees, flown from the flagstaff), visitors vacate the island by 1630 each day.

The pilotage of the islands is tricky, and is complicated by four factors: the strong tidal streams, the numerous dangerous rocks, the lack of good transits, and the fact that the charting of the islands (in 1847) was evidently not up to the Admiralty's usual high standard. The charts display a caution to the effect that positions differ by varying amounts from those on the smaller scale charts. Certain rocks, notably the Seven Heads and the rocks 3 cables NE of them, are shown as drying but in fact stand well above HW. The offset between AC2740 and WGS84 datum is officially unknown; this offset varies over the area of the chart and may be as much as a cable, the sense being as usual, i.e. GPS positions must be adjusted E and S before plotting on the chart. In any case, when navigating around the Saltees by GPS, allow an extra cable of margin for error, and do not depend upon chartplotters.

Be that as it may, the islands are a fascinating place to explore in good weather, home to several hundred species of birds, and offer reasonable temporary anchorages.

The main ship channel passes outside the Coningbeg buoy, 9M offshore, but with careful pilotage a yacht can pass between or north of the Saltees in any reasonable weather. The classic route is across St Patrick's Bridge, a gravel bar between the Little Saltee and the shore, with 2·4m at LAT and buoyed in summer. Saltee Sound, between the Great and Little Saltees, has 7m but is unmarked. There is deep water south of the Great Saltee, but the eastbound yacht must then take care to avoid the dangerous Bore and Brandies Rocks.

## ST PATRICK'S BRIDGE

52°09'·2N 6°35'·3W

**From the W**, steer to pass in mid-channel between Little Saltee and the shore, and note the positions of Murroch's Rock to the S and Forlorn Rock to the W. Identify the fairway buoy and the buoys marking the deepest water across St Patrick's Bridge. If the lateral buoys are not on station, hold mid-channel until well over the bar and in deeper water. **From Kilmore Quay**, keep the leading marks astern 008° to the fairway buoy before turning E.

## Saltee Sound

**From the W**, approach with the summit of Little Saltee bearing 095°. When the E tip of Great Saltee bears 185°, turn to starboard and steer 150° through the sound. Rounding the S point of Little Saltee and if bound E towards Carnsore Point, first steer NE, giving the island a berth of 4 cables until its N point is well abeam. This

*Plaque overlooking the N anchorage, Great Saltee*

*The anchorage on the SE side of Great Saltee*

leads clear N of Long Bohur. **From the SE**, and heading for Kilmore Quay, a bearing of 330° on the SW end of Little Saltee leads between The Bore and the Brandies. Give Little Saltee a berth of 3 cables and hold the course of 330° to pass midway between Jackeen Rock and Murroch's Rock. When the buoys on St Patrick's Bridge are abeam, head towards them until the Kilmore Quay leading beacons line up 008°.

## Anchorage

In settled conditions or moderate winds between NE and S, anchorage is available off the NW shore of Little Saltee in 4m, sand and boulders; and also off the N shore of Great Saltee, N of the buildings, in 2 to 4m, sand. In settled conditions with no swell, the bay (with 3·4m on the chart) on the SE side of Great Saltee 3 cables N of the Seven Heads Rocks provides an attractive temporary anchorage. The rocks on the E side of the bay, shown on the charts as drying but in fact 2m high, provide a landmark for entry *(see photograph)*. The Seven Heads rocks, to the SW, also stand well above HW.

## KILMORE QUAY TO ROSSLARE

*AC1787, 2049, 2740, SC5621, Imray C61*

The Tuskar Rock, 6M ENE of Carnsore Point, is the principal landfall for a vessel approaching the SE corner of Ireland. The lighthouse on the Tuskar, dating from 1815, marks the entrance to St George's Channel and the Irish Sea. The area is one of strong tides, irregular seabed contours and dangerous offshore rocks, while further offshore are busy shipping lanes. In settled weather, the waters around Carnsore Point can be like a millpond, but in adverse conditions the combination of wind over tide and the irregular bottom can throw up tumultuous seas.

Rosslare Europort, the busiest passenger port in Ireland, is fairly typical of its kind – a 19th-century railhead steam packet harbour enlarged, improved and developed to handle conventional and fast ferries up to 30,000 tons. These arrive at and leave from Rosslare around the clock, but the harbour can offer shelter to a yacht on passage, provided the proper courtesies are observed, and it is a handy place for crew changes.

## Tides

Streams run at up to 3 kn at springs between Carnsore Point and Greenore Point, and through Saltee Sound, and can reach 4·5 kn over St Patrick's Bridge; elsewhere at 1·5 to 2·5 kn, turning N and E at –0110 Cobh and S and W at +0510 Cobh. In heavy weather there are steep and dangerous breakers on The Bailies, between the Tuskar Rock and Carnsore Point. The stream sets NW–SE through the South Shear, SE of Rosslare, to join the main stream S of the offshore banks and NE of the Tuskar. Around the Tuskar the set is NNE–SSW. The spring rate here is 2 to 3 knots, turning N at –0100 Cobh and S at +0500 Cobh. The range at Rosslare is 1·6m at springs and 0·6m at neaps. Constant at Rosslare (HW) +0035 Cobh, (LW) +0005 Cobh, MHWS 1·9m, MHWN 1·4m, ML 1·1m.

## Dangers

*Between the Saltees and Carnsore Point:*

**Black Rock** (2m high), 2·5 M SW by W of Carnsore Point

**Tercheen** (dries at LW), 2 cables N of Black Rock

A **dangerous wreck** 2 cables N of Tercheen

**The Barrels** (dry 1·5m), 1·5M SW by S of Carnsore Point

**Nether Rock** (5m), 2 cables NW of the Barrels

*S of Rosslare:*

**Tuskar Rock**, 5m high, 6M ENE of Carnsore

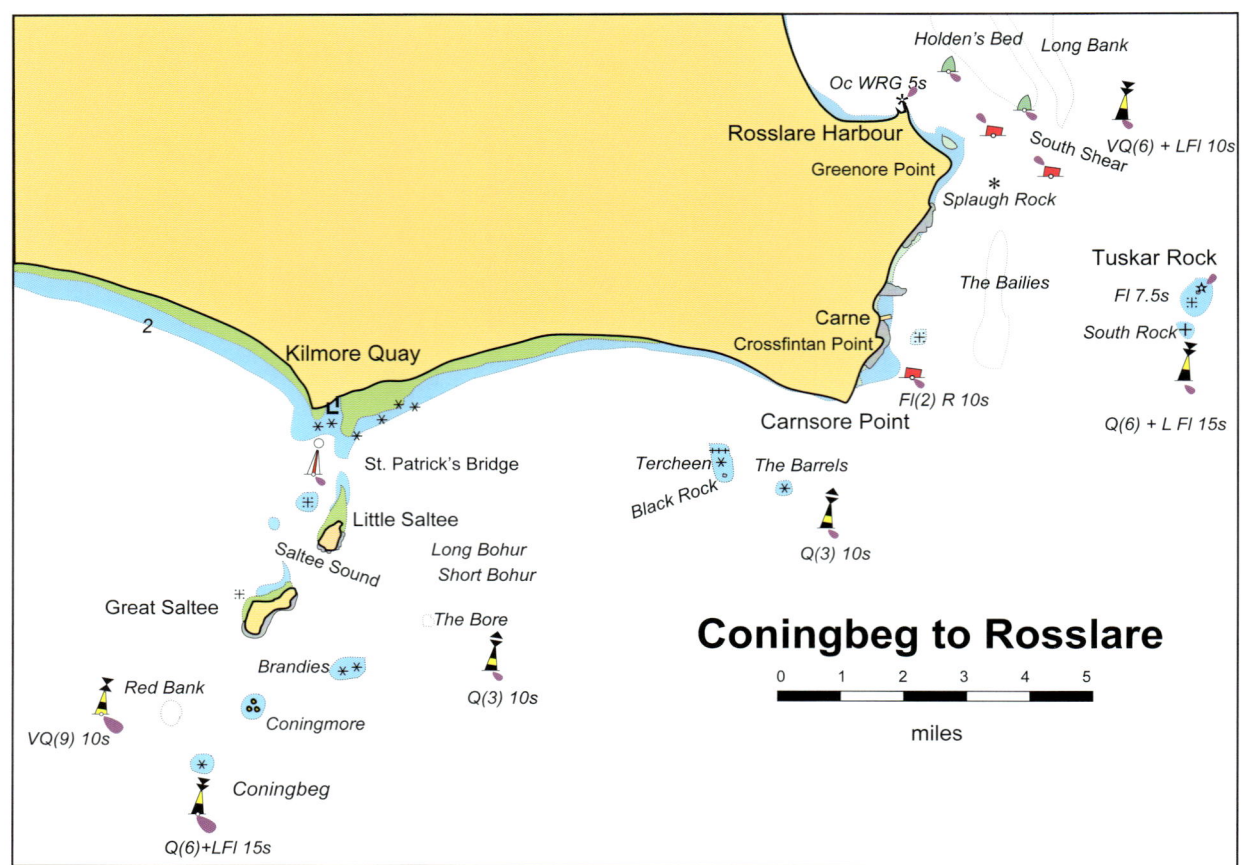

Point

**Gypsy Rock,** 2m, 2 cables NNW of the Tuskar

**Unnamed rock,** awash, 2·5 cables SSW of the Tuskar

**South Rock,** 2·4m, 6·5 cables SSW of the Tuskar

**Fundale Rock** (dries 1·2m), the outer end of a reef extending 5 cables SE from Crossfintan Point

**Collough Rock** (awash at LWS), 5 cables NW of Fundale Rock and 5 cables E of Crossfintan Point

**The Bailies,** 9 to 12m, 1M NE of Collough Rock

**Whilkeen Rock** (dries 2·5m), 4 cables offshore 2M SSW of Greenore Point

**Splaugh Rock** (extensive reef drying 0·3m), 6 cables SE of Greenore Point

**Wreck,** 3 cables N of Splaugh Rock

**Carrick Rock,** drying reef extending 3·5 cables ENE from Greenore Point

**Holden's Bed,** 6m, **Long Bank,** 2·8m and **Lucifer Bank,** 3·5m, NE of Greenore Point.

## Lights and Marks

**Barrels** buoy, E Card Q(3) 10s, 1M SE of the rocks

**Carnsore Point,** wind farm of 7 conspicuous turbines close inland of the point

**Fundale Rock** buoy, PHM Fl(2) R 10s, 2 cables SE of the rock

**Carne Pier,** metal col Fl R 3s 6m 4M

**Tuskar Rock,** white tower Q(2) 7·5s 33m 28M, Horn (4) 45s, Racon (T) 18M

**South Rock** buoy, S Card Q(6)+L Fl 15s, 1·5M S of the Tuskar

**Splaugh** buoy, PHM Fl R 6s

**Carrick Rock,** red PHM perch, unlit

**South Long** buoy, S Card VQ(6)+L Fl 10s

**Calmines** buoy, PHM Fl R 2s

**South Holdens** buoy, SHM Fl(2) G 6s

**West Holdens** buoy, SHM Fl(3) G 10s

**Lucifer** buoy, E Card VQ(3) 5s, 4M ENE of Greenore Point

**Rosslare Breakwater,** red tower, Oc WRG 5s 15m W13M R10M G10M; G 098°–188°, W 188°–208°, R 208°–246°, G 246°–283°, W 283°–286°, R 286°–320°. Shows a narrow white sector ESE over the main E approach through the South Shear channel, and white to the NNE over the North Shear channel. Red sectors show over the Long and Lucifer Banks to NE and between Splaugh and Greenore Point

*Ballytrent mast and Whilkeen Rock in line clears Collough Rock*

to the SE. Green sectors show inshore to N and NW and over Holden's Bed to the E.

**Ballygeary,** pole bn   Oc WR 1·7s 7m 4M, R shore −152°, W 152°−200°, W(unintens) 200°−205°. Shows red to W, white to N, unintensified white close to the breakwater end.

**Rosslare** buoy, SHM QG

## Traffic Separation Scheme

There is a TSS E and S of the Tuskar Rock. The S- and W-bound lane is 3 to 6M from the lighthouse, and the E- and N-bound lane 8 to 11M from the lighthouse. The lanes should be crossed at right angles, or as nearly as possible.

Yachts rounding the Tuskar should use the inshore traffic zone, between the TSS and the rock. The South Shear is the main channel for ships approaching the port of Rosslare.

## Directions – Kilmore Quay to Rosslare, inshore passage

From St Patrick's Bridge, steer 082° and identify the above-water Black Rock, 6M to the E. Leave Black Rock at least 7 cables to starboard to avoid Tercheen and the wreck N of it. Carnsore Point may be identified in moderate to good visibility by its conspicuous wind farm. The point is clean, and in calm weather it may be given a berth of one cable. The passage between the Bailies and Collough Rock is 1M wide, and the passage between the Bailies and the Tuskar is 2M wide. In settled weather, the straightforward route to Rosslare runs close E of the Fundale, Splaugh and Calmines buoys, staying E of the line between Fundale and Splaugh buoys to clear Collough Rock. There are however several short cuts: Black Rock just visible S of Carnsore Point 239° leads safely between Fundale Rock and its buoy, and also SE of Collough Rock, while a course of due N from Fundale buoy on longitude 6°20'·2W leads between Collough Rock and the shore. The red perch on Carrick Rock may be left half a cable to port, but beware then of the Calmines shoal and a shallow patch N of it. The tall white mast among the trees masking Ballytrent House, in line with Whilkeen Rock 340°, clears Collough Rock to the NE.

## Anchorage

Anchorage in winds between SW and NNW may be found in St Margaret's Bay, between Carnsore Point and Greenore Point. This is a useful and com-

### Map: Approaches to Rosslare

QG

Long Bank

North Shear

Rosslare Village

Holden's Bed

VQ(3) 5s

Rosslare Harbour

Oc WRG 5s

Fl(3) G 10s

Fl(2) G 6s

**Approaches to Rosslare**

Water tower

Greenore Point

Fl R 2s

South Shear

VQ(6) + L Fl 10s

Fl R 6s

A. Black Rock and Carnsore Point 239°
B. Whilkeen Rock and Ballytrent mast 340°

FS

Splaugh Rock

Ballytrent Bay

Whilkeen Rock

The

Tuskar Rock
Q(2) 7.5s 28M

Carne

St Margaret's Bay

Fl R 3s

Bailies

South Rock

Wind farm

Collough Rock

Fundale Rock

Q(6) + L Fl 15s

Fl(2) R 10s

Carnsore Point

0    1    2    3
miles

*Carne Pier*

fortable anchorage in strong NW winds, when Rosslare is exposed. There is a small drying pier at Carne (Carna on the charts), on the S side of the bay. **From the S**, pass close to Fundale buoy and from it steer due N to pass inside Collough Rock. When Carne pier bears 250°, turn in to the bay, steering NW. **From the N**, from a position 2 cables SE of Whilkeen Rock, steer towards the pier. Anchor 2 to 3 cables NE of the pier in 3 to 4m, sand. The pier is unsuitable as an alongside berth, and rocks extend 20m beyond the pier head. Shop, pub and restaurant at Carne.

Anchorage is also available in Ballytrent Bay, to the N.

**Directions – Kilmore Quay to Rosslare – offshore**

If the weather precludes the passage of St Patrick's Bridge, then a course either through Saltee Sound or close S of Great Saltee may be practicable, but in these cases the greatest care must be taken to avoid the rocks E and SE of the Saltees. In rough conditions, leave the Barrels buoy to port and give Carnsore Point a berth of 3M, then turn NNE, leaving the overfalls on The Bailies well to port. When Rosslare breakwater is open of Greenore Point, turn to port and steer to leave the Splaugh buoy close to port. For the passage outside Great Saltee, give the S end of the island a berth of 4 cables, then keep this distance off while rounding the island and steer to leave Little Saltee 4 cables to port as well. When the N end of Little Saltee is well abeam, turn E for the Barrels buoy. Note that a direct course from close S of the Great Saltee to the Bore Rocks

*Rosslare Harbour from the N (Iarnrod Eireann)*

buoy passes dangerously close to the Brandies.

These passages are considerably facilitated by careful use of appropriate and pre-programmed GPS waypoints (but see *Saltee Islands,* above, with reference to GPS/chart offsets) and in bad weather and darkness or fog the safest option is to stay south of the Coningbeg buoy, 52°03'·2N 6°38'·6W.

*Carrick Rock Perch from the N - Carnsore Point wind farm beyond*

**Tuskar Rock**

The Tuskar should be given a berth of 5 cables on its E, N and W sides, more in heavy weather. On the S side, South Rock buoy should be left on the proper hand.

**ROSSLARE**

52°15'·3N 6°21'W, *AC1787, 1772, SC5621·15, Imray C61 and Plan*

Rosslare Harbour lies opposite the southern end of the sandbanks which parallel the Irish coast from Dublin southwards. There is anchorage in the bay to the W. The harbour is sheltered from NE through S to SW but exposed from WNW to N. Very large conventional and fast ferries sail to Fishguard, Pembroke Dock, Roscoff and Cherbourg, and the harbour is also a busy RoRo cargo port. With recent heightened concerns on transport security, the Port Area is required to comply with the International Ship and Port Facility Code, which may mean restricted or prohibited access to the harbour. Subject to these provisos, it is possible for a yacht to be accommodated alongside the quay on the SW side, by permission of the HM.

**Directions**

**From the E** (South Shear Channel) leave the Tuskar light 2M to port, South Long, South Holdens and West Holdens buoys to starboard

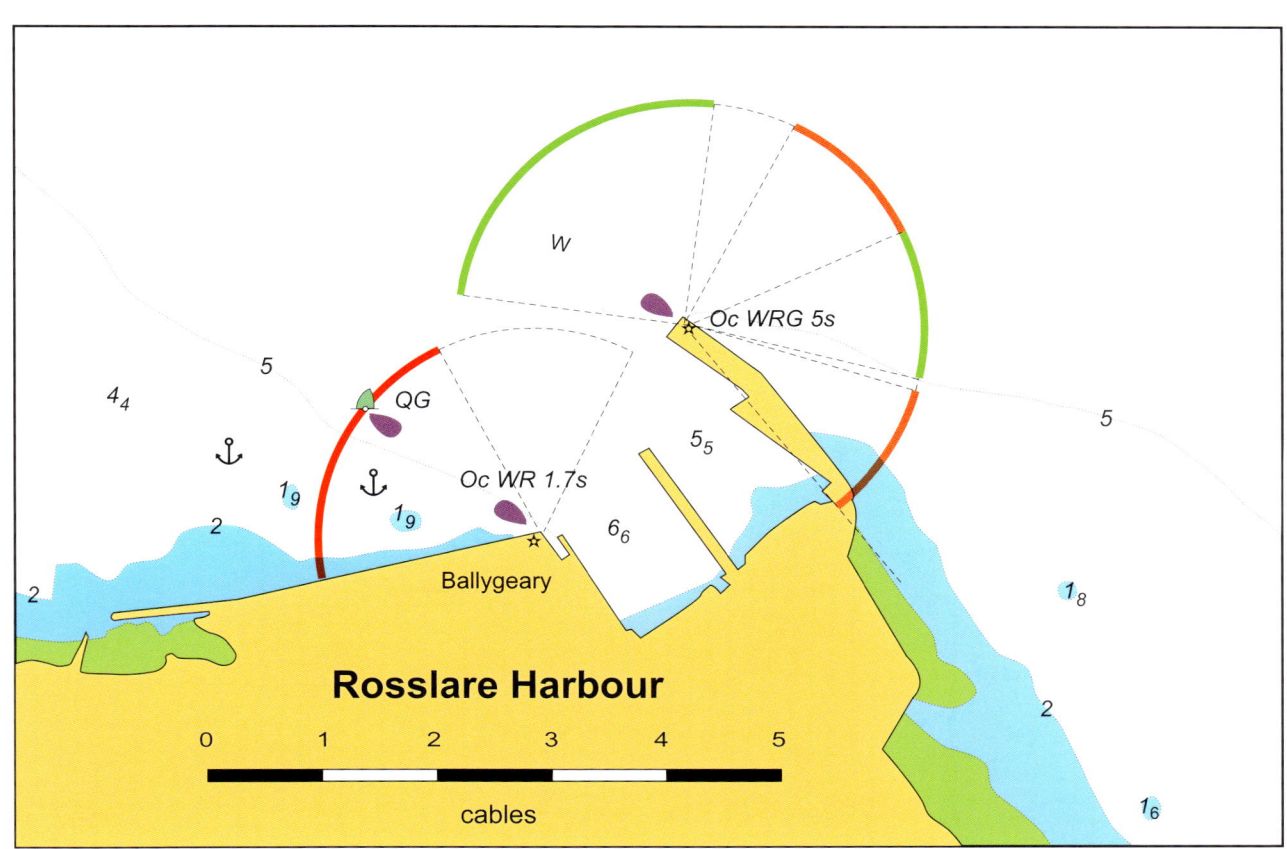

*Rosslare harbour from the N*

and Splaugh and Calmines buoys to port. Identify the breakwater light, and give the breakwater end a wide berth to allow space for ferries leaving. **From the S**, leave the Tuskar light 1M to starboard, then Splaugh to port and South Holdens to starboard as above. **From the N** (North Shear Channel), leave West Long and West Holdens buoys to port, then identify the breakwater light.

### Anchorage

Anchorage is available to the W of the harbour entrance, in 3m, sand, staying well out of the way of the ship channel and clear of moorings. Anchorage is prohibited within 5 cables to the N and E, and 3 cables to the W, of the breakwater head. Somewhat subject to swell.

### Harbour

For an alongside berth, permission must be obtained from the Port Operations tower; call Rosslare Harbour VHF Channel 14 or phone 05391 57929 or 087 232 0251. The SW quay has 3 to 5m. The RoRo berths on the central pier and the breakwater must not be obstructed. The harbour is managed by Iarnród Éireann (Irish Railways).

### Facilities

For mechanical and electrical repairs, check with the Port Operations tower. Filling stations, shops, pubs, restaurants, hotels. Train, bus and ferry connections, car rental. RNLI all-weather lifeboat station.

### ROSSLARE TO ARKLOW

*AC1410, 1787, 1772, SC5621, Imray C61*
The coast between Rosslare and Arklow is generally low-lying, with long stretches of sand and pebble beach and the low headlands of The Raven Point, Blackwater Head, Cahore Point and Kilmichael Point. Tara Hill (251m) and Arklow Rock (123m) are prominent landmarks. The salient feature is the offshore banks, which parallel the coast and continue north as far as Dublin Bay. These are variable in depth, and dry in places from time to time, but they are well marked and with due care are easily avoided. There are no good harbours between Rosslare and Arklow; there is a pier at Polduff and a small harbour at Courtown, but the once-significant port of Wexford, although it has an energetic sailing club, is now all but inaccessible to a visiting yacht due to its shallow water and shifting sandbanks.

### Tidal Streams

The tidal streams are strong and tend to dominate passage planning along the coast. In the North Shear, inside the Long Bank, the tide runs S for ten hours out of twelve; the S-going stream begins at -0235 Dublin and the N-going at -0435 Dublin, the rate reaching 2 kn at springs. Between Wexford and Cahore Point the SSW-going stream starts at -0235 Dublin and the NNE-going at +0355 Dublin, reaching 2 to 3 kn at springs. The NNE-going stream tends to set outward across the banks, and care must be taken to avoid being set on to the banks if using the inshore passage. Conversely the SSW-going stream sets inshore across the banks from seaward, and the corresponding allowance must be made when offshore. Close S of Cahore Point, in the Rusk Channel and the Sluice, the tidal stream reaches 3 to 4 kn.

### Dangers

**Holden's Bed,** sandbank 2M by 1M with 6m, 1·6M NE of Rosslare Harbour
**Long Bank,** sandbank with 2·5m and 3·4m

in places, extending for 6M from 52°15'N to 52°21'N in 6°16'W, NE of Rosslare

**Lucifer Bank,** sandbank with 3·5m in places, extending for 5M from 52°17'N to 52°22'N in 6°14'W, NE of and parallel to the Long Bank

**Blackwater** and **Money-weights Banks,** contiguous sandbanks drying in places, extending for 8M from 52°23'N to 52°32'N in 6°12'W, between Wexford and Cahore Point

**Rusk Bank,** sandbank with 2·4m in places, extending for 3M from 52°29'N to 52°32'N in 6°12'W, S of Cahore Point

**The Ram,** spit with 1·4m, extending 1M S from Cahore Point

**Glassgorman Bank,** sandbank with 3·7m in places, extending for 7M from 52°38'N to 52°45'N in 6°08'W, SE of Kilmichael Point

**Arklow Bank,** sandbank drying in places, extending for 13M from 52°41'N to 52°54'N in 5°57'W, E of Arklow. There is a wind farm of seven turbines on the bank, each turbine 73m high with 104m-diameter blades.

## Lights and Marks

**Lucifer** buoy, E Card VQ(3) 5s
**West Long** buoy, SHM QG
**North Long** buoy, N Card Q
**Wexford Bar** buoy, PHM Fl(2) R 10s, 1·8M SE of The Raven Point
**South Blackwater** buoy, S Card Q(6)+L Fl 15s
**South East Blackwater** buoy, PHM Fl R 10s
**West Blackwater** buoy, SHM Fl G 6s
**East Blackwater** buoy, E Card Q(3) 10s
**Rusk No 1** buoy, SHM Fl(2) G 5s
**Rusk No 2** buoy, PHM Fl(3) R 10s
**Rusk No 4** buoy, PHM Fl(2) R 5s
**Rusk No 6** buoy, PHM Fl R 3s
**North Blackwater** buoy, N Card Q
**Glassgorman No 1** buoy, PHM Fl(2) R 6s
**Glassgorman No 2** buoy, PHM Fl(4) R 10s
**Arklow** LANBY, Fl(2) 12s 12m 15M, Racon (O) 10M, Horn Mo (A) 30s
**South Arklow** buoy, S Card VQ(6)+L Fl 10s
**Arklow No 1** buoy, PHM Fl(3) R 10s
**Arklow Bank** wind farm, N and S turbines Fl Y 5s 14m 10M, other turbines Fl Y 5s
**Roadstone Jetty,** Oc R 10s 9m 9M
**Roadstone Breakwater,** QY
**Arklow South Pier,** white col Fl WR 6s 11m 13M, R shore–223° W223°–350° R350°–shore.

Shows white over the approach from SE, E and NE, red inshore to N and S
**Arklow North Pier,** L Fl G 7s 7m 10M

## Directions – Rosslare to Courtown
*AC1787, SC5621·11*

The passage inside the banks is well buoyed and lit, but should be used with caution at night or in poor visibility, bearing in mind that the N-going tide sets obliquely NE/SW over the banks. The shallows E of Wexford Harbour extend out to sea and up to 2M SE of The Raven Point. Pass not more than 1M W of West Long and North Long buoys, then leave West Blackwater buoy to starboard. There are two channels between the banks off Cahore Point. The wider of the two, the Rusk Channel, is marked by one starboard- and three port-hand buoys. No.4 Rusk buoy should be kept close aboard to port as the E side of the channel is shoal. Pass out between No.6 Rusk and North Blackwater buoys.

The channel between the Rusk Bank and the shore, 2M wide at is S end, narrows and shallows at its N end. **The Sluice** is the name given to the pass between Rusk Bank and the Ram, to the W. It is 5 cables wide with a least charted depth of 4·7m; the depth varies, and less water has been reported on several occasions, but in 2007 there was a least depth of 9m in mid-channel between the No.6 Rusk buoy and the shore, on a course of 030°–210°. The passage close inshore, W of the shallowest part of the Ram, cannot be recommended. The tidal streams run fast through the Sluice, with eddies and overfalls.

From here to Courtown there are no dangers if the coast is given a berth of 3 cables.

## WEXFORD HARBOUR
52°19'N 6°19'W. *AC1772, SC5621·15A (but see Caution, below) and Plan*

Wexford (16,000), at the head of a 3-mile-wide, shallow and partially drying lagoon where the River Slaney meets the sea, is an historic and fascinating town with a maritime tradition dating back to the dawn of history. It had once a significant seaborne trade, but in 1925 the sea swept away a mile and a half of the protecting Rosslare Point sandspit, and the writing was on the wall for the port. Regular dredging ceased many years ago. It was never deep; the name

*Wexford from the E; the River Slaney and training walls, with the Black Man beacon, R*

comes from the Old Norse *Waesfjord,* shallow inlet. The energetic Wexford Harbour Boat Club has recently succeeded in having the buoyage from the bar to the quays upgraded and lit to the Irish Lights' standards, and in settled or offshore weather a shallow-draft vessel can safely reach the town; but the limited depths and the small rise of tide mean that a yacht with 2m draft can navigate the channel only near HW springs, and the continuing accuracy of the buoyage depends on the dedication of the Boat Club members. For (voluntary) pilotage advice phone 087 242 5643.

**Caution**
The present hydrography and buoyage of the channel (with the exception of the bar buoy position) bear little resemblance to AC1772, AC1787 and SC5621·15A, all of which are based on surveys of 1932 and 1951. Do not depend upon a GPS chartplotter in Wexford Harbour, but follow the buoys, proceed at moderate speed and keep a constant watch on the echosounder.

**Directions**
The channel to Wexford town is marked by 13 port- and 4 starboard-hand buoys, Fl R and Fl G respectively, and by the **Black Man**, green stone pillar, with S Card topmark, on the end of the N training wall.

The channel and buoyage in 2007 were as shown on the plan. Entry should only be attempted is settled weather on a high and rising tide. Bear in mind that the channel from the bar buoy to the town is 5M long and will take time to transit, the least depth is only 0·5m, and the rise of tide is very small. **From the S,** it is safe to steer 350° from Rosslare breakwater towards The Raven Point, with its conspicuous woods *(see photograph).* The depths on this line decrease slowly and steadily to 3·8m where the buoyed channel to Wexford crosses this track in 52°19'·3N; at this point turn W and follow the buoys. **From the N,** stay 1·5M E of The Raven Point until the bar buoy is identified. There is a derelict perch 3 cables N of the channel, marking the former position of Rosslare Point and the ruins of the pier which once stood on it. The shallowest point in the channel is 1M ESE of the Black Man beacon, and there is also a shallow patch SW of the Black Man. The Ballast Bank, an artificial island in mid-stream off the town, is navigable on either side, and there is deep water NW of it. The enclosed basin on the S side of the river has silted to less than 0·3m, and the berths at the town quays are currently monopolised by mussel dredgers. Anchor clear of the moorings, or berth at the quays on the NE side of the river. The mussel dredgers use the buoyed channel frequently and anchoring in it is hazardous.

Constant (Wexford Bar) springs +0225 Cobh, neaps +0010 Cobh, MHWS 1·7m, MHWN

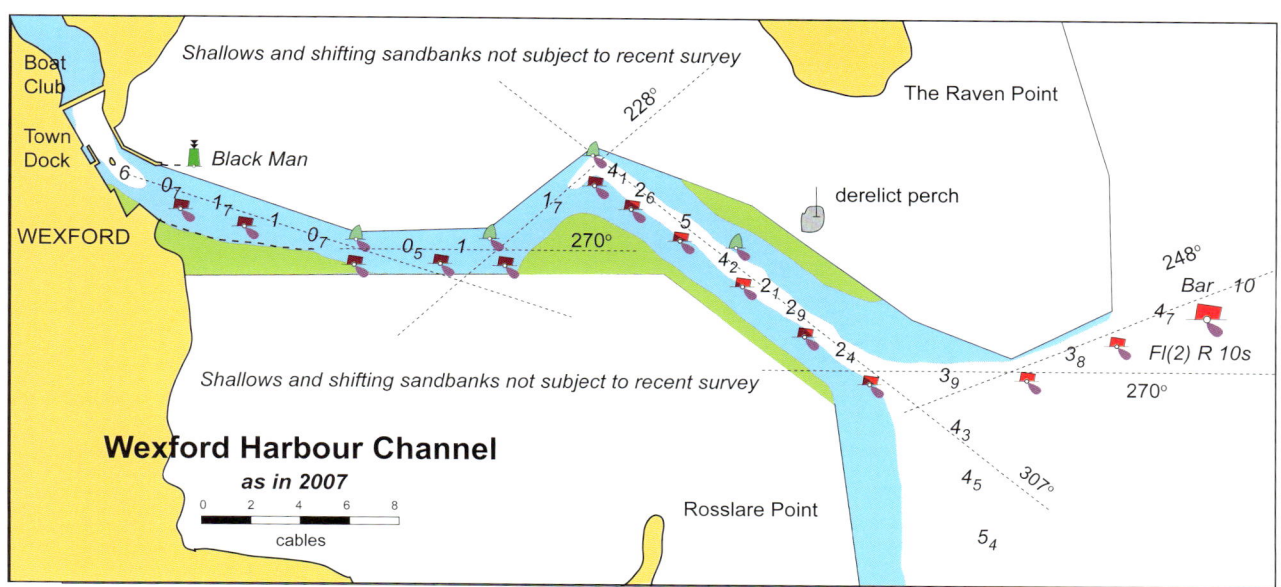

**Wexford Harbour Channel**
*as in 2007*

1·4m, MLWN 0·5m, MLWS 0·4m. HW at the quay is an hour later.

**Facilities**
All the facilities of a large town. Bus and train connections to Rosslare Harbour, Waterford and Dublin. Wexford Harbour Boat Club (05391 22039), on the S bank above the bridge, welcomes visitors and has bar and showers. RNLI inshore lifeboat station.

**River Slaney**
Wexford Bridge has headroom 5·8m at MHWS, and there are three more low bridges, but for small shallow-draft vessels the Slaney is navigable as far as Enniscorthy, 14M upstream.

**Pollduff**
52°34'N 6°11·4'W, *AC1787*
This bay, with its pier close NW of Cahore Point, offers a pleasant temporary or passage anchorage in offshore winds and is a handy place to lie over if awaiting a fair tide. From the S, give the shore SE of the pier a berth of a cable to avoid rocks with 1m in the bay. From the N, keep the pierhead bearing not less than 210° to avoid a sandspit with 0.8m and a rock at its outer end, off Glascarrig Point, 5 cables N. Anchor N or NE of the pierhead in 2 to 3m. The pier has 1m at its outer end and may offer a temporary alongside berth with sufficient rise of tide, although the range is very small. Constant −0400 Dublin, MHWS 1·2m, MHWN 0·8m.

*The Raven Point from the S*

*Wexford from the approach channel - Black Man beacon, R*

*Polduff pier from the NE*

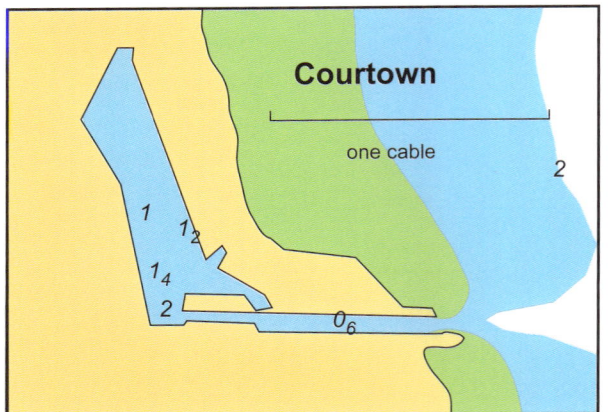

Pub near the pier, shop 400m, filling station 1·5 km. Temporary anchorage in offshore winds is also feasible NW of Roney Rock, 2M N of Pollduff.

## COURTOWN

52°38'·6N 6°13'W, *AC1787 and Plan*

This little harbour 4·5M N of Pollduff provides good shelter and an interesting port of call, but the approach is dangerous in strong onshore winds or any onshore swell. The entrance channel is 30m wide and has 0·6m, and the S part of the inner harbour has 1·0m alongside the walls. After heavy onshore winds, depths in the approach may be reduced. The N half of the inner harbour is entirely taken up with moorings. In winds between SW and NW, anchorage is available 2 cables off the piers in 6 to 7m, sand. Constant –0330

*Courtown Harbour entrance from the E*

*Courtown from the SE*

Dublin, MHWS 1·1m, MHWN 0·6m.

Shops, PO, pubs, restaurants, filling station, laundry. RNLI inshore lifeboat station. Courtown Sailing Club, phone 055 25307, www.courtownsc.com.

**Courtown to Arklow**

In daylight, the passage inside Glassgorman Bank is straightforward. Head for Kilmichael Point, and when Tara Hill bears W, stay 5 cables off the shore. If passing close outside Glassgorman Bank, make sure the tide does not set the yacht W of the line between the two port-hand buoys. Arklow Rock, to the SE of the town, has been half quarried away, and the stone is shipped out from the Roadstone Harbour, which is not available to yachts.

**ARKLOW**

52°47'·7N 6°08'W, *AC1787, 1468, 633*

The harbour area of the once-busy port of Arklow (8500), at the mouth of the Avoca River, is undergoing major redevelopment at the time of writing in 2007. Its boatyard was world-famous, and built the sail training ship *Asgard II* and Francis Chichester's *Gypsy Moth IV.* Two piers projecting NE from the river mouth protect the harbour, quays line the river banks for half a mile, and there is a dock 0·5 cable by 1 cable on the S side. The 50-berth marina occupies a smaller dock on the N side, and there is a 100m-long pontoon upstream of the marina entrance. Arklow no longer handles cargo vessels. Check www.irishcruisingclub.com for the latest information on the redevelopment work. The entrance is hazardous in strong winds between NE and S, and a swell from the N or NE can penetrate right into the river. Strong SE to SW winds raise tidal levels, while strong NW to NE winds lower them.

The small marina has limited manoeuvring space, and yachts of 12m and above should berth on the pontoon in the river in preference. The S side of the channel upstream of the marina entrance and opposite the pontoon is shoal, and a conical red buoy marks the limit of the deep

*Arklow Harbour from the NW; pontoon and marina centre L, dock upper R*

*Arklow entrance from the NE*

channel. An alongside berth may be available in the dock; contact the HM. The SW side of the dock is shallow and partly occupied by the ship lift. The lifeboat berth is in the S corner.

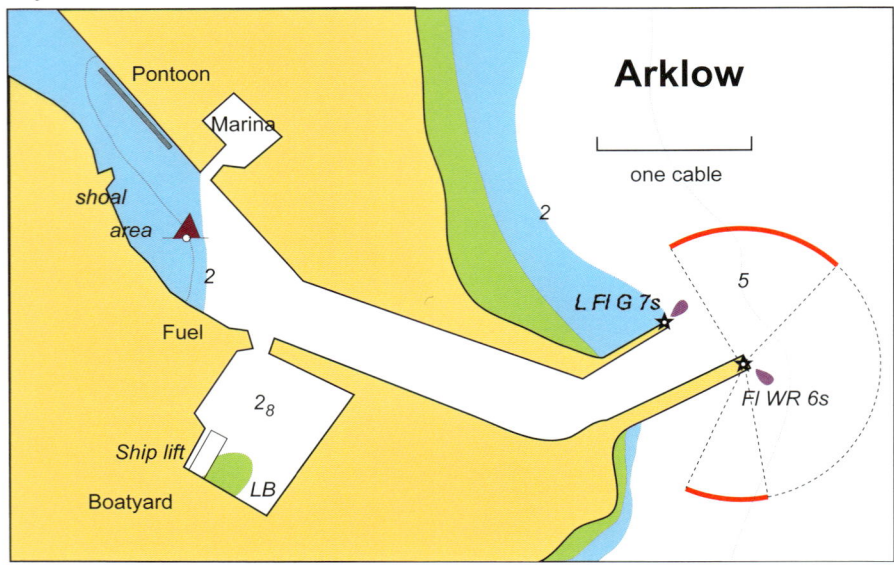

### Facilities

Water on the pontoons. Diesel on the quayside in front of the harbour office. Some chandlery available at the hardware shop on the quay. Supermarkets, shops, pubs, restaurants, banks, ATMs, Internet access, doctors in town, 1 km. Bus and train connections to Dublin and Rosslare. RNLI all-weather lifeboat station.

Constant –0230 Dublin, MHWS 1·7m, MHWN 1·4m, MLWN 1·2m, MLWS 0·8m.

### ARKLOW TO DALKEY

*AC 1787, 1468, Imray C61*

The coast continues in sandy bays and rocky headlands, of which Wicklow Head and Bray Head are the boldest. Here and there are significant coast-protection works; this part of Ireland suffers the most from erosion by the sea. The offshore banks are a salient feature all the way to Dublin Bay.

The pleasant town of Wicklow (6400) sits close N of Wicklow Head, at the mouth of the Leitrim River. Wicklow's most celebrated son was Captain Robert Halpin, a distinguished 19th century seafarer who was master of Brunel's *Great Eastern* when she laid the first transatlantic telegraph cable. The Captain's fine house, Tinakilly, is now a hotel.

The small harbour at Greystones incorporates a wide circular pier-head called the Kish Base, a legacy of the construction project for the Kish Bank lighthouse in 1965. The sections of the revolutionary telescopic concrete structure had each to be cast in one piece, and they had to be flawless. When it came to the lowest and largest

*Arklow pontoon. The marina entrance is to the R of the red light mast*

*Wicklow Head from the NW*

casting, the first attempt cracked, and so was downgraded from lighthouse base to harbour breakwater.

## Tidal Streams

The streams close S of Wicklow Head and across the N end of the Arklow Bank are among the strongest on this section of coast, reaching 4 kn at springs, turning N at approximately LW Dublin and S at HW Dublin. These rates may also be attained between Bray Head and the Codling Bank; between the South Codling and North India buoys; and within 5 cables of the W side of the India Bank. There are also strong streams and eddies between Wicklow Head and Wicklow harbour entrance.

## Dangers

**Arklow Bank**, sandbank drying in places, extending for 13M from 52°41'N to 52°54'N in 5°57'W, E of Arklow. There is a wind farm of seven turbines on the bank, each turbine 73m high with 104m diameter blades.

**Wolf Rock,** dries 1m, 5 cables offshore 3M S of Wicklow Head

**Horse Shoe Shoal**, 0·5m, 1M S of Wicklow Head

**India Bank**, sandbank with 3·5m, 6M NE of Wicklow Head

**Codling Bank**, with 2·6m, 8M E by S of Greystones. The rocky bottom here is covered with narrow ridges of gravel and large boulders

**Breaches Shoal,** 5m, 1·3M offshore 4M SE of Greystones

**Moulditch Shoal,** 3·8m, 7 cables offshore 1·4M SE of Greystones

**Bray Bank** and **Kish Bank**, contiguous sandbanks forming a shoal with 1·6m in places,

extending 10M from 53°09'N to 53°19'N in 5°56'W, E of Bray Head and Sorrento Point

## Lights and Marks

*Arklow and Approaches:*
**No 2 Arklow** buoy, PHM Fl R 6s
**North Arklow** buoy, N Card Q
**Arklow Bank Wind Farm,** seven turbines each Fl Y 5s and a **Mast** 2Fl Y 3s 40m to the south of the turbines
*Wicklow and Approaches:*
**Horseshoe** buoy, PHM Fl R 3s
**Wicklow Head,** white tower Fl(3) 15s 37m 23M
**Wicklow** outfall**,** Fl(4) Y 10s
**Wicklow West Pier,** Iso G 4s 5m 6M
**Wicklow East Pier,** white tower with red base, Fl WR 5s 11m 6M, R136°–293° W293°–136°. Shows red to N and E over the approach from seaward, white inshore and over the harbour
**West Packet Quay,** Fl WG 10s 5m 6M, G076–256° W256°–076°. Shows green to N, white to S
*Wicklow to Dalkey Island:*
**South India** buoy, S Card Q(6)+L Fl 15s
**North India** buoy, N Card Q
**Codling,** LANBY Fl 4s 12m 15M, Horn 20s, Racon (G) 10M
**South Codling** buoy, S Card VQ(6)+L Fl 10s
**East Codling** buoy, PHM Fl(4) R 10s
**West Codling** buoy, SHM Fl G 10s
**Breaches Shoal** buoy, PHM Fl(2) R 6s
**Moulditch Bank** buoy, PHM Fl R 10s
**Greystones** outfall buoy, Fl Y 5s
**Bray** outfall buoy, Fl (4) Y 10s
**Killiney** outfall buoy, Fl Y 3s
**East Kish** buoy, PHM Fl(2) R 10s
**North Kish** buoy, N Card VQ
**Kish Bank,** white tower, red band, Fl(2) 20s 29m 22M, Horn (2) 30s, Racon (T) 15M, AIS
**Bennett Bank** buoy, S Card Q(6)+L Fl 15s
**Muglins** beacon, white tower, red band Fl 5s 14m 11M

## Directions

North of Arklow a berth of 4 cables clears all dangers as far as Jack's Hole, 8M from Arklow,

*Wolf Rock (breaking) from the SE*

but the unmarked Wolf Rock is 5 cables offshore 1M further N. It lies opposite the largest of the conspicuous sand dunes on shore *(see photograph)*. The Horseshoe Shoal, 1M S of Wicklow Head, is marked by a port-hand buoy which should normally be left to port; but a least depth of 8m inside the Horseshoe Shoal may be found, in settled or offshore weather, by staying a cable from the cliffs S of Wicklow Head.

Temporary anchorage in fine weather may be found in any of the bays. Jack's Hole is perhaps the most attractive of these anchorages; beware the drying reef extending NNE from the point.

## WICKLOW
52°59'·1N 6°02'W, *AC1468, 633*
Wicklow Harbour lies 1·5M NW of Wicklow Head, and is protected by 250m-long breakwaters extending NW and NE from the shores on either side of the mouth of the Leitrim River. The harbour is a significant commercial port, typically handling two or three cargo vessels a week. The principal trade is in coal and building materials. The energetic and hospitable Wicklow Sailing Club organises the prestigious biennial Round Ireland Race, and the race starts and finishes here.

### Directions
The harbour is almost always accessible. Approching from the S, beware Planet Rock, 0·8m, 0·5 cable to seaward of the mid-point of the E breakwater, and beware also of the strong tidal streams NW of Wicklow Head, which can set a vessel inshore. The area inside the harbour to the S of the W breakwater is occupied by moorings, and the remaining space in the outer harbour is required by commercial vessels for manoeuvring, so there is no room to anchor. Visiting yachts should berth alongside the East Pier and contact the HM for advice. Do not obstruct the lifeboat slip. In heavy weather it may be possible to secure a temporary berth out of the swell, in the river upstream of the Packet Quay. HM phone 0404 67455. Constant −0045 Dublin, MHWS 2·7m, MHWN 2·3m, MLWN 0·9m, MLWS 0·5m.

### Facilities
Supermarkets, shops, pubs, restaurants, PO, banks, ATMs, Internet access, doctors. RNLI all-weather lifeboat station. Bus and train connections to Dublin and Rosslare.

*Wicklow Harbour from the SW*

*Wicklow Harbour entrance from the NE*

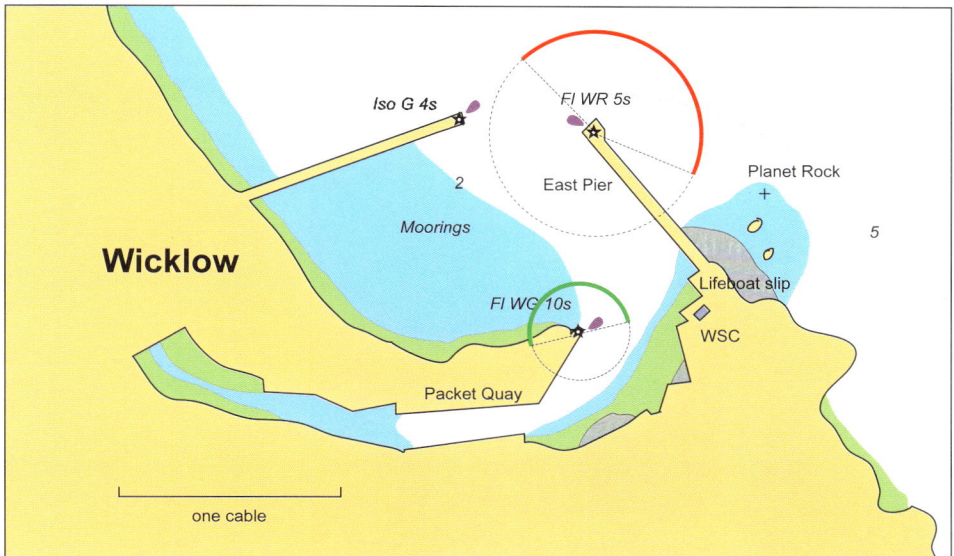

Iso G 4s
Fl WR 5s
East Pier
Planet Rock
Moorings
**Wicklow**
5
Fl WG 10s
Lifeboat slip
WSC
Packet Quay
one cable

## Greystones

53°09'·2N 6°03'·4W, *AC1468, SC5621·7*

Greystones harbour is small, and crowded with small craft, but the inside of the large circular pierhead of the E pier has 2m. The rest of the harbour dries. Greystones Sailing Club (01 287 4628) welcomes visitors. Supermarkets, shops, PO, pubs, restaurants, filling station, banks, ATMs, doctors in Greystones.

*Greystones Harbour from the S*

*Bray Harbour entrance from the NE*

## Bray

53°12'·7N 6°05'·7W, *AC1468, SC5621·7*

The entrance to the small harbour at Bray faces N and has 1·5m, but the harbour almost entirely dries out, and has many moored boats which can take the ground. The outermost berth on the N pier has 0·1m and that on the S pier dries 0·2m, but the centre of the harbour is shallower. There is a strong outflow from the river which runs through the harbour, even on the flood tide. Constant –0006 Dublin.

Bray Sailing Club (01 286 0272) has bar and showers, and welcomes visitors. Bray has all the facilities of a town of 25,000 people. Buses to Dublin, train connections to Dublin and Rosslare.

## Killiney Bay

53°16'N 6°06'W

Anchorage is available in offshore winds at the N end of Killiney Bay, but it is very much subject to swell.

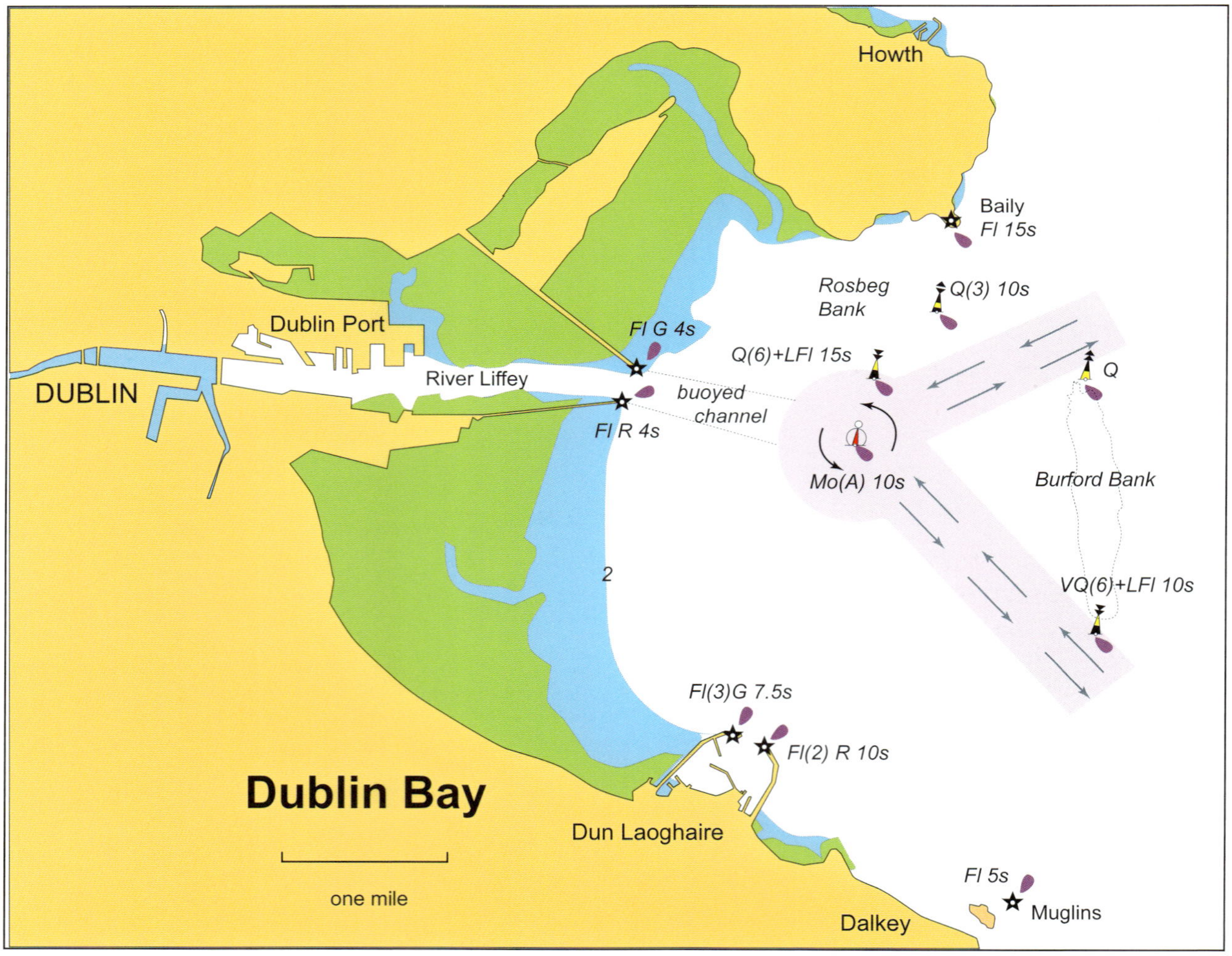

*Dalkey Sound from the SW; Sorrento Point centre L, Dalkey Island and Muglins centre R, Howth top L*

## DUBLIN BAY

*AC1468, 1415, SC5621, Imray C61; see Plan*
Dublin Bay, extending from Dalkey Island to the Baily of Howth, is one of Ireland's most popular sailing areas and also includes the approaches to the port of Dublin, the busiest on the island. Dublin handles ferries up to 50,000 tons, container ships, bulk carriers, car carriers and tankers. Dun Laoghaire, on the S side of the bay, is a terminus for a high speed ferry, the base of operations for the Irish Lights, and the home of four of Ireland's senior yacht clubs. Dun Laoghaire Harbour, a quarter of a square mile in area with breakwaters almost a mile long, was built as the Royal Navy's Irish Sea base, and at the time of its completion in 1847 was one of the largest man-made harbours in the world.

### Tidal Streams

The flood tide sweeps round the bay from Dalkey Island to rejoin the main stream outside the Rosbeg Bank. Along the S shore the stream turns N at +0315 Dublin and S at -0310 Dublin. Along the N shore, the tide runs seaward for 9 hours out of 12, turning NE at +0315 Dublin and SW at -0015 Dublin. There is little stream in the centre of the bay, but at the Kish Bank the tide reaches 3·25 kn at springs, turning N at LW Dublin and S at HW Dublin. At the Baily, the E-going stream causes overfalls, which can be significant, where it meets the main stream.

Dublin (North Wall) is the Tidal Standard Port for the coast from Cahore Point to Carlingford Lough.

### Dangers

**Leac Buidhe,** dries about 1m, 2 cables N of Dalkey Island

**Burford Bank**, with 4·6m in places, extending 2M N-S between 53°18'·5N and 53°20'·5N in 6°01'·5W

**Rosbeg Bank,** with 4·6m in places, 7 cables SW of the Baily

*Sorrento Point, Dalkey; Dalkey Island R with the Howth peninsula beyond.*

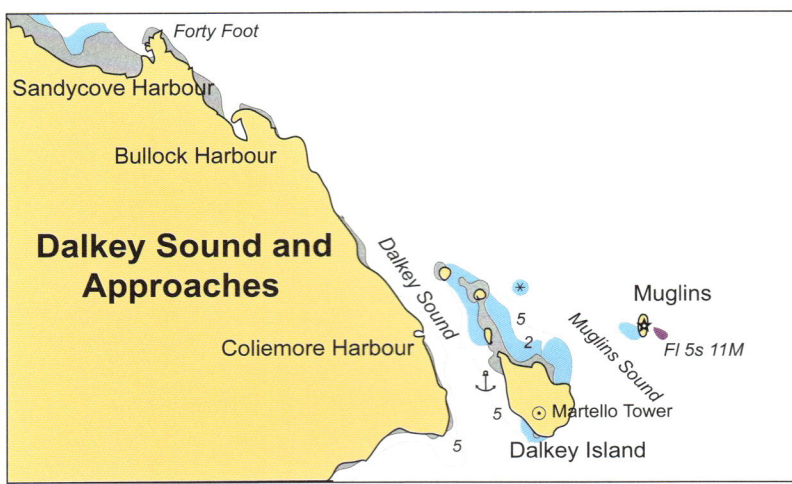

**Dalkey Sound and Approaches**

*Dublin and Approaches*

**Dublin Bay** buoy, safe water mark RWVS, Mo(A) 10s, Racon (M)
**No 1** buoy, SHM Fl(3) G 5s
**No 3** buoy, SHM QG
**No 4** buoy, PHM IQR
**No 5** buoy, SHM Fl G 5s
**No 6** buoy, PHM Fl R 2s
**Poolbeg**, red tower Fl R 4s 20m 10M
**North Bull**, green tower Fl G 4s 15m 10M
The Liffey channel is marked by port-and starboard-hand buoys, Fl R and Fl G, and by
**North Bank**, green tower Oc G 8s 10m 16M.

**South Burford** buoy, S Card VQ(6)+L Fl 10s
**North Burford** buoy, N Card Q
**Rosbeg South** buoy, S Card Q(6)+LFl 15s
**Rosbeg East** buoy, E Card Q(3) 10s
**Baily,** grey tower, Fl 15s 41m 26M

**Obstructions** variable in depth, close N of the dredged channel 1·2M E of the North Bull light

**Rubble breakwater** drying 1.4m, extending 5 cables SE from the Bull Wall and forming the N side of the entrance to the River Liffey

**Lights and Marks**

*Dun Laoghaire*

**East Breakwater Head**, grey tower Fl(2) R 10s 16m 17M, Horn 30s

**Outfall**, Fl Y 5s

**West Breakwater Head**, grey tower Fl(3) G 8s 11m 7M

**West Marina Breakwater**, pole beacon, 2×FG vert

**East Marina Breakwater**, pole beacon, 2×FR vert

**No 2 (Marina) fairway** buoys, PHM and SHM, Fl R and Fl G respectively

**Traffic Separation Scheme**

There are two short Traffic Separation Schemes in the entrance to Dublin Bay, close SW and NW of the Burford Bank. The former scheme is centred 2·5M NE of Dalkey Island and the latter 1·2M SE of the Baily. These schemes lead to a third, rotatory anticlockwise, centred on the Dublin Bay buoy. For directions see *Port of Dublin Small Craft (Leisure) Regulations,* below.

*Dalkey Island from the Sound; the white-painted well is visible between the church and the Martello tower*

*Coliemore Harbour from the SE*

*Dun Laoghaire Harbour from the SW; the marina, centre L and St Michael's Pier ferry terminal, centre. The Great South Wall at the entrance to the Liffey, upper L; Howth peninsula and Lambay island upper R*

## Dalkey
53°16'·1N 6°05'W

Dalkey Sound is clean on the mainland side and a berth of a cable clears all the dangers on the island side. Muglins Sound is also easily navigable over a width of 1·5 cables but beware Leac Buidhe, a cable NE of the string of islets and rocks stretching NW from Dalkey Island. Anchorage is available on the SW side of Dalkey Island, in 4m, off the white-painted well SE of the landing place.

There are three tiny harbours near Dalkey: Coliemore, Bullock and Sandycove. None of them is safe for a stranger to enter. Adjacent to Sandycove Harbour is the Forty Foot, a natural swimming-pool where it is traditional for gentlemen (and more recently ladies as well) to take their daily dip, often without the benefit of clothing. In onshore weather, a close approach to the coast here may be hazardous.

## DUN LAOGHAIRE
53°18'·3N 6°07'·7W *AC1415, SC5621·13*

Dun Laoghaire Harbour is home to four yacht clubs – the Royal Irish, the Royal St George,
the National, and Dun Laoghaire Motor Yacht Club – and also an 820-berth marina, an all-weather lifeboat and the Irish Lights Vessel *Granuaile*. The Irish Lights' headquarters and principal engineering depot adjoin the harbour. A 25,000-ton high speed ferry runs from Dun Laoghaire to Holyhead.

### Directions
The pierheads are conspicuous from seaward. The main fairway, used by the ferry, runs NE from the RoRo terminal at St Michael's Pier and extends 3 cables beyond the entrance, into Dublin Bay. When entering, keep a good lookout for traffic movements and keep a listening watch on VHF Ch 14. Do not obstruct the ferry, and give the pierheads a good berth. Drying boulders extend 8m W from the head of the E pier. There is a speed limit of 8 knots in the harbour. The marina entrance (No 2 fairway) is marked by a pair of lateral buoys. Anchoring is prohibited within the harbour.

Const as Dublin, MHWS 4·1m, MHWN 3·4m, MLWN 1·5m, MLWS 0·6m

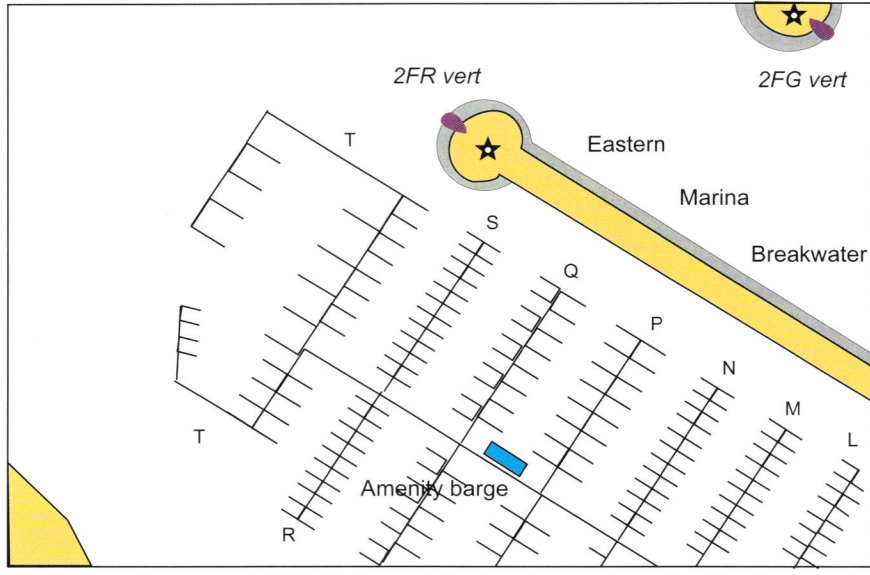

## Marina

The marina monitors VHF Ch 37 and 80 (M1 and M2), phone 01 202 0040, www. dlmarina.com. Visitors are normally accommodated on the outer hammerheads P, Q, S and T. The pontoons between the West Marina Breakwater and the West Pier are for resident berth-holders only.

When she is in Dun Laoghaire, ILV *Granuaile* uses berths near the root of the E pier and at the CIL depot on the SW side of the harbour, behind the marina. She is an extremely manoeu-

*Dun Laoghaire Harbour entrance from the NE*

*The Liffey, looking up-river; Poolbeg Marina, foreground, East Link bridge beyond, Dublin City Moorings and the Macken Street bridge works top centre. Ringsend basin, top L.*

vrable ship, but it is essential not to obstruct the No.2 Fairway or the area to the W of the marina pontoons.

## Facilities

Water, shore power, diesel, petrol, laundry at the marina. Apart from the facilities in the main marina building, there is a barge with toilets and showers alongside the main gangway between piers P and Q. The four yacht clubs are open to visitors who are members of clubs with reciprocal arrangements, and they all have dining and bar facilities. Chandlery, Viking Marine 01 280 6654, Windmill Marine 01 280 5325, Western Marine 01 280 0321; sailmakers, Downers 01 280 4826; boatyard services, MGM Marine 01 280 2020 and 087 135 2189; for rigging and electrical specialists, contact the marina. Electronic repairs, Marine Electronic Services (Raymarine agents), 086 254 7550. Taxis, 01 285 7777 and 01 285 5444; bus and train services to Dublin and Rosslare. RNLI all-weather lifeboat station.

## Yacht Clubs

National YC, 01 280 5725; Royal St George YC, 01 280 1811; Royal Irish YC, 01 280 9452; Dun Laoghaire Motor YC, 01 280 1370.

## Anchorage

Anchorage is available in Scotsman's Bay, a cable SE of the E pier, in 6m, well sheltered from winds between WNW and SSE.

## DUBLIN

53°20'·3N 6°07'W
*AC1415, SC5621·10*

Ireland's capital city was founded by the Vikings in 988 AD, but the site at the mouth of the Liffey was inhabited long before that. The name derives from the Irish *dubh linn,* "black pool", but the modern Irish name, Baile Atha Cliath, means "township at the ford of the hurdles" and commemorates the ancient crossing point here, the lowest on the river. Dublin, the city of James Joyce, Jonathan Swift and Oscar Wilde, the birthplace of Bram Stoker and the Duke of Wellington, is renowned worldwide for its cultural and historical treasures and its overflowing welcome.

The Liffey flows into Dublin Bay between the projecting breakwaters of the Great South Wall and the North Bull, the latter covering at HW. The port area starts 1M inside the pier heads and extends for 1·5M to the opening East Link Bridge. Close downstream of the bridge

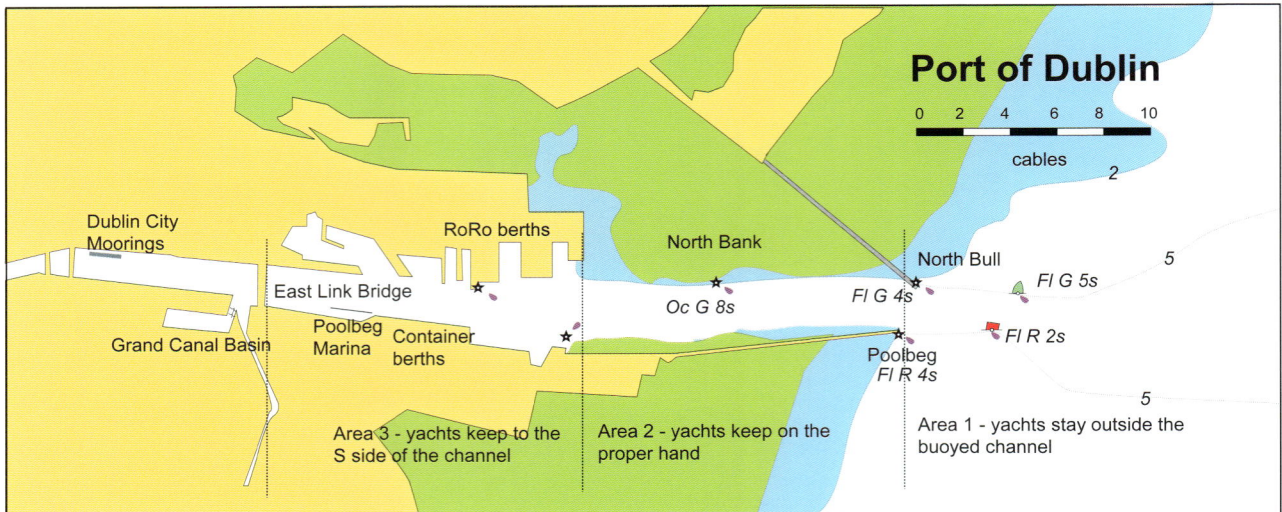

is Poolbeg Marina, and 5 cables upstream are the Dublin City Moorings. The river is then spanned by the Sean O'Casey Bridge, the first of the city's many low bridges.

## Caution

Dublin is Ireland's busiest port, and large passenger and cargo vessels arrive and leave around the clock. The fairway from the Dublin Bay buoy to the East Link Bridge is a "narrow channel" within the meaning of IRPCS Rule 9, which specifies that in such a channel vessels under 20m in length, and sailing vessels, shall not impede large vessels which can safely navigate only within the channel. The Port Company's jurisdiction extends out to a line joining the Baily, the Burford Bank and Dalkey Island and includes the fairway, and the Traffic Separation Schemes NE and SW of the Dublin Bay buoy.

## Port of Dublin Small Craft (Leisure) Regulations *(see Plan)*

The following rules must be observed at all times by leisure craft navigating within the Port area defined above.

- Stay out of the TSS areas by passing either within 1M SE of the Baily or within 2M NE of Dalkey Island. Do not sail over the Burford Bank or otherwise between the two TSS areas.
- Between the Dublin Bay Buoy and Poolbeg Lighthouse, stay outside the buoyed channel.
- Between Poolbeg Lighthouse and the No.14 buoy (in front of the power station) keep well to starboard; N side inbound, S side outbound.
- Upstream of the No.14 buoy, keep to the S side of the channel, beside the container berths here and away from the docks and RoRo berths on the N side. Do not enter any of these docks.
- When obliged to cross the channel, do so as nearly as possible at right angles.
- When in the channel, proceed under power only.
- High-speed power craft must not exceed a moderate speed (10 knots or so) while within the port area.
- Inform Dublin Port Radio on VHF Ch 12 of your position and intentions before entering or leaving the port, obey any instructions given, and maintain a listening watch on Ch 12 while transiting the port.

Copies of the full Regulations are available from the

*River Liffey entrance from the E; Poolbeg lighthouse and the conspicuous chimneys of Poolbeg power station*

*Port of Dublin, looking up-river, from close W of the No.14 buoy. Leisure craft must keep to the S side of the river in this zone. Poolbeg Marina is immediately beyond the container berths, extreme L*

HM, 01 887 6000, www.dublinport.ie, or from any of the Dublin area marinas.

## POOLBEG MARINA

The 100-berth marina is situated on the S side immediately upstream of the container terminal. It is operated by Poolbeg Yacht and Boat Club. There is a minimum depth of 3m alongside. Phone 01 668 9983 for a berth or tie up to the long outside pontoon.

## Facilities

Water, diesel, pumpout, shore power, use of clubhouse facilities including bar, dining room and showers. Shops, PO, laundry, banks, ATMs, doctor at Ringsend, 1 km; bus services to Dublin city centre.

## East Link Bridge

The bridge has headroom 2·25m when closed, and opens, on request, at 1100, 1500 and 2100 daily. The lifting span, immediately N of the

*Poolbeg Marina*

*East Link Bridge, looking up-river*

*Dublin City Moorings*

bridge cabin and marked by high-visibility orange panels, is 31m wide. Requests for opening should be made in advance (by at least 20 minutes, but much more is appreciated) to Dublin Port on VHF Ch 12 or phone 01 887 6070. The bridge operator may be contacted direct on Ch.12 at callsign "East Link". The bridge shows traffic signals:

• 3 red lights – vessels may not proceed
• 3 green lights – vessels may proceed, one way at a time
• 3 flashing red lights – emergency; all vessels stop or divert.

Dublin City Moorings are 5 cables upstream of the bridge.

## Dublin City Moorings
This is a 175m-long pontoon parallel to Custom House Quay on the north bank of the Liffey in the city centre. The facility is operated by Dublin Docklands Development Authority; phone 01 818 3300 or mobile 086 856 8113 to arrange a berth. There is 4·2m of water at the pontoon, which can accommodate vessels up to 1000t and has 24-hour security.

## Facilities
Water and shore power on the pontoon, showers and toilets. Ashore, all the facilities of a capital city and major international business and tourist centre. Train and bus connections to all parts of Ireland. Taxis at Busáras, 200m N from Sean O'Casey Bridge. See under Dun Laoghaire and Howth for specific marine services in the greater Dublin area.

Dublin (North Wall) is a Tidal Standard Port; MHWS 4·1m, MHWN 3·4m, MLWN 1·5m, MLWS 0·6m.

## Macken Street Bridge
At the the time of writing (late 2007) a new bridge is under construction at Macken Street, midway between the East Link Bridge and the Dublin City Moorings. When completed the new bridge will have an opening span and will be operated in concert with the East Link Bridge.

## Grand Canal
The Grand Canal, linking the Liffey with the Shannon, is entered via a lock on the south side close upstream of the East Link Bridge and leading to Ringsend Basin. The canal runs for 71M to Shannon Harbour, S of Athlone, with 36 locks, and has the following restrictions: length 18·5m, beam 3·9m, draft 1·2m, air draft 2·7m. Refer to *The Inland Waterways of Ireland* by Jane Cumberlidge, published in 2002 by Imrays, and contact Waterways Ireland 071 965 0898 for further information.

## Clontarf
Clontarf Yacht and Boat Club operates from a slip on the N shore, inside the Bull Wall, reached via a shallow creek running N and W around the main Port area. This is difficult of access to a stranger.

## Bellingham
Anchorage on the N side of Dublin Bay may be found off Bellingham, a tiny harbour 4 cables NW of Drumleck Point, the S tip of the Howth peninsula. Anchor not less than a cable off the harbour in 3 to 5m, well sheltered from NW to ENE, slightly tiderode.

*The Liffey, looking seaward, and Dublin Bay; East Link Bridge, foreground, Ringsend basin and the River Dodder, lower R. Further downriver are Poolbeg Marina, the container berths, Poolbeg power station and the Great South Wall on the S bank, and the main docks and the North Bull on the N bank. Dun Laoghaire harbour (R) and Howth peninsula (L) in the distance.*

# Chapter 2

## Howth to Ardglass

*Howth Harbour and marina from the SW; Ireland's Eye upper L and Lambay beyond*

The harbour at Howth was built 200 years ago, and achieved lasting fame in the annals of Irish national aspirations when in 1914 Erskine Childers, the author of *The Riddle of the Sands,* landed 900 rifles there from his yacht *Asgard* to arm the Republican Volunteers. Today, Howth is a fashionable suburb of Dublin, home to a fine marina and prestigious yacht club, and still a significant fishing port; the original *Asgard* languishes ashore awaiting long-deserved restoration, but in the meantime the fine brigantine *Asgard II* is the national Sail Training ship.

Drogheda was founded in the 10th century at the lowest ford on the Boyne, and by the 1400's was an important fortified city. In 1649, the year of King Charles I's execution, the army of Oliver Cromwell massacred 3000 citizens of the town in one of the worst atrocities in Ireland's long and chequered history; and in 1690 what is perhaps the best-known battle in that history was fought on the banks of the river, 12 miles upstream. Dundalk takes its name from Dún Dealgan, the home of the legendary hero Cúchulainn, and the Cooley Peninsula was the setting for the Táin Bó Cuailnge, the Cattle-Raid of Cooley, among the most celebrated sagas of Celtic mythology, in which Cúchulainn played a starring role.

The scenic Carlingford Lough provides some of the best sailing water on the east coast, but it is also an important commercial waterway. The thriving port of Warrenpoint, on the Newry River at the head of the Lough, took over from the much older port of Newry, five miles further north by river and canal, when the latter lost its vital lock gates in 1974. The gates, and the canal, were re-opened in 2007, the refurbished Albert Basin at Newry is now accessible once again, and the passage up from Warrenpoint is an unexpected delight.

Carlingford Lough bridges the two jurisdictions: Greenore, Carlingford and Omeath are in County Louth, while Newry, Warrenpoint, Rostrevor and Greencastle are in County Down.

Where the Mountains of Mourne sweep down to the sea are the important fishing harbour of Kilkeel, the picturesque harbour of Annalong, and the holiday harbour of Newcastle. The broad sweep of Dundrum Bay ends in the low and rocky headland of St John's Point, where in 1950 the eminent author Brendan Behan was fired as a lighthousekeeper for opening paint tins with the blunt end of a hammer.

**Charts**

SC5621 and SC5612 cover the coastwise passage and Carlingford Lough, but not Drogheda or Dundalk. In terms of individual charts, AC44 Nose of Howth to Ballyquintin Point covers the whole area of this chapter and is adequate if merely passagemaking. AC1431 is needed if going into Drogheda or Dundalk, and AC2800 is essential for Carlingford Lough. AC633 has plans of Howth, Malahide, Rogerstown, Skerries, Killough and Ardglass. Imray's C62 Irish Sea includes plans of Malahide, Skerries, Carlingford Entrance, Kilkeel and Ardglass. At the time of writing there is no published chart of the Newry River and Canal above Warrenpoint.

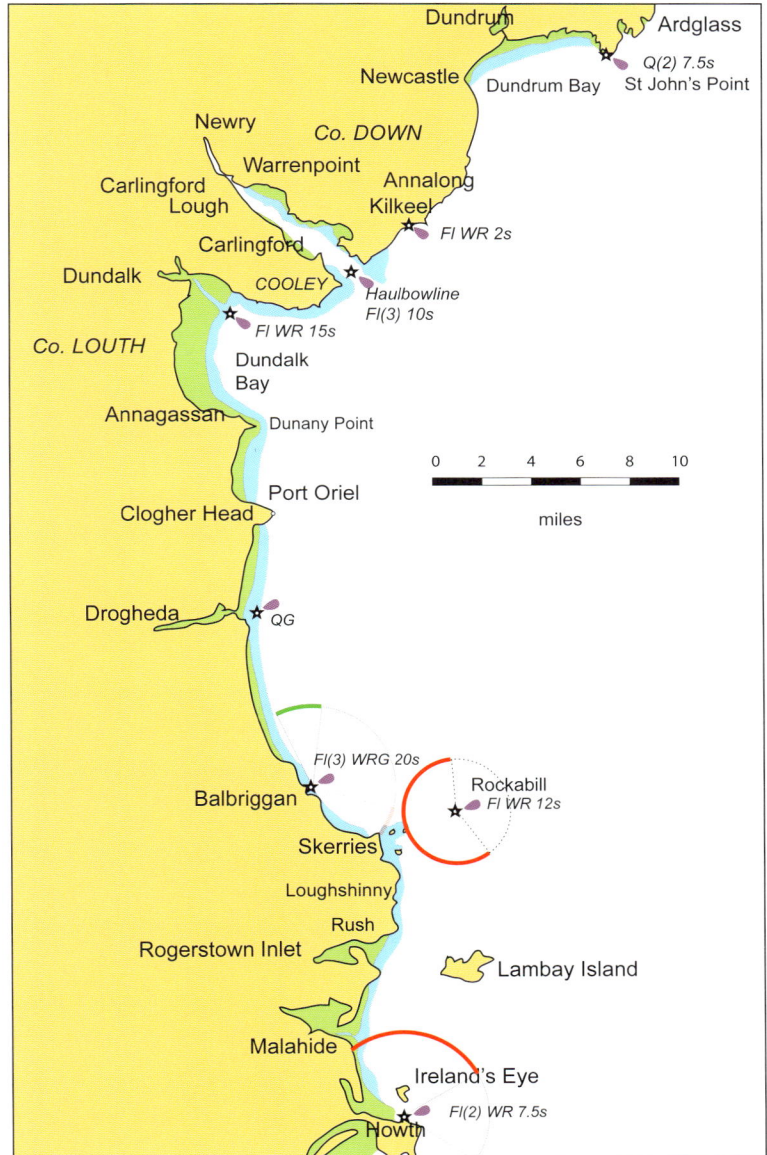

## HOWTH TO SKERRIES

Howth Head consists of three headlands – the Baily, Piper Head and the Nose of Howth, all cliffbound and steep-to. Ireland's Eye is a rugged little island to the N, with cliffs and stacks on its E side, reefs to the S and a shallow bay to the W. Howth Sound, with least depth 2·4m, separates Ireland's Eye from Baldoyle Spit to the W. North of Howth harbour are three wide sandy bays, with Malahide and Rogerstown inlets opening into two of them, and Lambay Island 2M offshore. The coast from here to Skerries is rocky, with the village and pier at Loughshinny standing on a small bay. The Skerries Islands, with shallow sounds between them, lie to the N.

In addition to the navigation marks, the Martello towers – there are no less than seven of them on this short stretch of coast – form useful landmarks, although care must be taken to distinguish which is which.

### Tidal Streams

Close inshore on the N side of the Howth peninsula, the stream turns N at HW Dublin +0445 and S at HW Dublin –0115, and runs at 2 knots at springs. The N-going stream divides at Ireland's Eye, and runs N through

Lambay Sound and NE through Howth Sound, where the S-going ebb begins 15 minutes earlier. Rates attain 2 knots in Howth Sound and 2·5 knots in Lambay Sound.

## Dangers

*Approaches to Howth:*

**Rowan Rocks,** drying up to 1·1m, in two groups extending 2 cables SE and SW of Thulla, at the S end of Ireland's Eye

**Flat Rock,** dries 0·2m, 1 cable NE of Thulla

**Rock** drying 2m, 0·5 cable NE of The Steer, at the N end of Ireland's Eye

**Rock** with c.1m, c.0·3 cable W of The Steer

**Baldoyle Spit,** drying sandbank 7 cables NW of Howth harbour

*Lambay:*

**Burren Rocks,** drying 0·6m, off the W point of Lambay

**Unnamed rock** with 1·2m, 1 cable offshore 1 cable N of Lambay Harbour

**Tayleur (Tailor's) Rocks,** drying, 1·5 cables NNW of Scotch Point, the NW point of Lambay

*Approaches to Skerries:*

**Punch Oak Rock,** with less than 2m, 3 cables SSE of Shenick's Island

**Flat Rock,** dries 0·3m, 2 cables N of Shenick's Island

**Plough Rock,** dries 2·1m, and **Roaring Rock,** with less than 2m, extending 3 cables S of St Patrick's Island

**Unnamed rock** drying 1·5m, 2 cables S of Colt Island

**Dthaun Spit,** 0·6m, extending 1 cable WSW from St Patrick's Island

**Cross Rock,** drying reef extending 2 cables N of Skerries Pier.

## Lights and Marks

*Howth:*

**Rowan Rocks** buoy, E Card Q(3) 10s

**South Rowan** buoy, SHM QG

**Howth** buoy, SHM Fl G 5s

**East Pier,** Fl(2) WR 7·5s 13m W12M R9M, W256°–295° R295°–256°. Shows white over the approach from the E, red elsewhere

**West Pier Extension, Mole Head** Fl G 3s 7m 6M

**Trawler Pier Head,** QR 7m 6M

*Malahide, Rogerstown and Loughshinny:*

**Malahide Fairway** buoy, RWVS L Fl 10s

**Malahide Channel** is marked by four pairs of lateral beacons and two pairs of lateral buoys, Fl R and Fl G

**Rogerstown Channel** buoys, fairway RWVS, and lateral buoys, four pairs red and green, unlit

**Loughshinny,** bent iron perch on the reef, unlit

*Lambay Island:*

**Burren Rocks** perch, W Card, unlit

**Tailor's Rocks** buoy, N Card Q

*Skerries:*

**Cross Rock** buoy, PHM Fl R 10s

**Skerries Pier Head,** white tower Oc R 6s 7m 7M, visible 103°–154°

## HOWTH

53°23'·7N 6°04'·1W

*AC633 and SC5621·10, see Plan*

Howth is a designated fishing harbour and has one of Ireland's premier marinas. The harbour is

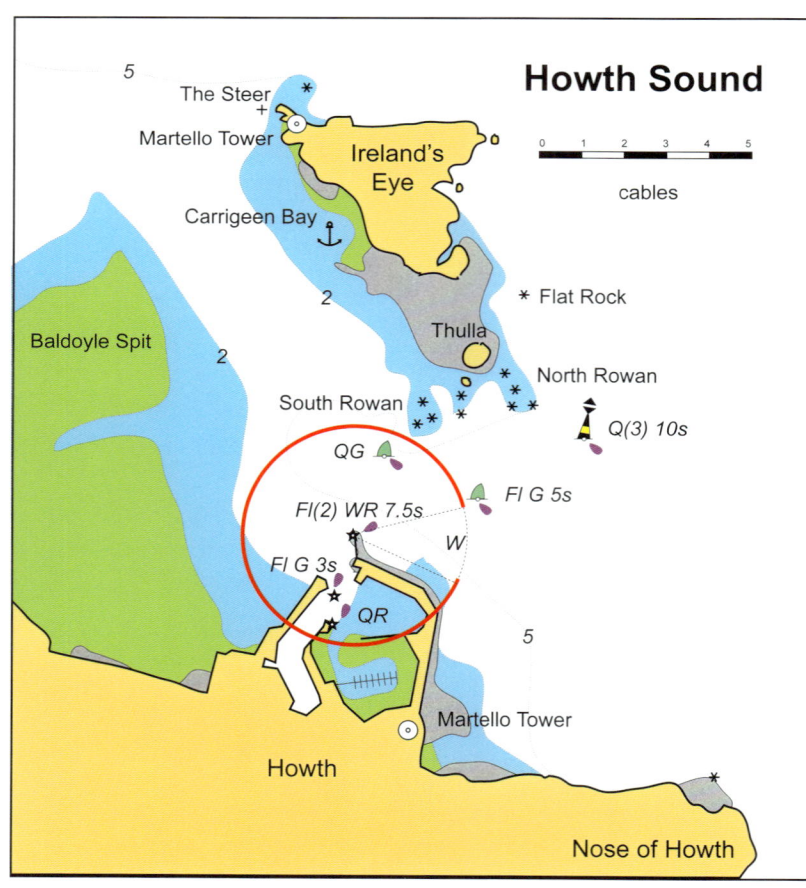

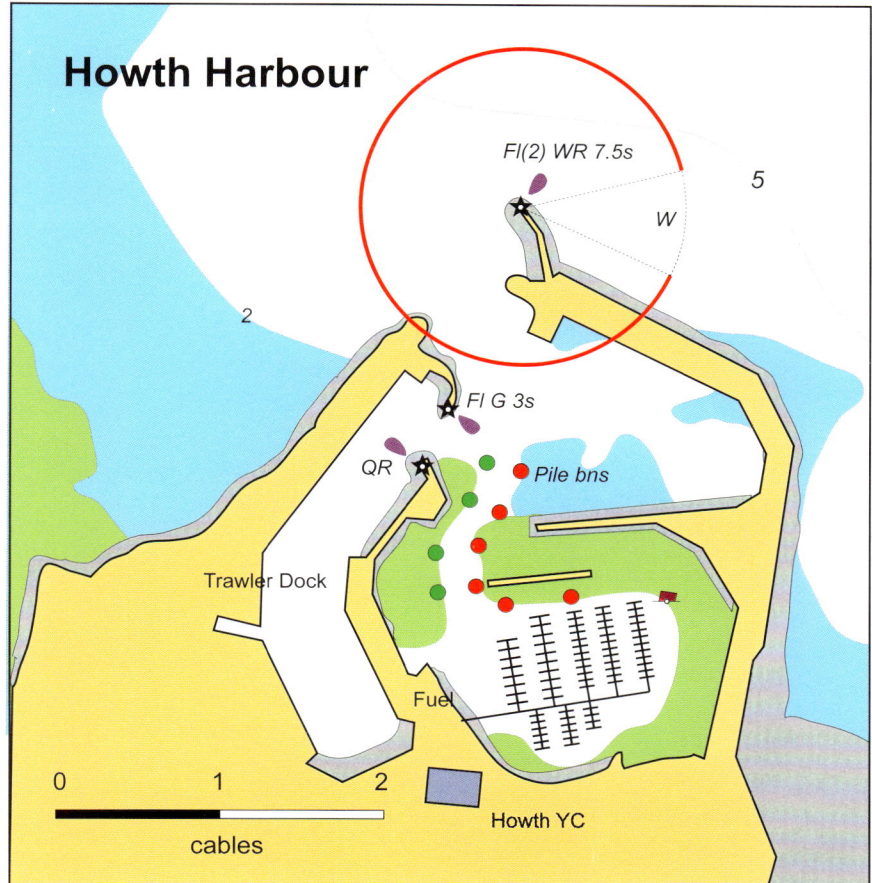

**Howth Harbour**

Fl(2) WR 7.5s

5

W

Fl G 3s

QR

Pile bns

Trawler Dock

Fuel

0    1    2

cables

Howth YC

showers. Visitors have access to the facilities of the YC including bar and restaurant. Diesel (by hose), petrol (in cans), 15t crane, Laundry at the marina. Shops, pubs, restaurants, PO in Howth. Masts & Rigging (Ireland) 086 389 2614; electrical and electronic repairs, Yachtronics 01 839 5222 or 086 254 7700. Chandlery, MPD (Swords) 01 807 5144, Dinghy Supplies 01 832 2312, or Marine Suppliers, Howth 01 832 5835. Taxis, 087 829 5003 or 01 839 6020. Howth is an RNLI all-weather lifeboat station.

**Ireland's Eye**

The island is a nature reserve, privately owned but uninhabited, and the owners have no objection to visitors landing provided common-sense rules and courtesy are observed. They request that visitors behave responsibly, do not stay ashore overnight, do not light fires or leave litter on the island and do not disturb seabirds' nests. The Martello tower and the ruins of St Nessan's Church are protected buildings and must not be interfered with. An intending visitor with a specific good reason to stay on the island should consult Howth YC or HM for advice, and to obtain contact details for the owners.

Howth Sound may be hazardous around LW in gale force winds from the E. Carrigeen Bay, on the SW side of the island, offers attractive temporary anchorage in offshore winds or settled conditions, especially around HW.

managed by the Department of Communications, Energy and Natural Resources and the marina by Howth YC. From the E, leave the Howth and South Rowan buoys to starboard and identify the breakwater end. From the N via Howth Sound, give Ireland's Eye a berth of 2 cables and leave the South Rowan buoy to port. The trawler dock, on the W side of the harbour, is clearly marked as not open to leisure craft. The channel to the marina is marked by green and red pile beacons. Contact the marina on VHF Ch 80 or phone 01 839 2777 for a berth. Constant –0010 Dublin, MHWS 4·1m, MHWN 3·4m, MLWN 1·2m, MLWS 0·5m.

**Facilities**

Water and shore power on the pontoons,

*Howth Harbour entrance from the E; the larger light tower (centre) is unlit*

*Ireland's Eye from the N, with Howth beyond*

# MALAHIDE

53°27'·1N 6°06'·8W

*AC633, SC5621·4, see Plan*

Malahide Inlet is a channel between sand dunes and banks in the centre of the bay 4M NNW of Howth, leading to a large drying lagoon. The channel is shallow and requires occasional maintenance dredging, but is navigable by day or night except around LWS, and well marked and lit. It leads to Malahide village and its fine marina, which has 350 berths and all services.

## Directions

Identify the lit fairway buoy, which is conspicuous 3·2M NNW of Ireland's Eye. The channel runs 1·4M W then WNW, between four pairs of pole beacons and two pairs of buoys, to the marina entrance. The least depth

is 1·6m (2007), so the marina is accessible in reasonable weather at all times except around LWS; but the depths can change. Care must be taken not to confuse Rogerstown inlet, to the N, with Malahide; the two bays are similar in appearance from seaward, but Rogerstown inlet is shallower and unlit.

## Marina

Call the marina on VHF Ch 37 (M1) or 80 (M2) or phone 01 845 4129 for a berth. The visitors' berths are on the finger pontoons along the N breakwater. The breakwaters are floating, and the tidal stream runs strongly through the marina.

## Facilities

Water and shore power on the pontoons,

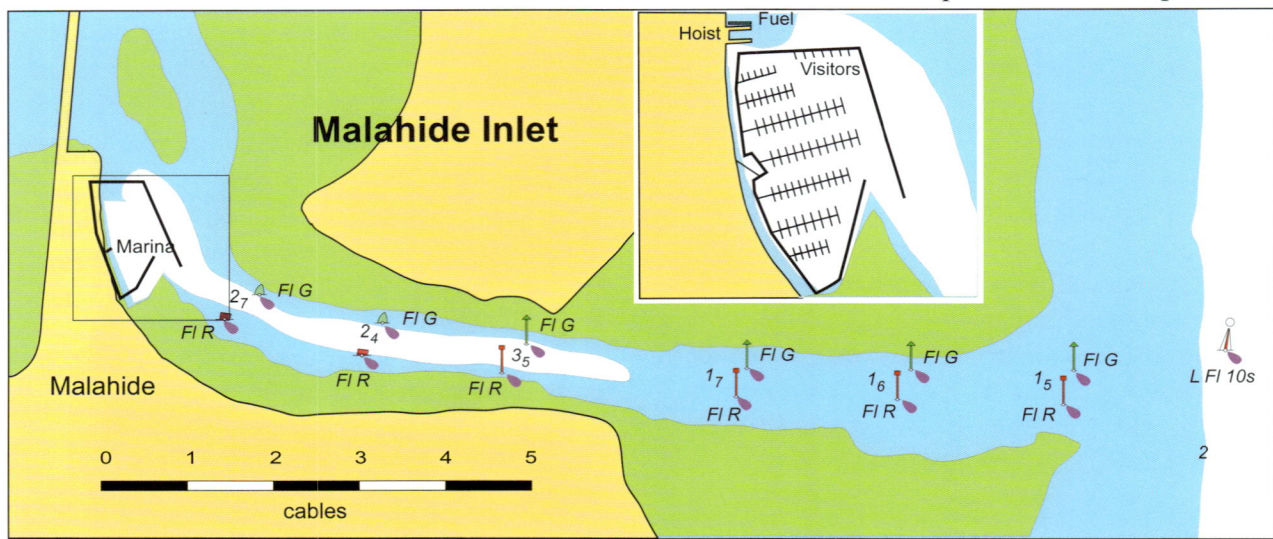

*Malahide Inlet from seaward*

*Malahide Inlet from the ESE; marina at top.*

*Malahide Marina. The lagoon beyond the railway bridge largely dries.*

pumpout station, laundry, diesel (by hose), petrol (in cans), 30-tonne travelhoist. Chandlery, BJ Marine; mechanical, electronic and rigging repairs (contact the marina); GRP repairs, Colin Coady 087 677 9605; sailmaker, Philip Watson, pwatson@indigo.ie. Malahide YC (01 845 3372) welcomes visitors. Shops, pubs, restaurants, PO, banks, ATMs, Internet access, doctors in Malahide village.

Constant –0015 Dublin, MHWS 4·5m, MHWN 3·3m, MLWN 1·7m, MLWS 0·3m.

## Lambay Island

53°29'·5N 6°03'W
*AC44, SC5621 and Plan*

The only inhabited island on Ireland's east coast is privately owned, and visitors are – regrettably – unwelcome. Landing may be regarded as out of the question. There are however several bays around the island offering at least temporary anchorage in offshore winds or settled conditions. The island is farmed, and has a resident population of 6. Evidence has been found of occupation in Mesolithic times, and the island has a fascinating history. In 1853 the White Star Line ship *Tayleur*, on her maiden voyage, was wrecked on the rocks N of Lambay, with the loss of 370 lives. The rocks are now named after her, although the charts use the spelling "Tailor's Rocks".

*Lambay harbour from the W*

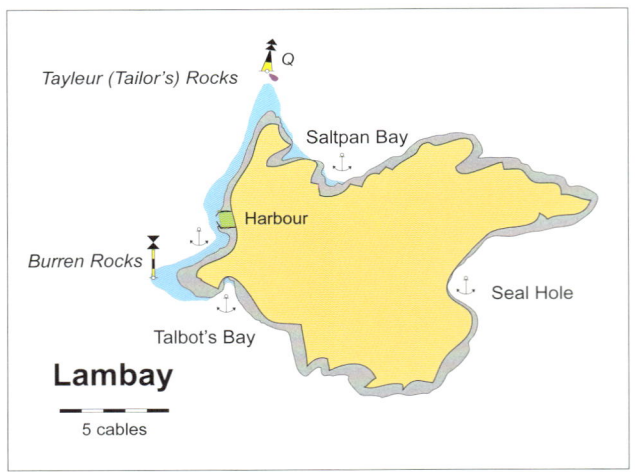

**Anchorages**

In winds between NE and S, the bay close S of the harbour offers good shelter. Talbot's Bay is sheltered from N to ESE, and Saltpan Bay is relatively swell-free in winds from the S quarter. All these bays have 3 to 4m on sand. Seal Hole, on the E side, provides a temporary anchorage close to the cliffs.

**ROGERSTOWN INLET**

53°30'·2N 6°05'·8W

*AC633, SC5621·4 and Plan*

Rush Sailing Club has its clubhouse and slip on the N side of this inlet 3·4M N by E of Malahide. The inlet, between drying banks and sand dunes, has a channel well marked

*Rogerstown Inlet from the S; pier, centre L*

*Rogerstown Inlet from seaward*

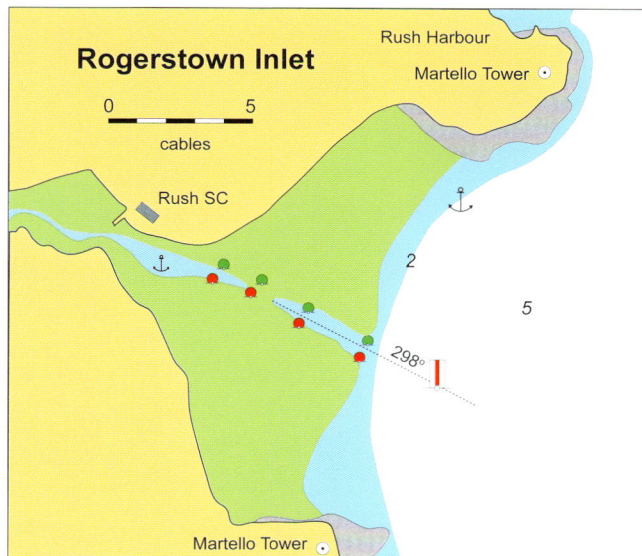

**Rogerstown Inlet**

Rush Harbour

Martello Tower ⊙

0     5
cables

Rush SC

2

5

298°

Martello Tower ⊙

(in summer) by the Club with a small fairway buoy and four pairs of red and green markers, all unlit, and is accessible above half tide. The sandbars give protection from the E, and the inlet is most attractive, tranquil and rural in its ambience. However it is also very crowded with moorings and anchoring space is limited.

The Club may be able to provide a mooring for a visitor.

**Directions**
The channel changes from time to time, and the buoys are not on station in the winter months, but the following directions were applicable in 2007. The fairway buoy is slightly S of the midway point between the Martello towers on the N and S arms of the bay. From the buoy, steer approximately 300° for the first pair of channel marks, then 298° for the second pair, then 307° for the third pair, then 296° for the fourth pair. The inlet opens up between the headlands at this point, and has 1·3m to the pier; the channel dries 0·2m, E of the third pair of buoys. The club (01 843 0695) has bar and showers, and welcomes visitors.

There is temporary anchorage in offshore winds on the N side of Rogerstown Bay and also off Rush Harbour, N of the Martello tower. The small harbour dries at half tide but is convenient for landing. Shops and filling station 1 km.

*Loughshinny from the SW*

*Loughshinny Pier*

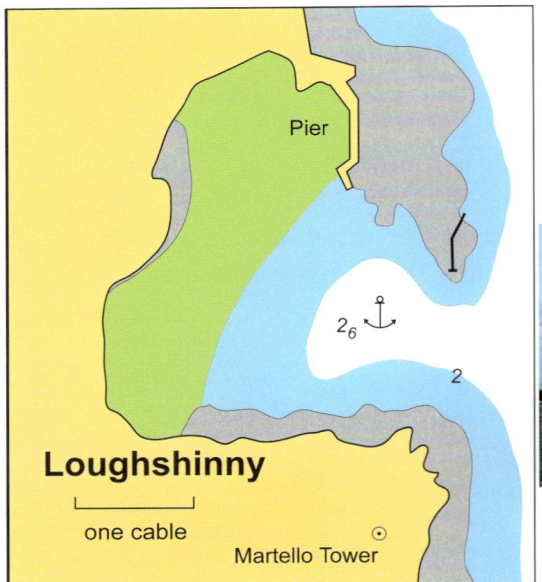

## Loughshinny
53°32'·6N 6°04'·6W, *AC44, SC5621 and Plan*
This cove 1·5M N of Rush Point offers good shelter in winds between SSW and NNW. The end of the pier has 0·3m and the centre of the bay 2·6m. Drying reefs, marked by a bent iron perch, extend for a cable SE of the pierhead. Shop and pub.

*Loughshinny perch from the S; Shenick's Island with its Martello tower L, St Patrick's Island R, and the mountains of Mourne and the Cooley peninsula beyond*

*Skerries from the NW, with Colt Island and St Patrick's Island beyond; Shenick's Island, top R*

*Shenick's Island Martello tower in line with Popeshall Hill leads between Colt and St Patrick's Islands*

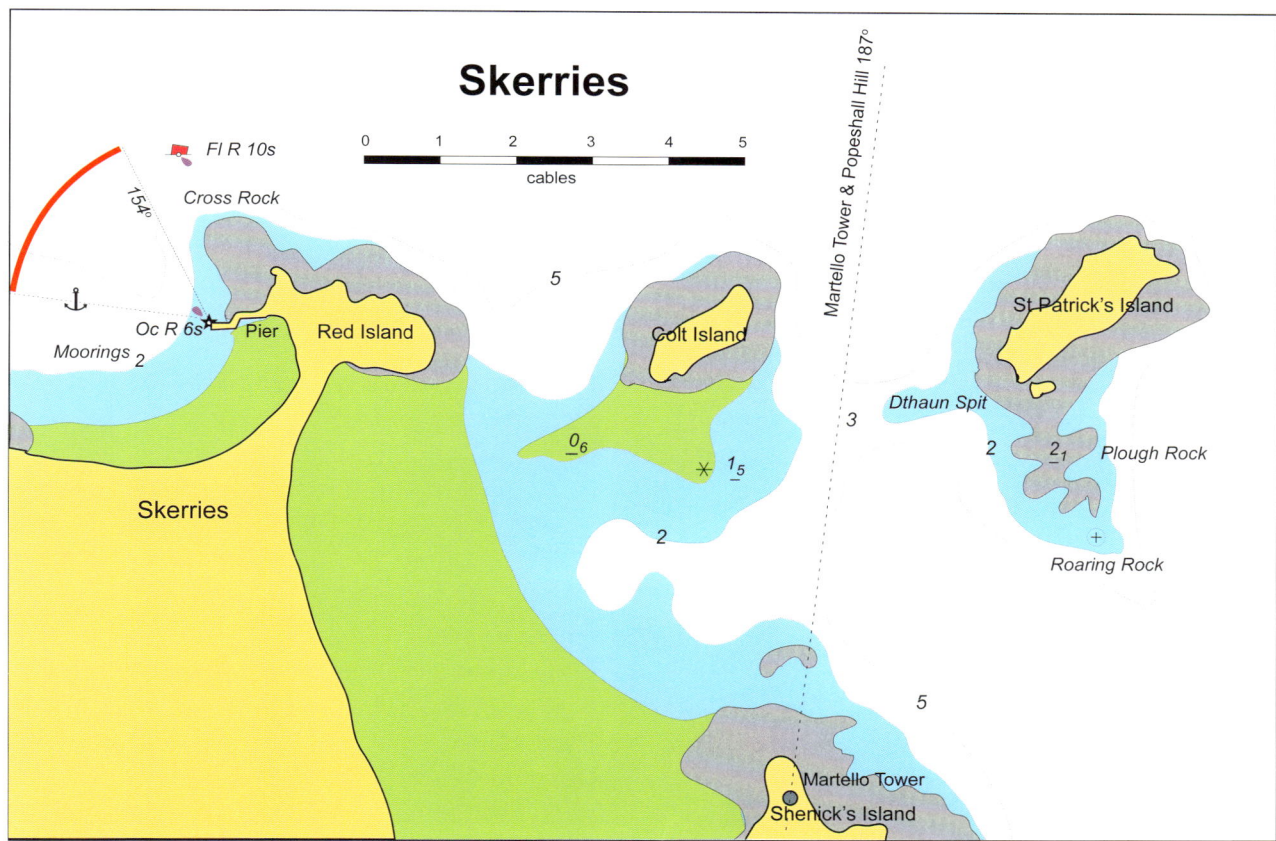

## Skerries Islands

53°35'N 6°03'·7W, *AC633, SC5621·4 and Plan*
St Patrick's Island has drying reefs extending 2·5 cables from its S end, and Dthaun Spit, with 0·6m, extends 2 cables WSW of the island. The channel between St Patrick's Island and Colt Island, to the W, has least depth 3m and is navigable by keeping the Martello tower on Shenick's Island, to the S, in line 187° with Popeshall Hill to the S *(see photograph)*. The channel between Colt Island and the shore almost dries, but is navigable near HW, favouring the mainland side. The Admiralty charts, although based on a survey of 1907, still provide a fair picture of the hydrography.

## Skerries Bay

Skerries Bay is sheltered from ESE through S to NW. From the S, give Colt Island and Red Island a berth of 2 cables and leave the Cross Rock buoy to port, then steer due S into the bay until the pierhead bears 154° (at night, until the pierhead light becomes visible) before turning towards the pier. The pier is used by fishing vessels and has 1·5m at the second berth beyond the head; an alongside berth may be available. Anchor E to NE of the pier in 3 to 4m, clear of the moorings.

## Facilities

Shops, pubs, restaurants, PO. Skerries Sailing Club has bar and showers, and welcomes visitors. RNLI inshore lifeboat station.

## SKERRIES TO CARLINGFORD LOUGH
*AC44, Imray C62*

North of Skerries the coast sweeps in wide sandy bays to the high ground of the Cooley Peninsula and the Mountains of Mourne, which – in good visibility – dominate the view to the north.

### Tides

This stretch has the weakest coastwise streams on the east coast, seldom exceeding 1·5 knots, but in the entrance to Carlingford Lough the tide runs at up to 5 knots. Between Skerries and Rockabill the flood runs NNW, starting at HW Dublin +0540, and the ebb SSE, starting at HW Dublin –0030. Inshore at this point, the ebb starts half an hour earlier and runs for 7 hours, and the stream runs faster between the Skerries Islands. The streams run into and out of Dundalk Bay round both headlands. Dundalk and Warrenpoint have among the highest tidal ranges – 4·5m at springs – on the east coast. For details of streams in Carlingford Lough, see below.

### Dangers - coastwise passage

**Rockabill,** two rocks 9m high, 2·5M E by N of St Patrick's Island

**Cardy Rocks,** dry 2m, 1M N of Balbriggan

**Dunany Shoals,** 2m, extending 2M NE of Dunany Point

**Rocks** with less than 2m, within 1M ESE, SE and SSW of Cooley Point, including **Imogene Rock** (0·3m) and **Castle Rocks** (0·6m).

**Ballagan Spit,** less than 2m, extending 8 cables E from Ballagan Point

**Hellyhunter Rock,** 1·4m, 1·3M ESE of Cranfield Point

### Lights and Marks

**Rockabill,** white tower, black band Fl WR 12s 45m W17M R13M, W178°–329° R329°–178°. Shows white to seaward, red towards the coast.

**Cross Rock** buoy, PHM Fl R 10s

**Skerries Bay Pier Head,** white column Oc R 6s 7m 7M

**Outfall** buoy, yellow, Fl Y 5s, 8 cables NW of Skerries pier head

**Balbriggan,** white tower Fl(3) WRG 20s 12m W13M R10M G10M, G159°–193° W193°–288° R288°–305°. Shows white to seaward to the E and NE, green over Cardy Rocks and inshore to the N, red over Skerries Islands to the SE

**Cardy Rocks,** red perch, unlit

*Drogheda and Approaches:*

**Aleria** beacon, black stone tower with white top, QG 18m 3M

**Lyons** beacon, Fl(3) R 5s 10m 3M

**Port Approach, Port Entry Light** Dir WRG 10m W19M R15M G15M, FG 268°–269° AltWG 269°–269·5° F 269·5°–270·5° AltWR 270·5°–271° FR 271°–272°

The channel to Drogheda is marked by pile beacons Fl R and Fl G.

*Clogher Head, Port Oriel Harbour:*

**Leading Beacons,** orange triangles on poles, Fl 3s synchronised 4M, front 4m, rear 8m

**Pier Head,** red pole beacon PHM Fl(2) R 5s 5m 3M

**Port Oriel Harbour** buoy, SHM Fl G 3s

*Dundalk and Approaches:*

**Dunany** buoy, PHM Fl R 3s

**Pile Light,** white hut on green piled structure Fl WR 15s 10m W21M R18M, W 124°–151° R 151°–284° W 284°–313° R 313°–124°. Horn (3) 60s. Shows white to SE and up-river to NW, red elsewhere

The channel to Dundalk is marked by pile beacons Fl R and Fl G

**Giles Quay,** Fl G 3s

**Imogene** buoy, PHM Fl(2) R 10s

**Hellyhunter** buoy, S Card, Q(6)+L Fl 15s, AIS

For details of tides, dangers, lights and marks in Carlingford Lough, see page 61.

### Coast – Skerries to Carlingford Lough

The coast consists chiefly of broad sandy bays, with shallow water extending well out to sea. The direct course from Skerries or Howth to Carlingford Lough is free of dangers until within 4M of the entrance to the Lough. Between Skerries and Drogheda or Clogher Head, a berth of a mile clears all dangers; but coming N from Balbriggan, take care to avoid the Cardy Rocks. Clogher Head is clean, but Dunany Point must be given a berth of a mile. On the N side of Dundalk Bay, identify the Imogene buoy and steer 045° from it towards the Hellyhunter buoy to clear The Ridge, S of Ballagan Point.

## Balbriggan

53°37'N 6°10'W, *AC44 and Plan*

Balbriggan Harbour is 3M NW of Skerries. The harbour consists of inner and outer basins, and just dries. The entrance faces W into the drying bay. A stream runs through the harbour, which helps to keep it scoured, but sandbanks tend to build up extending about 50m NW from the end of the E pier, and 30m N from the W side of the W pier. Approach steering SW for the middle of the bay, and when the harbour entrance opens up, turn and steer for the centre of the entrance, approximately SE. When 50m from the entrance, turn to port and head for the end of the E pier, on the port hand, to avoid the bank off the W pier. Keep the E pierhead close aboard on entering.

Shops, pubs, restaurants in Balbriggan. Constant −0020 Dublin, MHWS 4·4m, MHWN 3·6m.

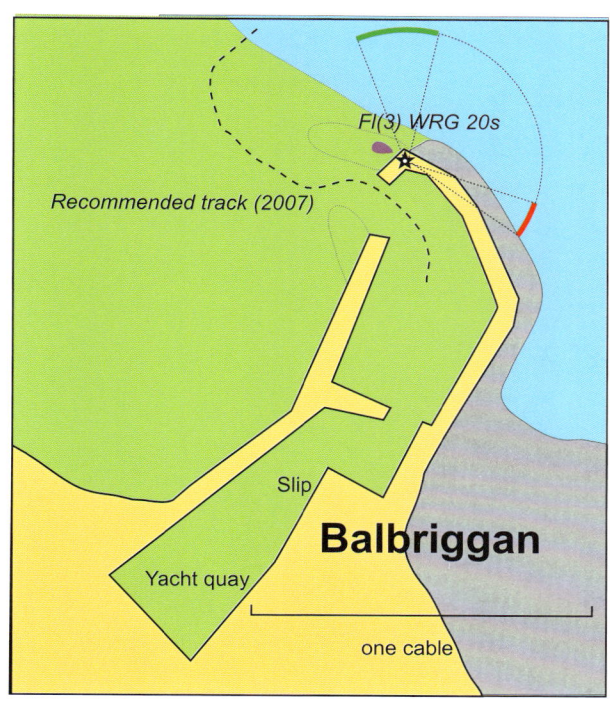

River Boyne entrance; Aleria beacon centre R

*Balbriggan entrance from the NW (Ed Wheeler)*

### Bremore Port (proposed development)

Drogheda Port Company has proposals to build a new deepwater port at Bremore (Braymore on the chart), 1M N of Balbriggan. The outline plans involve a breakwater extending N from Braymore Point, with 11m depth alongside and container and RoRo capacity for 10 million tonnes of cargo annually. Check www.droghedaport.ie for updates on progress.

## DROGHEDA

53°43'·3N 6°13'·4W, *AC44, 1431 and Plan*

The busy port of Drogheda (25,000) stands on the River Boyne 5M from its mouth. The river reaches the sea between rubble breakwaters projecting E into the bay, 5M S of Clogher Head. The entrance and river channel have a maintained depth of 2·2m; the entrance should not be attempted in winds of F5 and above between NE and SE, particularly on the ebb

*River Boyne entrance; Aleria beacon centre R*

*River Boyne entrance from the SE; Aleria beacon, R*

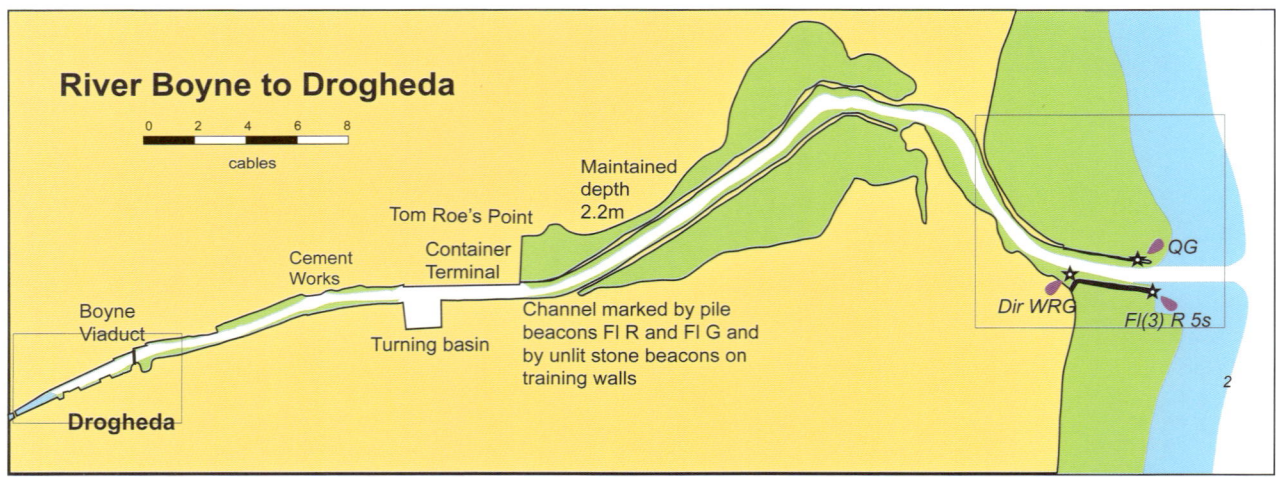

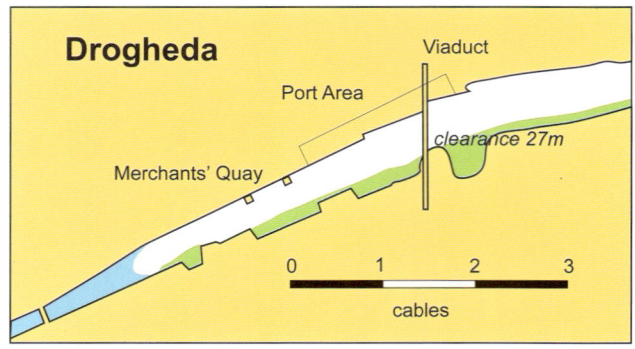

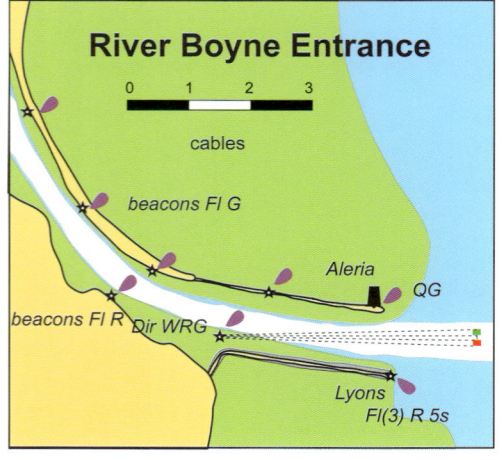

tide. Aleria beacon, on the N breakwater, is conspicuous; approaching from the N, the remains of the wreck (the fore part of a ship) on the sandy beach 1M N of the river mouth are also conspicuous.

Approach with the leading beacons in line 270°, in the narrow white sector of the Port Entry Light, which is clearly visible by day. Hold mid-channel between the training walls, which are marked by port- and starboard-hand

*Drogheda; Merchant's Quay and the Boyne Viaduct, looking down-river*

beacons, Fl R and Fl G respectively. There is a container terminal at Tom Roe's Point, 3M within the river, with a turning basin opposite, and a cement works with jetty 3 cables further W. The main port area is on the N bank immediately upstream of the Boyne Viaduct (clearance 27m), and the river is spanned by a low footbridge 3 cables further W. The Harbour office monitors VHF Ch 11 (HM phone 04198 38378 or 086 254 7827) and should be contacted in advance to obtain clearance, information on shipping movements and advice on berthing.

**Caution**

The River Boyne is a "narrow channel" within the meaning of IRPCS Rule 9, and vessels under 20m in length, and sailing vessels, must not impede large ships in the river. Shipping movements normally take place only around the time of high water but skippers should check with Drogheda Harbour Radio before entering and leaving.

**Berthing**

There are no specific facilities for yachts in Drogheda. Yachts are normally advised to

*Drogheda from the W*

berth under the viaduct on the N bank; this is within the secure Port area, and access to the town can be awkward from here; but there are also two small jetties along Merchants' Quay, where an alongside berth is normally available, but without security. The ebb tide runs past the quays at up to 3 knots. There is no anchorage in the river.

## Facilities

All the facilities of a large town; supermarkets, shops, PO, pubs, restaurants, banks, ATMs, Internet access, doctors. Diesel by tanker, phone Tiger Oil 041 983 4888. Bus and train connections to Dublin and Belfast.

Constant (River Boyne entrance) –0020 Dublin, MHWS 5·4m, MHWN 4·1m.

## PORT ORIEL

53°48'N 6°13'·3W, *AC44 and Plan*

On the N side of Clogher Head, the harbour at Port Oriel is a handy overnight stop when passagemaking. The old pier was extended in 2007 to form a harbour half a cable each way, offering good shelter from winds between N and SW. The entrance faces W, and strong winds between W and NW make the harbour uncomfortable. There is 4m alongside the pier and between it and the starboard-hand buoy. Approach on the line of the leading beacons

*Port Oriel entrance from the N; pierhead beacon and starboard-hand buoy, centre, leading beacons R*

*Port Oriel from the NW*

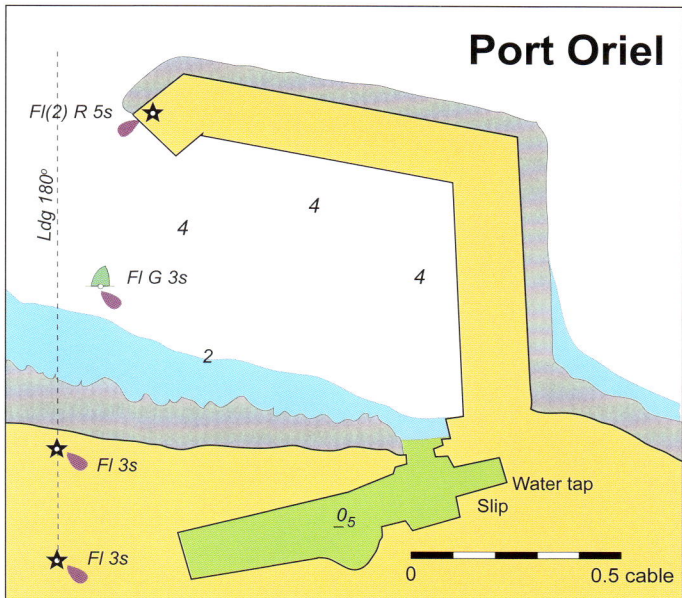

**Port Oriel**

Fl(2) R 5s

Ldg 180°

Fl G 3s

4

4

4

2

Fl 3s

Water tap
Slip

0·5

Fl 3s

0          0.5 cable

180°. Berth near the root of the pier or raft up to a fishing boat with permission. In the SE corner of the harbour is the old dock, which dries about 0·5m with a firm level bottom. Water tap beside the old dock; shop and pubs at Clogherhead village, 1·5 km.

Anchorage in settled weather is possible in 3 to 4m, SW of Clogher Head. RNLI all-weather lifeboat station (Clogherhead), 1M SW of the

Head. Constant –0025 Dublin, MHWS 4·8m, MHWN 4·3m.

**DUNDALK BAY**
Dundalk Bay, 7M long and 7M wide between Dunany Point and Cooley Point, has less than 16m of water anywhere and shelves steadily to drying sands extending 2M from the HW mark. The Castletown River in the NW corner of the bay provides a navigable channel to the port of Dundalk, and there are drying piers on the N and S shores of the bay.

**Annagassan Quay**
The approach to the drying quay at Annagassan on the S side of Dundalk Bay lies across extensive drying sandbanks, and although there are leading lights, the quay is difficult of access and effectively inaccessible to a stranger.

**Dundalk**
53°57'·4N 6°16'·4W, *AC44, 1431 and Plan*
The channel to Dundalk dries 0·9m at its shallowest point but is well marked and lit, and (since Dundalk has one of the highest tidal ranges on

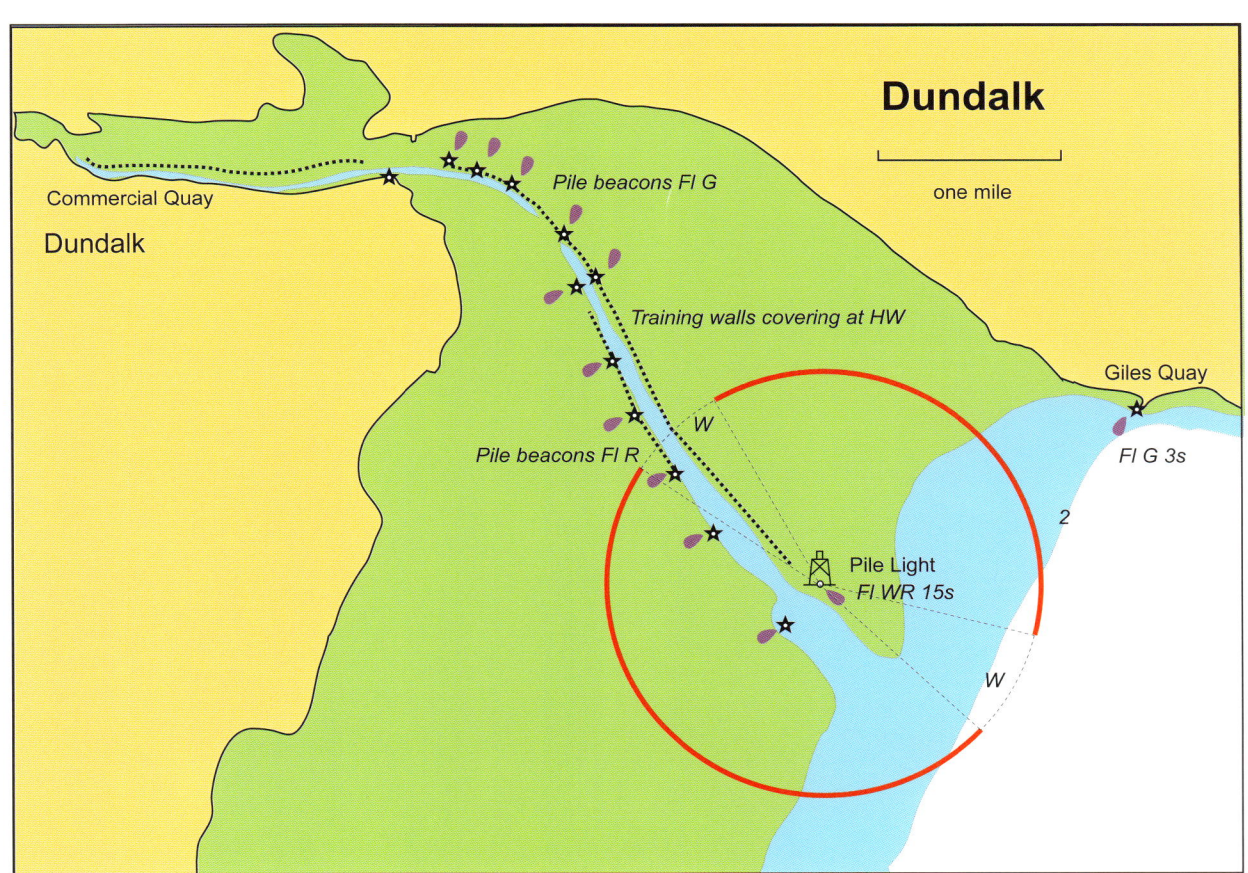

**Dundalk**

Commercial Quay
Dundalk

one mile

Pile beacons Fl G

Training walls covering at HW

Giles Quay

Pile beacons Fl R

W

Fl G 3s

2

Pile Light
Fl.WR 15s

W

the E coast) is navigable above half tide; but the entrance is hazardous in winds over F5 between NNE and SW, and entry at night cannot be recommended. The port handles imports of building materials and animal feeds, and exports scrap metal. The channel is entered at the Pile Light, and is bordered by old training walls which cover at half tide. These are marked by port- and starboard-hand piles, but (for most of the channel's length) these are not paired. It is therefore essential to

*Dundalk Pile Light*

stay close to, but inside, the line of successive beacons in order to stay clear of the submerged wall on the opposite side. Contact the HM on VHF Ch 12 or phone 04293 34096 to check on traffic movements. Under IRPCS Rule 9, small vessels and sailing vessels must not impede larger ships using the channel.

The commercial quay, on the S side of the river 5M from the Pile Light, has 2m. An alongside berth may be available; consult the HM. Supermarket 300m from the quay; shops, PO, pubs, restaurants, banks, ATMs, doctors in town, 1 km.

Constant –0010 Dublin, MHWS 5·5m, MHWN 4·0m, MLWN 1·6m, MLWS 0·4m.

**Giles Quay**
53°58'·6N 6°14'·5W
This pier on the N side of the bay 2M NE of the Pile Light just dries at its head, but offers a temporary berth to a yacht above half tide in settled weather. Anchorage is available a cable S of the pierhead in 2m, sand.

**CARLINGFORD LOUGH**
Carlingford Lough is one of the two areas of enclosed seawater on the east coast; Strangford is drowned drumlin country, but Carlingford is a true fjord, with deep water between steep mountains, and a relatively shallow threshold. Its name derives from the Old Norse and

*Dundalk Commercial Quay*

*Giles Quay. The yellow pillar is part of a piling barge moored alongside*

means "the inlet of the hag." The Lough was a port from earliest times, but it was not until the 19th century that the entrance was dredged and large-scale commercial operations began. These were centred at Newry, 5M above the head of the Lough by river and canal. Newry (27,000) was a commercial port until 1974, but was supplanted by Warrenpoint (6,000) and Greenore, and it was only in 2007 that the Newry Canal was re-opened, now with a view to recreational traffic. The Lough is a major sailing centre, and the backdrop to the annual Carlingford Oyster Festival, which takes place in August.

**Tidal Streams**
The flood starts about –0500 Dublin and the ebb about +0020 Dublin, but the best predictor is the tide tables for Liverpool; the flood starting at LW Liverpool and the ebb at HW Liverpool (the same applies to Dundrum). These streams are not felt at the Hellyhunter buoy, where the tide runs coastwise. In the channel, the streams reach 3·5 knots in the approach, 4·5 knots E of Haulbowline Rocks, 5 knots off Greenore, 2·5 knots between Stalka and Watson Rocks, and

1·5 knots off Carlingford. They are only just perceptible off Rostrevor. During the flood, the tide tends to run anticlockwise around Haulbowline lighthouse; N between the lighthouse and the No. 5 buoy, and S between the lighthouse and Blockhouse Island.

**Dangers**
**Ballagan Spit**, less than 2m, extending 8 cables E from Ballagan Point
**Hellyhunter Rock**, 1·4m, 1·3M ESE of Cranfield Point
**The Breast**, 1·8m, 9 cables SSW of Cranfield Point
**Morgan Pladdy,** 1·3m, 7 cables SW of Cranfield Point
Dangerous **wrecks** within 3 cables S of Cranfield Point
**Limestone Rocks**, area of reefs 1M by 7 cables, extending from the SW shore, drying up to 2·8m at Cooley Long Rock and showing above HW at Block House Island, 8 cables E by S of Cranfield Point.
**Haulbowline Rocks,** drying 2·5m, 2 to 3 cables ESE of Block House Island

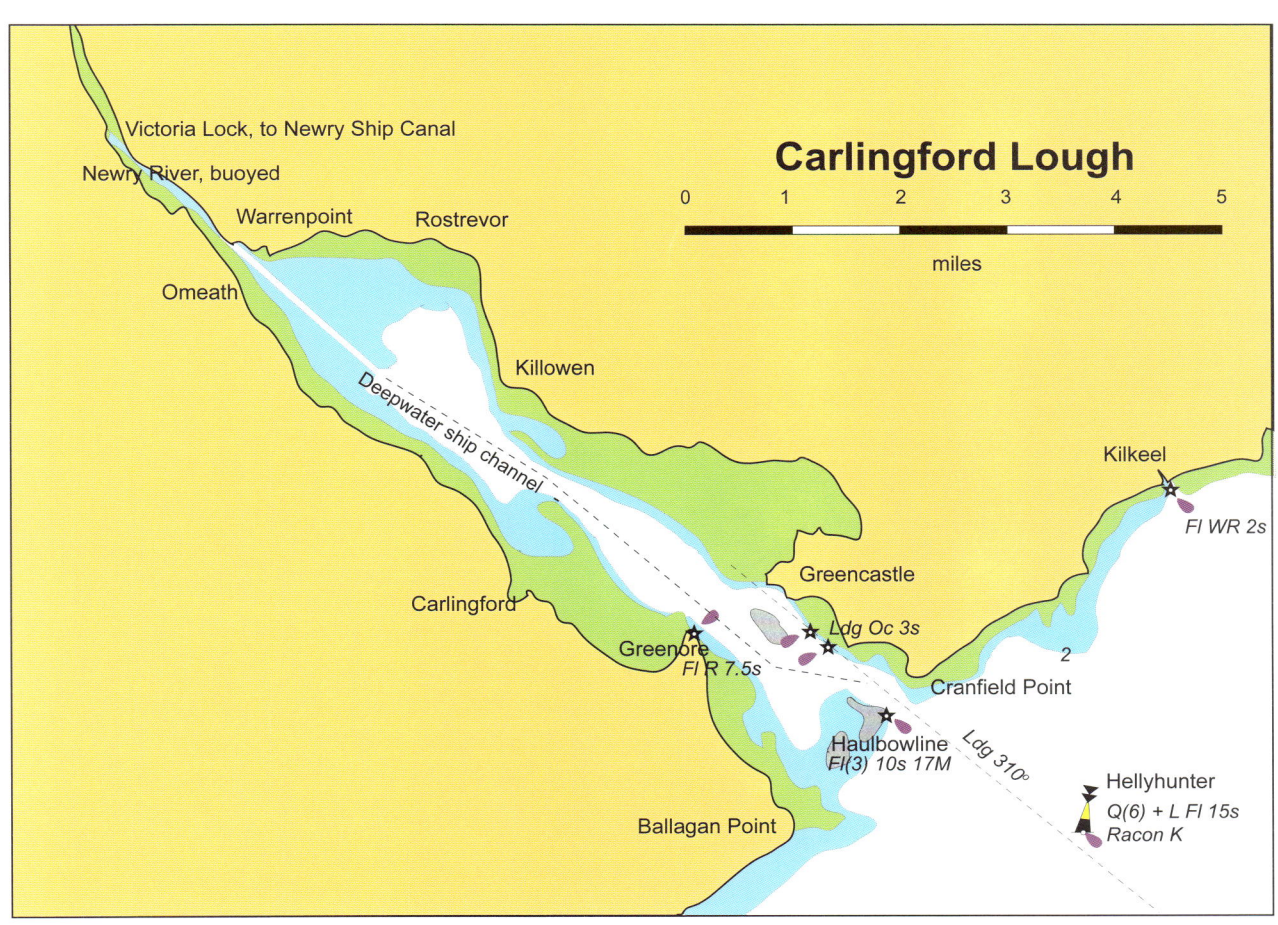

*Carlingford Lough entrance from the SSE; Haulbowline lighthouse R foreground, Block House Island L centre with Greencastle beyond.*

**Vidal Rock**, 1·7m, 4 cables NW of Block House Island

**The Breast**, 1·8m, 9 cables SSW of Cranfield Point

**Drying rocks** E and NE of Green Island

**Drying and below-water rocks** extending 1·1M NW from Green Island and including **Earl Rock** and **Stalka Rock**

**Watson Rocks**, 1·5m, 4 to 7 cables NW of Greenore Point

*The tides run fast in the entrance to Carlingford Lough*

**Lights and Marks**

**Carlingford Fairway**, safe water mark RWVS, L Fl 10s

**Hellyhunter** buoy, S Card Q(6)+LFl 15s, AIS

**No 1** buoy, SHM Fl(3) G 8s

**No 2** buoy, PHM Fl(4) R 8s

**No 3** buoy, SHM Fl G

**No 4** buoy, PHM Fl R

**No 5** buoy, SHM Fl G 2s

**No 6** buoy, PHM Fl R 2s

**Haulbowline**, grey tower Fl(3) 10s 32m 17M, Horn 30s

**Carlingford Entrance** leading lights 310·4° Oc 3s 11M, orange triangles on green piled structures with white huts, front 7m rear 12m

**Greenore Point**, Fl R 7·5s 10m 5M

The channel between Haulbowline and Warrenpoint is marked by port- and starboard-hand buoys, Fl R and Fl G

**Carlingford W pierhead**, Fl G 3s 5m 3M

**Carlingford E pierhead**. Oc R 4s 5m 3M

**Newry River** leading lights 310·4° Iso 4s 2M, stone cols, front 5m rear 15m

**Warrenpoint breakwater**, Fl G 3s 6m 3M

**Warrenpoint Container Terminal**, Fl G 5s

The Newry River to Victoria Lock is marked by port- and starboard-hand buoys, Fl R and Fl G.

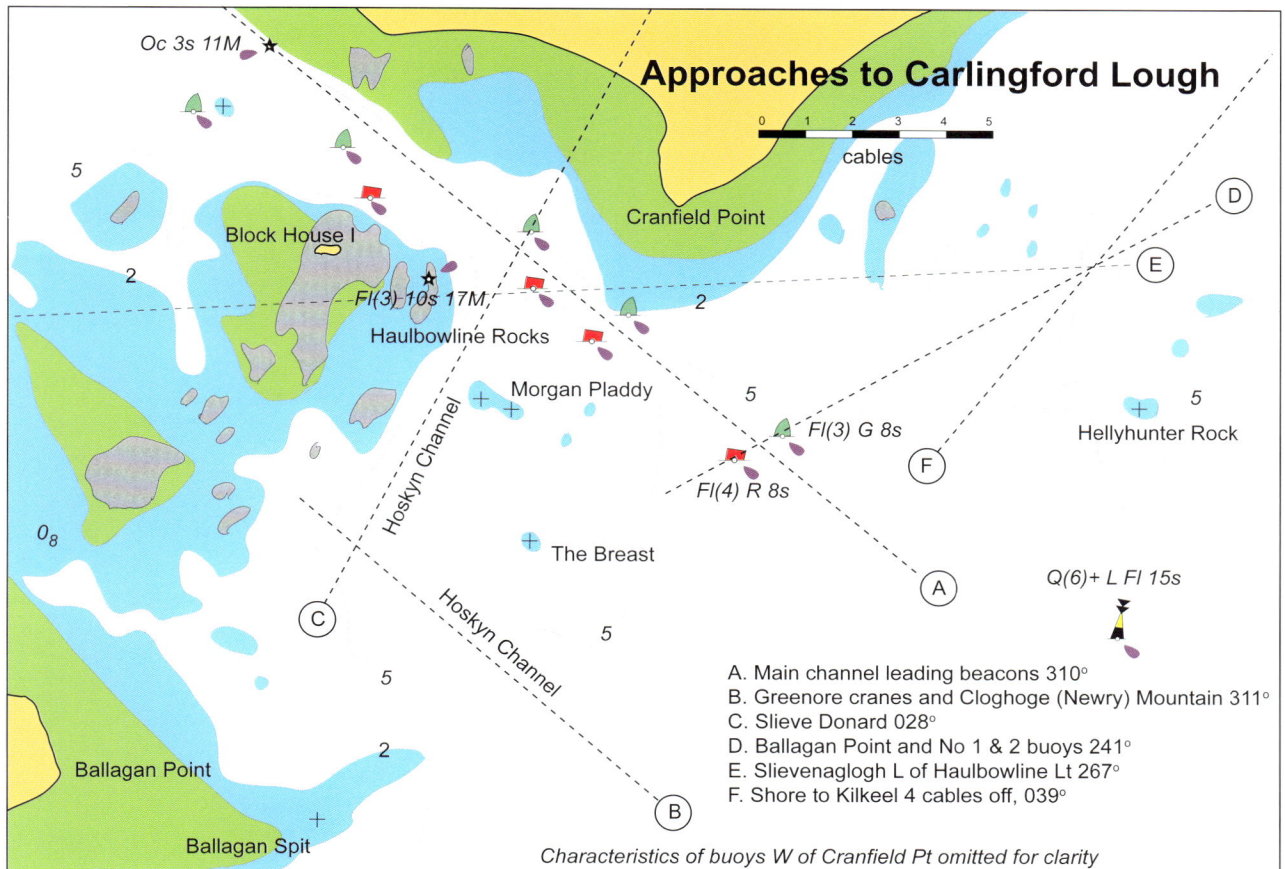

**Approaches to Carlingford Lough**

Oc 3s 11M

5

2

Block House I

Fl(3) 10s 17M

Haulbowline Rocks

Morgan Pladdy

Hoskyn Channel

0·8

The Breast

C

Hoskyn Channel

5

5

Ballagan Point

2

Ballagan Spit

B

cables

Cranfield Point

2

5

Fl(3) G 8s

Fl(4) R 8s

F

A

D

E

5

Hellyhunter Rock

Q(6)+ L Fl 15s

A. Main channel leading beacons 310°
B. Greenore cranes and Cloghoge (Newry) Mountain 311°
C. Slieve Donard 028°
D. Ballagan Point and No 1 & 2 buoys 241°
E. Slievenaglogh L of Haulbowline Lt 267°
F. Shore to Kilkeel 4 cables off, 039°

*Characteristics of buoys W of Cranfield Pt omitted for clarity*

## Carlingford Lough Entrance

54°00'·8N 6°03'·4W, *AC2800, SC5621 and Plan*

The main channel is entered between the No.1 and No.2 buoys, S of Cranfield Point, and runs NW to pass 2 cables NE of Haulbowline light, then turning WNW and passing close NE of Greenore Point. The harbour cranes at Greenore are conspicuous. Past Greenore Point the channel turns NW again and then WNW towards Warrenpoint. In moderate to good visibility the next buoy is always visible, but care must be taken (especially between Haulbowline and Greenore) to avoid being swept out of the channel by the tide. NW of Greenore, the channel widens, and while there is navigable water for a yacht over a width of 2 cables at Greenore, there is half a mile at Killowen and a mile at Rostrevor.

A yacht should not attempt to leave Carlingford Lough with the ebb tide in S or SE winds over F5.

Constant –0020 Dublin, MHWS 4·8m, MHWN 4·3m, MLWN 1·8m, MLWS 0·7m.

### Caution

The ship channel from the Hellyhunter buoy to Greenore and Warrenpoint is a "narrow

*Carlingford Entrance leading beacons; Warrenpoint in the distance*

*Greenore cranes in line with Cloghoge Mountain 311 leads through the S part of the Hoskyn Channel*

*View NE through the N part of the Hoskyn Channel; No.6 channel buoy, centre R*

channel" within the meaning of IRPCS Rule 9, and vessels under 20m in length, and sailing vessels, must not impede large ships in the channel. Note that the many fish farm symbols on the charts indicate shellfish beds rather than fish cages. The beds do not impede navigation of the Lough but anchoring on them should be avoided.

## Hoskyn Channel
54°00'N 6°04'·2W, *AC2800, SC5621·6*

The southern entrance to Carlingford Lough is named after Richard Hoskyn, Master RN, who surveyed the Lough in 1857. The channel offers a short cut to and from the south and avoids the strongest of the tidal streams; but since a section of it runs SW-NE across the tide, great care must be taken to stay on the transit line. The channel is unmarked, has least depth 5m, and makes a dog-leg S and W of the shallows surrounding The Breast (1·8m) and Morgan Pladdy (1·3m) before joining the main channel NE of Haulbowline Rocks. It should not be attempted in strong SE winds, or if the tide is running and the transits cannot be clearly seen.

## Directions
From the Imogene buoy, steer 031°, with the Hellyhunter buoy on the starboard bow, to clear Ballagan Spit. When the cranes at Greenore port come in line with Cloghoge Mountain 311° *(see photograph)* turn and steer on this transit until the peak of Slieve Donard bears 028°. Turn to starboard and keep Slieve Donard on this bearing, steering N or S of the heading as required to maintain the course over the ground. The photograph shows the view on this course, with a prominent house behind the caravan park at Cranfield Point in line with the valley between Slieve Binnian and Chimney Rock Mountain. Keep the No.6 port-hand buoy fine on the starboard bow, and leave it close to starboard, joining the main channel E of Haulbowline lighthouse.

*Greencastle from the ESE; Green Island L with Earl Rock beacon beyond, Greencastle Point centre R. The main channel rear leading beacon, lower L*

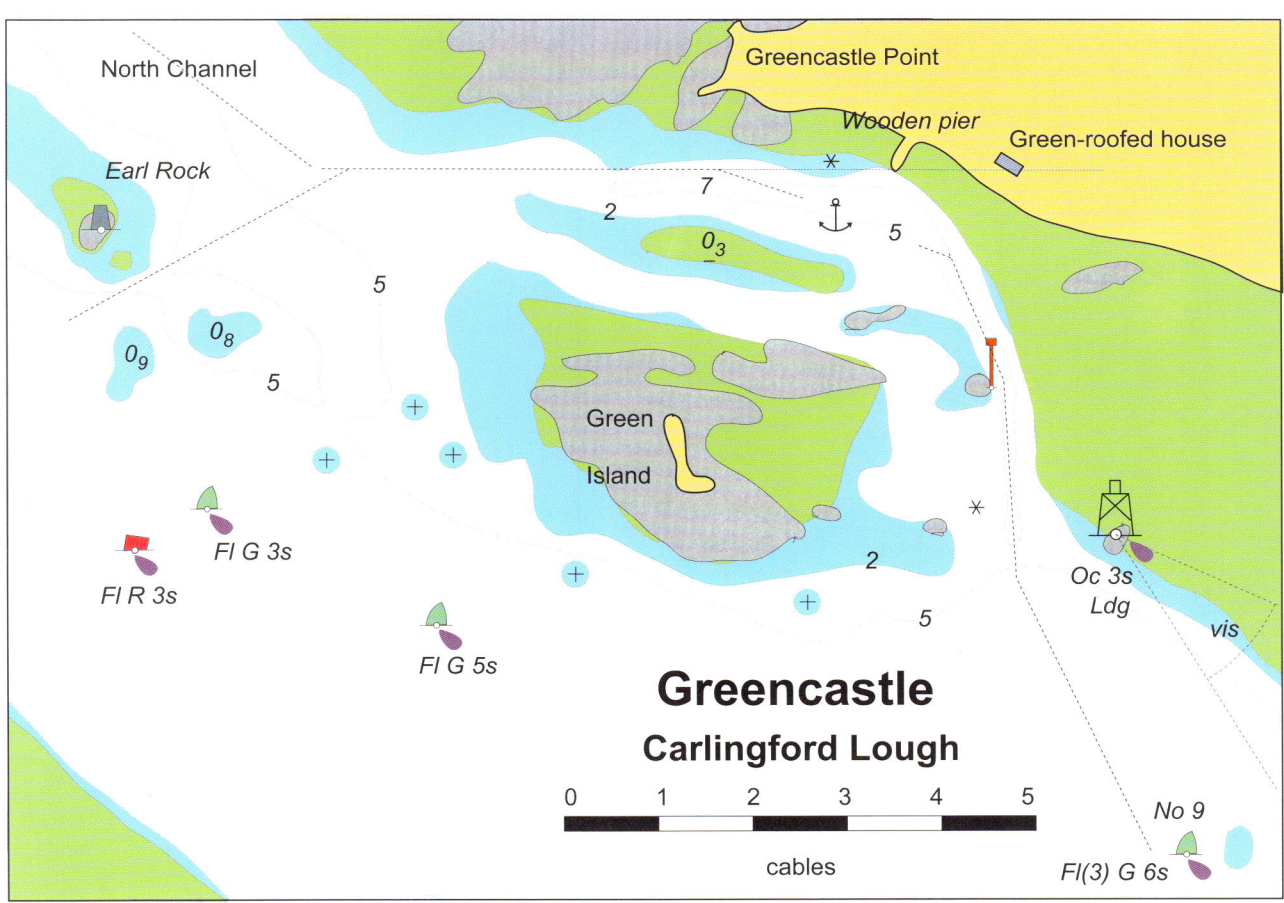

North Channel

Greencastle Point

*Wooden pier*

Green-roofed house

Earl Rock

7

2

0<sub>3</sub>

5

5

0<sub>8</sub>

0<sub>9</sub>

5

Green

Island

Fl G 3s

Fl R 3s

2

Oc 3s
Ldg

vis

Fl G 5s

**Greencastle**

**Carlingford Lough**

5

0   1   2   3   4   5

cables

*No 9*

*Fl(3) G 6s*

*Greencastle approach from the S: the port-hand perch, foreground, and the wooden pier, centre*

## GREENCASTLE

54°01'·9N 6°05'·8W, *AC2800, SC5621·6 and Plan*

The channel between Green Island and Greencastle Point, on the N shore 1·5M from Cranfield Point, offers good anchorage although yachts will normally be tide-rode. From the main channel to the E, leave the No.9 buoy close to starboard and then steer for the houses on Greencastle Point. This course leads within a cable W of the rear leading beacon tower for the main channel; when this tower comes abeam to starboard, identify the slim PHM perch on the rock E of Green Island, and leave it 15m to port. Then steer for the root of the wooden pier at Greencastle, and follow the line of the moorings *(see photograph)*. Note that there is a drying bank close S of the moorings.

From the upper Lough, approach either via the N channel (NE of Stalka and Earl Rocks); or from the main channel by passing close SE of Earl Rock. In the latter case leave Earl Rock half a cable to port to avoid the rocks (with 0·9 and 0·8m) to the SE. When a green-roofed two-storey house comes in line with the end of the wooden Greencastle pier *(see photograph)* steer in on this transit and follow the line of moorings. (On the N side, one starboard- and two port-hand perches mark the channel to the concrete pier at Greencastle Point).

Anchor W of the moorings, staying S of the transit of the green-roofed house and the pier. The reefs around the low Green Island cover at HW; it is much easier to make the passage near LW, when the reefs show.

### Greenore

Greenore harbour consists of a single cargo berth, and cannot accommodate yachts.

*Earl Rock beacon*

*Greencastle from the W; the two-storey green-roofed house in line with the end of the wooden pier leads in to the anchorage*

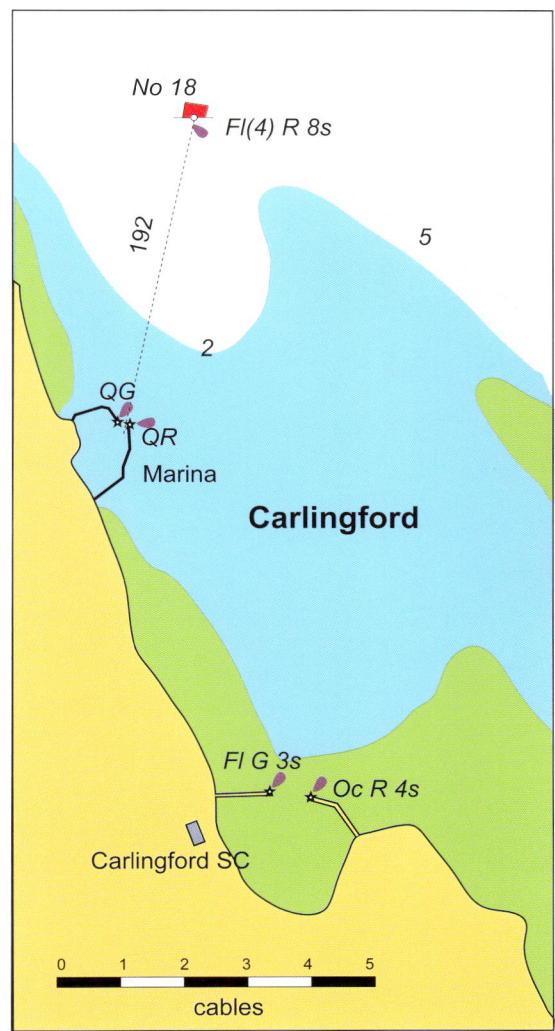

*Greencastle Point from the SE*

## CARLINGFORD
54°03'·6N 6°11'·2W, *AC2800, SC5621·6 and Plan*

Carlingford harbour, 2M WNW of Greenore Point, is approached from the N across extensive shallows, and the harbour itself dries 1·5 to 2m. The E wall is reported to have the better bottom for drying out alongside. The harbour is close to the village, but its wide entrance is exposed to winds between NW and NE and the whole area is subject to heavy squalls off the hills in NW winds. Carlingford marina, 6 cables further NW, has 160 berths. Approach the marina steering 192° from the No.18 channel buoy. The marina monitors VHF Ch.M (0900–2000), phone 04293 73073. The vicinity of the marina is also subject to squalls, and it is reported that the breakwaters may be overwhelmed in heavy weather.

### Facilities
Shops, PO, pubs, restaurants in Carlingford village. Bar and restaurant at the marina. Carlingford Sailing Club, in the village, welcomes visitors and has bar and showers.

*Carlingford Marina from the No.18 buoy*

*Carlingford from the SE; harbour, lower L, and marina, top centre*

## WARRENPOINT

54°05'·6N 6°14'·9W, *AC2800 and Plan*

Warrenpoint Harbour, on the NE bank of the Newry River where it flows into the head of Carlingford Lough, consists of a RoRo terminal and a container berth, the Town Dock with a pontoon facility, and a basin enclosed by two breakwaters. There are daily freight services to Heysham, and the port handles many container and general cargo ships. The Town Dock pontoons are provided principally for the use of mussel dredgers, but the dredgers do not operate in summer, and between June and September the Town Dock is open to visiting yachts. The basin between the breakwaters, to the SE, has (at the time of writing in 2007) works in progress with a view to marina development;

check www.irishcruisingclub.com for updates. There is also a pontoon on the NW side of the outer breakwater. The harbour welcomes yachts, but commercial shipping takes precedence and visitors must obtain clearance from the harbour office before berthing, or transiting the harbour.

### Directions

The cranes at the container berth are conspicuous from several miles down the Lough, and the channel to Warrenpoint is well buoyed and lit. At or before the No.23 buoy, call the Harbour on VHF Ch 12 to obtain clearance and a berth, and to check that no large ships are about to leave. Harbour regulations prohibit transiting under sail, and vessels may not pass each other

*Warrenpoint from the W; Town Dock, centre*

in the dredged channel; but above half tide there is adequate depth close outside the line of the buoys until within a cable of the breakwater. The channel has 5·4m to the RoRo berth, but it shallows rapidly on either side. Gannaway Rock (dries 3m) close NE of the channel, is marked by a slim pole beacon, and there are below-water rocks and obstructions close SE of the breakwater.

### Harbour
There is a small starboard-hand buoy in the entrance to the Town Dock, marking a shoal extending W from the pierhead. Berth as directed. The Town Dock pontoons have a security gate.

The pontoon inside the SE breakwater is also available to visitors but has no gate; it is owned by the District Council rather than the Harbour. The deep channel beside this pontoon is only 20m wide.

### Facilities
Showers at the Town Dock office building. Warrenpoint has supermarkets, shops, PO, pubs, restaurants, banks, ATMs, filling stations, Internet access, doctors. Buses to Newry and Belfast. Passenger ferry to Omeath.

Constant −0010 Dublin, MHWS 5·4m, MHWN 3·9m, MLWN 1·4m, MLWS 0·2m.

*Newry River entrance; leading marks centre L, Warrenpoint cargo berths R*

## NEWRY RIVER AND CANAL
*See Plan*

NW of Warrenpoint Harbour, the river quite suddenly becomes rural and scenic. A major project, completed in 2007, dredged and marked the river, cleaned out and recommissioned the Newry Ship Canal, and refurbished the Victoria Lock and Newry's Albert Basin. The lock, 60m by 10m, is entered 2M above Warrenpoint, and the canal, 25m wide with 3·3m of water, runs 3·2M from there to Newry. The basin has 200m of quayside and ample turning room. There are no headroom restrictions. The river and canal are managed by Newry & Mourne District Council. The transit of the canal is a delightful experience, and the basin affords direct access to a large shopping centre.

### Directions

The lock is operated on request, in daylight, up to an hour either side of HW, and (at the time of writing) at 48 hours' notice; but the last two of these restrictions may well be relaxed as operating experience and traffic volume accumulate (check the website for updates). To request opening, phone Newry Tourist Information Centre (028 3031 3170) or e-mail newrytic@newryandmourne.gov.uk.

From Warrenpoint, the leading marks (stone towers with white daymarks, *see photograph*) are conspicuous. Follow their line and then stay between the buoys. Keep the first green buoy above Warrenpoint close aboard since there is a spit extending from the SW shore opposite. The river channel dries 0·5m, but where the channel to the lock joins the river, close S of the lock entrance, there is a sandbar drying 1·4m. This translates to a depth of at least 2·5m in the approaches to the lock at HW±0100 at neaps and HW±0200 at springs.

The lift in the lock is 2 to 3m depending on the height of HW in the river. There is a speed limit of 4 knots in the canal. Berth as convenient alongside the quay at the Albert Basin.

### Facilities

Newry has all the facilities of a large town. Chandlery, CH Marine, 028 3083 5870. Train and bus connections to Belfast and Dublin.

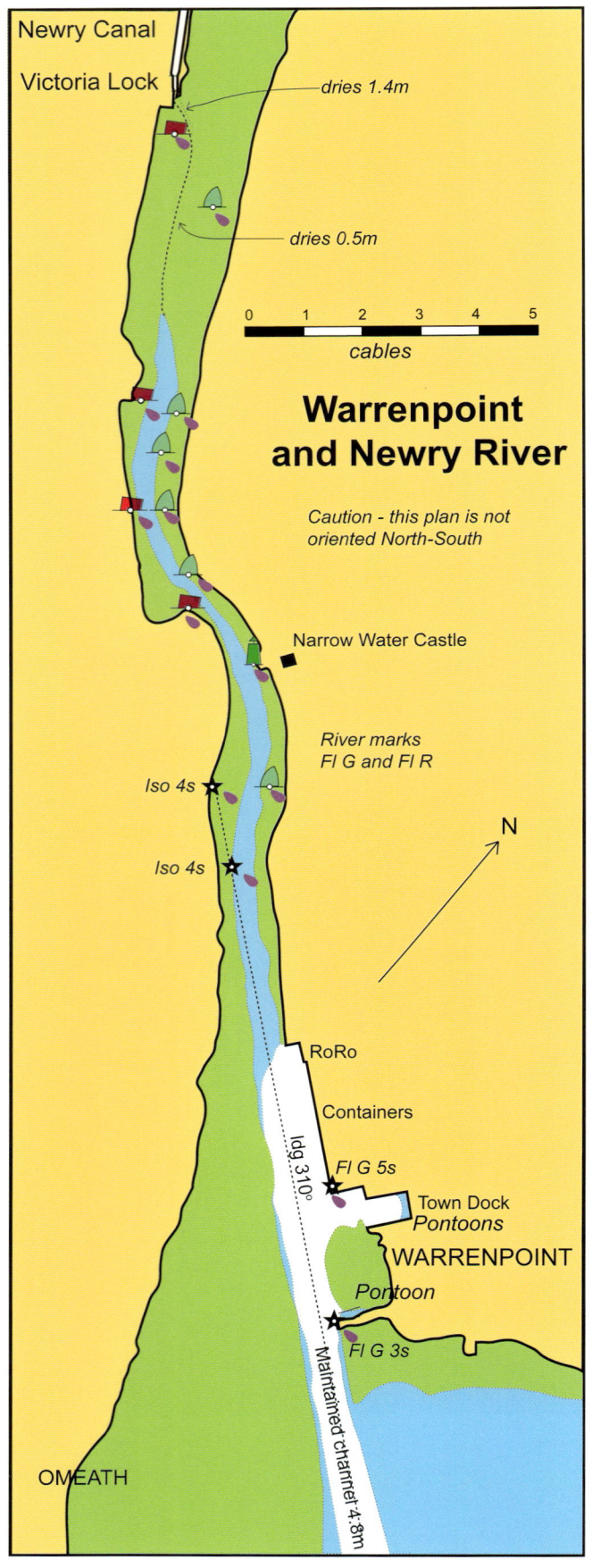

Newry Canal

Victoria Lock

dries 1.4m

dries 0.5m

0   1   2   3   4   5
*cables*

**Warrenpoint and Newry River**

Caution - this plan is not oriented North-South

Narrow Water Castle

River marks
Fl G and Fl R

Iso 4s

Iso 4s

N

RoRo

Containers

Ldg.310°

Fl G 5s

Town Dock
*Pontoons*

WARRENPOINT

*Pontoon*

Fl G 3s

Maintained channel 4·8m

OMEATH

*Victoria Lock from the Newry River*

*Newry Canal, looking S; the river, L, runs parallel*

*Albert Basin, Newry*

## CARLINGFORD LOUGH TO DUNDRUM BAY

The coast from Cranfield Point to Lee Stone Point, NE of Kilkeel, is foul with rocks and wrecks up to 1·3M offshore, with the Hellyhunter buoy marking the S end of the foul ground. In fresh to strong onshore winds or a heavy swell, the safe course is to pass S of the buoy. In settled conditions or offshore winds there is an inshore passage with at least 3m, N of the Hellyhunter Rock. From the Hellyhunter to Annalong the coast should be given a berth of a mile. N of Annalong, the coast is generally clean, but needs a berth of 3 cables to clear Roaring Rock.

### Charts

SC5612 covers this section of the coast. AC2800 and SC5621 have a detail plan of Kilkeel, and AC633 and SC5612 one of Ardglass and Killough, but for the other harbours the largest-scale chart is AC44 or SC5612·3 on a scale of 1:100,000.

### Tidal Streams

The streams offshore are generally weak, and close S of St John's Point are imperceptible, but there is a considerable run in the entrance to Dundrum.

### Dangers

**Hellyhunter Rock**, 1·4m, 1·3M ESE of Cranfield Point
Dangerous **wrecks** within 3 cables S of Cranfield Point
**Roaring Rock**, dries 0·5m, 2·5 cables offshore 2·5M N of Annalong
**Long Rocks**, dry 2m, **Pladdies**, dry 0·6m, and the **Cow and Calf**, awash at LAT, extending 1M offshore in Dundrum Bay, 3·5M W of St John's Point
**Water Rocks,** dry 3·1m, in the entrance to Killough Harbour
**St Patrick's Rock,** dries about 3·1m, 3·5 cables SE of Killard Point

### Lights and Marks

**Kilkeel Pier,** Fl WR 2s 8m 8M, R296°–313° W313°–017°. Shows white over the approach from the S, red over the shallows to the SE
**Meeney's Pier,** Fl G 3s 6m 2M

**Kilkeel Outfall** buoy, yellow, Fl(4) Y 12s
**Annalong** E breakwater, Oc WRG 5s 8m 9M G204°–249° W249°–309° R309°–024°. Shows white to the E, green to the NE, red to the S and SE
**DZ East** buoy, yellow, unlit
**DZ Middle** buoy, yellow, unlit
**DZ West** buoy, yellow, unlit
**St John's Point**, black tower, yellow bands, Q(2) 7·5s 37m 25M, Horn (2) 60s

*Killough*
**Water Rocks**, bent iron perch with cage topmark, unlit

*Ardglass*
**Ardglass South Pier,** Fl R 3s 10m 5M
**Ardtole,** grey pyramid beacon on the point opposite the South Pier, unlit
**Ardglass Inner Pier,** white tower, Iso WRG 4s 10m W8M R7M G5M, G shore–308° W308°–314° R314°–shore
**Churn Rock** beacon, disused E Card, unlit, in the middle of Ardglass harbour
**Inner Breakwater** buoy, E Card VQ(3) 4s
**No 2** buoy, PHM QR
**No 3** buoy, SHM QG
**No 4** buoy, PHM Fl R 4s
**No 5** buoy, SHM Fl G 4s
In addition there are 3 × S Card and 1× N Card perches, unlit, on the inner breakwater and the reef to the SW, and unlit port- and starboard-hand perches marking the channel to the marina and inner harbour.

**Guns Island,** white pyramid beacon with cage topmark, unlit.

### Passage N from Carlingford Lough

*(AC44, 2800, SC5612.3; refer to Plan on p 63)*
In heavy onshore weather, the safe passage lies outside the Hellyhunter buoy, but in moderate conditions there is a short cut inside the rock in a least depth of 3m, which helps to avoid some of the otherwise inevitable overfalls in the main channel. From the main channel at the No.1 and No.2 lateral buoys (in 54°00'·7N) steer 061°, with Ballagan Point directly astern, until the summit of Slievenaglogh (on the Cooley peninsula to the W, *see photograph*) is just left of Haulbowline lighthouse 267°. Then steer

*Slievenaglogh just left of Haulbowline lighthouse*

039° for a point 4 cables S of the entrance to Kilkeel, giving the coast a berth of 4 cables at Crawford's Point, SW of Kilkeel. AC2800 is essential for the short cut; SC5621·6 does not extend far enough E. The transits are easier to use when S-bound.

## KILKEEL
54°03'·3N 5°59'·2W, *AC44, 2800, SC5621·6 and Plan*

The bustling town of Kilkeel has Northern Ireland's largest fishing fleet. The harbour is run by the NI Fishery Harbour Authority, but responsibility is shortly (2007) to be transferred to Newry & Mourne District Council. The man-made harbour, extending 3 cables inland from the pierheads, offers perfect shelter and is accessible in all weathers except in winds over F5 between E and S. The entrance tends to shoal, particularly as a result of SW gales, and is regularly dredged to maintain a least depth of 1·5m in the approach; there is 1·3m in the harbour.

There are shoals close NE and SW of the entrance channel.

**Directions**
Approach with the S pierhead bearing 340°. From the N, give Lee Stone Point and the shore between there and Kilkeel a berth of 6 cables (steering due W for the outfall buoy clears all dangers) then approach as above. Keep a sharp lookout for vessels leaving. The NE wall of the basin is not available for berthing, but space is usually available on the SW wall, or raft up to a fishing boat, with permission. Consult the HM for advice and directions; phone 028 4176 2287, VHF Ch 12, 0900-2000. There are outline plans for yacht pontoons in the harbour.

**Facilities**
Water at the harbour, diesel by tanker. Showers at Nautilus Centre, at the head of the harbour. Chandlery, KTS Sea Safety, 028 4176 2655. All repairs, except sails, available. Engine repairs, Dr Diesel 028 4176 9777, 0777 082 3004. Supermarkets, shops, PO, pubs, restaurants, banks, ATMs, Internet access, doctors. RNLI inshore lifeboat station. Buses to Newry and Belfast.

HW as Belfast, MHWS 5·3m, MHWN 4·4m, MLWN 1·9m, MLWS 0·7m.

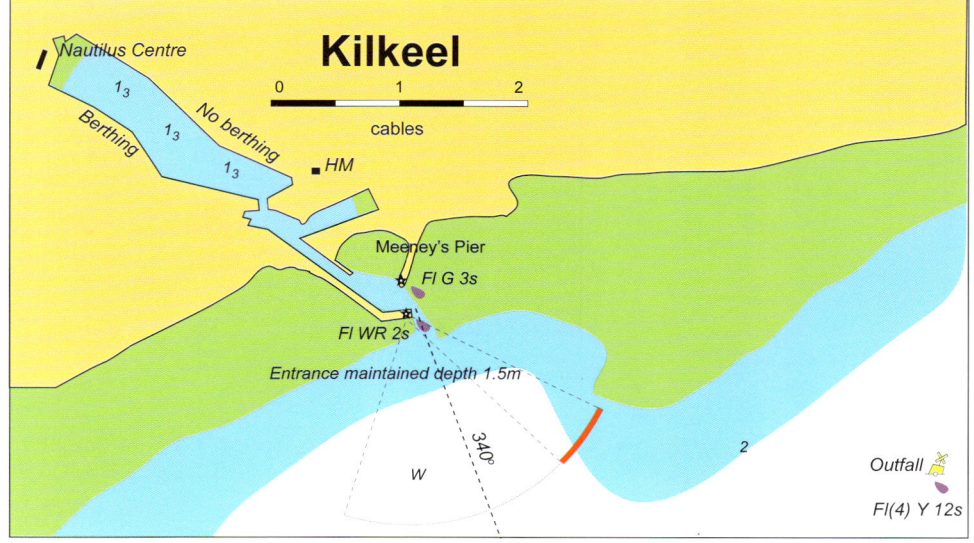

*Kilkeel Harbour from the SE*

*Kilkeel breakwater from the SSE*

*Kilkeel Harbour from the NW*

## ANNALONG

54°06'·4N 5°53'·3W, *AC44, SC5612·3 and Plan*

Annalong Harbour has a short breakwater projecting E and a narrow entrance to a basin 100m by 25m, and is accessible except around LWS. The basin has 2·5m at its SE end and 0·5m at its NE end, and the entrance channel has a least depth of 0·9m. The basin can be closed by a surge barrier in heavy weather. There is a 20m-long pontoon on the SW wall. The basin has many small craft, and a visiting yacht of more than 10m might have trouble manoeuvring in the remaining tight space. Larger vessels can find a temporary berth alongside the SW wall in the entrance in settled or offshore weather. Entry is hazardous in SE winds above F5. The shore is rocky to N and S, and a shoal patch extends ESE for half a cable from the breakwater head. Approach from a cable offshore keeping the N side of the breakwater just open, and enter at slow speed, since manoeuvring room is limited.

*Annalong*

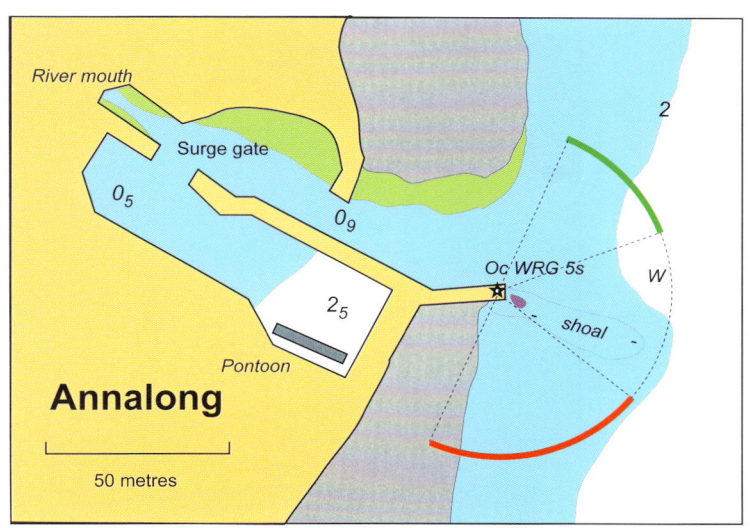

*Annalong entrance, looking seaward*

HM phone 0773 952 7036.

**Facilities**
Water on the pontoon. Shop, pubs, restaurant, filling station, ATM, Internet access. Buses to Downpatrick and Belfast.

*Annalong basin; the pontoon, L*

## DUNDRUM BAY

The 8M-wide bay between Newcastle and St John's Point is completely exposed to S and SE, and shallow water extends in places a mile out to sea. The direct course across the bay from Annalong or Newcastle is free of dangers, but if coasting, or heading for Dundrum from the NE, beware the reefs in the E half of the bay of which the Cow and Calf are the most S'ly. Keep St John's Point bearing N of E, or stay S of 54°13·5N, to avoid these rocks. St John's Point, with its conspicuous black-and-yellow lighthouse, should be given a berth of 2 cables.

## Newcastle

54°12'N 5°52'·5W, *AC44, SC5612·3*

The resort town of Newcastle (7200) nestles in the W corner of Dundrum Bay, at the foot of the Mourne Mountains. Its harbour entirely dries at least a metre, but may offer an attractive temporary alongside berth with sufficient rise of tide. The entrance faces N and the harbour is subject to scend in winds between SE and NE. There are many small-craft moorings. The best berth is at the N pier, between the end and the steps, clean sand bottom. Newcastle has all the facilities of a seaside town. Newcastle Sailing Club, at the harbour, has showers. RNLI all-weather lifeboat station. HM phone 028 4372 2106. Constant +0010 Belfast, MHWS 5·1m, MHWN 4·1m, MLWN 1·5m, MLWS 0·5m.

## Dundrum

54°14'N 5°49'W, *AC44, SC5612·3 and Plan*

The pretty village of Dundrum, once a commercial port, lies on a tidal lagoon connected to the sea at the head of Dundrum Bay by a narrow channel and a hazardous bar. The channel is unbuoyed and should only be attempted by shallow-draft yachts in settled conditions with no swell, on a high and rising tide, in which conditions Dundrum offers a charming temporary port of call. The E side of the channel is part of the Ballykinler firing range, and the resultant freedom from human interference has led to its becoming a large seal colony. The bar is subject to shifting of the sand. The following directions are based on a visit in 2007 at HWS by a yacht drawing 1·8m.

## Directions

AC44 shows a line for crossing the bar with Dundrum Castle bearing 330°. This is still valid, and approaching the shore from latitude 54°14'N on this line gives a least depth of 0·3m at LAT. On this line the church E of the quay is visible in the centre of the entrance. The shore to the E is grassy, and to the W, wooded. When within a cable of the spit on the E side, borrow a little to the W to bring the church into transit with the W point of the entrance. This is closer to the mid-point of the channel here (but further out to sea this line leads across the sandspit on the W side). There are two derelict pile struc-

*Newcastle Harbour from the SE*

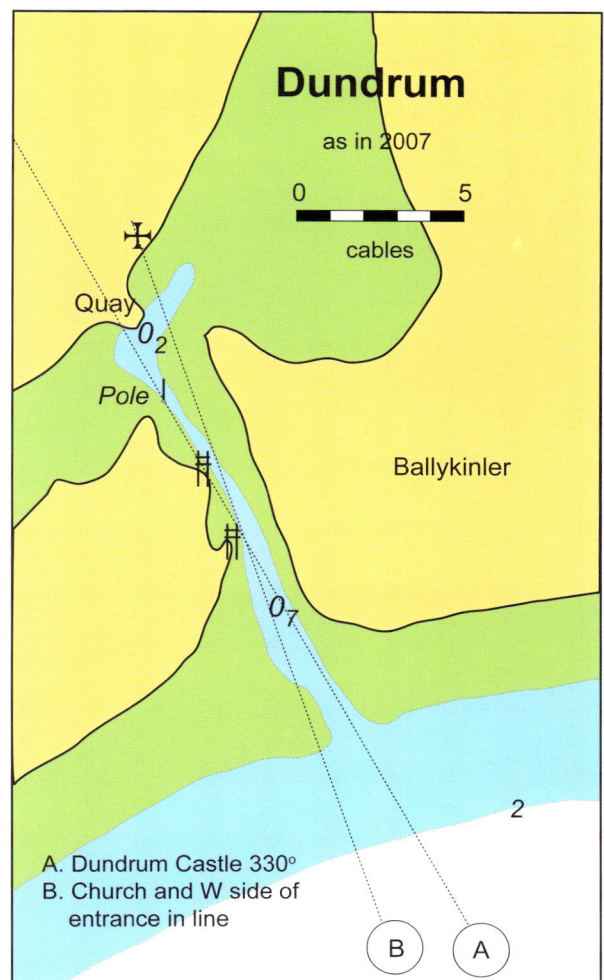

Dundrum

as in 2007

0      5

cables

Quay

0·2

Pole

Ballykinler

0·7

2

A. Dundrum Castle 330°
B. Church and W side of
   entrance in line

B    A

tures on the W side; leave them 50m to port. Leave the derelict pole beacon at the inner end of the channel close to port and steer for the quay, which has 0·2m. Strong tidal streams run in the channel and across the quay.

Shops, pubs and restaurants in Dundrum village. Constant +0005 Belfast, MHWS 4·8m, MHWN 3·8m, MLWN 1·8m, MLWS 0·8m.

## ST JOHN'S POINT TO ARDGLASS

Killough Bay opens a mile NE of St John's Point, and Phennick Cove, with the important fishing harbour of Ardglass, a mile further NE.

### Killough

54°14'·5N 5°36'·9W, *AC633 or SC5612·3 essential*

The inner bay dries out, and the outer bay has a number of drying rocks, of which only the outermost, Water Rocks, are marked. **From the S,** leave the Water Rocks perch a cable to port and steer for Ringfad Point until the distinctive castellated building at the root of Killough pier comes in line 304° with Castle Bright, a mansion 2M to the NW. Turn on to this line, which leads NE of the Plate and Carter Rocks and SW of the rocks off Crane Point. **From the N,** give Ringfad Point a berth of 2 cables. Once past Crane Point, steer for the outer end of the pier. The entrance to the inner harbour, between the stone pier to the W and the rubble remains of an old pier to the E, has 0·6m, and the inner face of the pier dries.

*Dundrum; the Castle, centre skyline*

*Dundrum Church and W side of the channel in line; derelict pile marker, L*

*St John's Point and the Mountains of Mourne from the NE*

*Killough approach and pier; note the castellated building, L centre*

Anchorage in suitable weather is available in Coney Island Bay, E of Crane Point. Subject to swell. Killough has shop and pubs. The pier is unsuitable as an alongside berth.

*Water Rocks perch, Killough*

## ARDGLASS

54°15'·4N 5°35'·8W, *AC44, 633, SC5612·3 and Plan*

The village of Ardglass lies on the S side of Phennick Cove, and has a fishery harbour and a small marina. The cove is much smaller and much less conspicuous from seaward than the nearby Killough Harbour, particularly when approaching from the S, and care should be taken not to enter Killough by mistake. Ardglass may be recognised by the conspicuous high breakwater of the South Pier; the harbour entrance is well lit. The entrance is straightforward by day or night, but should not be attempted in a SE gale. The buoyed channel to the marina was dredged to 3·3m, but in 2006 a yacht drawing 1·5m reported running aground in the channel abreast the No.4 port-hand buoy at LWS when the predicted tidal height was 0·7m.

### Directions

Approach steering NW and give the headlands on either side a berth of at least a cable. At night, approach in the white sector of the harbour light. Once past the end of the S pier, leave the small E Card buoy to port and follow the

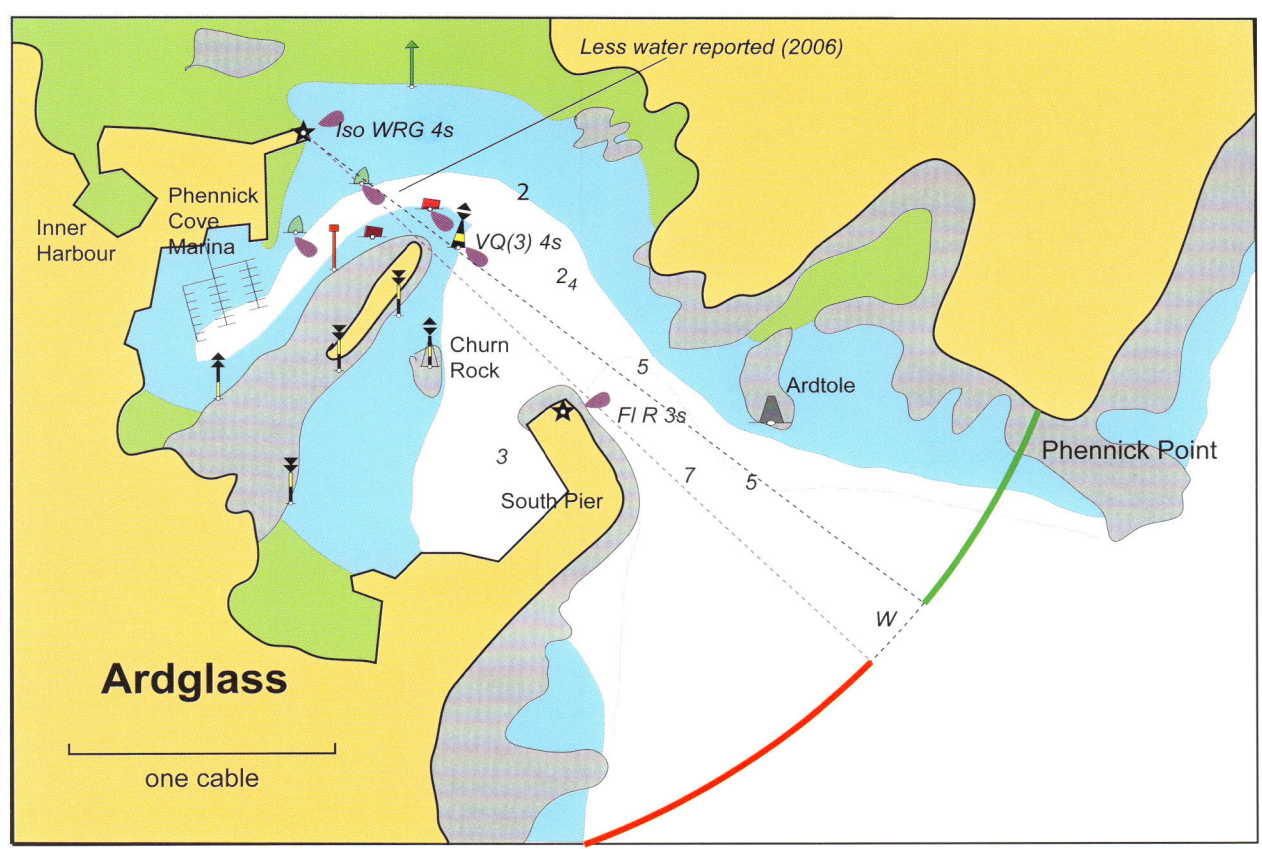

Less water reported (2006)

Iso WRG 4s

Phennick
Cove
Marina

Inner
Harbour

2

VQ(3) 4s

2₄

Churn
Rock

5

Ardtole

Fl R 3s

Phennick Point

3

7

5

South Pier

W

**Ardglass**

one cable

*Phennick Cove Marina, Ardglass; the buoyed entrance channel, R*

buoyed channel round into the marina. There is no anchorage in the harbour; a temporary alongside berth is available for fuelling from a tanker; call the HM on 028 4484 1291. The harbour is managed by the NI Fishery Harbour Authority, but is to be transferred to Down District Council.

## Marina

The marina has 80 berths and depths of 1·7 to 3·2m. Manoeuvring space can be a little tight for yachts over 13m in strong winds. VHF Ch M and 80 (office hours), phone 028 4484 2332.

## Inner Harbour

Leaving the white lighthouse tower close to port leads to the old inner harbour. The wall on the port hand dries 1m with a bottom of firm mud and small stones, and the inner harbour, once known by the delightful name of "God's pocket", dries 2m on soft mud.

## Facilities

Water and shore power on the marina pontoons; laundry; diesel in cans at the marina. Diesel by tanker, phone 028 4484 1494. Supermarket, shops, pubs, restaurant, doctor, bank, ATM, Internet access. Buses to Downpatrick and Belfast.

Constant +0010 Belfast, MHWS 5·3m, MHWN 4·2m, MLWN 1·7m, MLWS 0·7m.

## Bays between Guns Island and Killard Point

Ballyhornan Bay, N of Guns Island, offers attractive temporary or passage anchorage in 4 to 5m, sand; avoid anchoring in the S half of the bay due to underwater cables. Benderg Bay, to the NE, is sheltered from the NE by Killard Point and Craiglewey Rocks and also offers temporary anchorage in suitable conditions. Entering from the E, give Craiglewey Rocks a wide berth and do not turn in until Benderg Beach is well open.

**Killard Point** Constant +0005 Belfast.

*Ardglass Harbour from the S; Phennick Cove Marina, L*

# Chapter 3

## Strangford Lough to Fair Head

*Strangford Narrows; Strangford village and harbour, foreground, Portaferry at top*

Strangford Lough, the 12M by 2M stretch of water enclosed by the Ards Peninsula, is the finest sheltered sailing area in Ireland, and in its geology and ecology is quite unique in Europe. In geological terms, it is drowned drumlin country, debris left by the glaciers of the great Ice Ages and inundated by the sea. The bottom is extremely irregular, here flat and muddy, there steep-to and rocky. The glacial boulder clay has been eroded by the sea, leaving only the boulders in layers upon the shore and in heaps below water; where these great natural cairns are hazards to navigation they are known as pladdies, the word being derived from the Old Norse for "flat island". The west shore of the Lough, and the northern part of the Ards peninsula, fall within the commuter belt of greater Belfast, but the Lough has neverthe-

less a remote feel, and is ringed by small communities, each with its own distinctive character and charm; in keeping with that, there are no less than eleven sailing clubs on Strangford Lough, each one distinct in its aims and ambience. Strangford Lough is simply a delight.

The area is steeped in history, and the Lough is ringed by ancient castles and fine old houses. Daft Eddy's pub on Sketrick Island commemorates a famous character of two centuries ago who met his end during a gun battle between the smugglers and the Revenue men.

There was once a healthy export trade in farm produce from the small ports of Strangford Lough, but now the only commercial traffic is the ferry which crosses the Narrows. The peaceful and uncrowded ambience of the Lough is treasured by all those who live around its shores

Black Head — Fl 3s

Belfast Lough

Carrickfergus

L Fl 10s

Iso R 12s

Mew Island
Fl(4) 30s

Copeland
Islands

Cultra

Bangor

Donaghadee

Iso WR 4s

BELFAST

Ards Peninsula

Ballyferris Point

Skullmartin
L Fl 10s

Ballywalter

Strangford

Burial I

Lough

Portavogie

Iso WRG 5s

South
Rock LF
Fl(3) R 30s

0  2  4  6  8
miles

**Strangford Lough
to
Belfast Lough**

Ballyquintin Point

Angus Rock
Fl R 5s

Guns I — L Fl 10s

tion. Streams reach eight knots, with vigorous eddies of which the Routen Wheel is one of the only two named whirlpools in Ireland. An ebb tide against an onshore wind, the hospitable sailing clubs, and pubs like Daft Eddy's, are merely a few of the factors which can make Strangford Lough a difficult place to leave.

The North Channel coast of the Ards Peninsula is rocky and tideswept, with the fishing village of Portavogie, the resort town of Donaghadee, and the Copeland Islands at the entrance to Belfast Lough. The Lough is a busy commercial waterway and an important sailing centre, with large marinas at Bangor and Carrickfergus. Further north is the busy port of Larne, and the charming villages of Glenarm, Carnlough and Cushendall at the foot of the Glens of Antrim.

The North Channel, with its strong tides, can raise steep and dangerous seas in storm conditions. On January 31, 1953, the 2600-ton ferry *Princess Victoria,* on passage from Stranraer to Larne, foundered in heavy seas east of Belfast Lough, with the loss of 125 lives. The Donaghadee lifeboat *Sir Samuel Kelly* rescued 32 people that night. The same lifeboat later served at Courtmacsherry in County Cork, from where in August 1979 she rescued the crew of the yacht *Casse Tete V* during the disastrous Fastnet Race of that year. She is now preserved at Donaghadee.

and sail its waters, and its wildlife and underwater flora and fauna are diverse and often unique. The Lough is a Marine Nature Reserve; there are no fish farms and no large marina developments, and it is unlikely that there will ever be either.

The Lough is connected to the sea by a channel three miles in length and half a mile wide though which the tide flows with considerable force, and is being harnessed for power genera-

*The Routen Wheel;
Gowland Rocks
beacon, R*

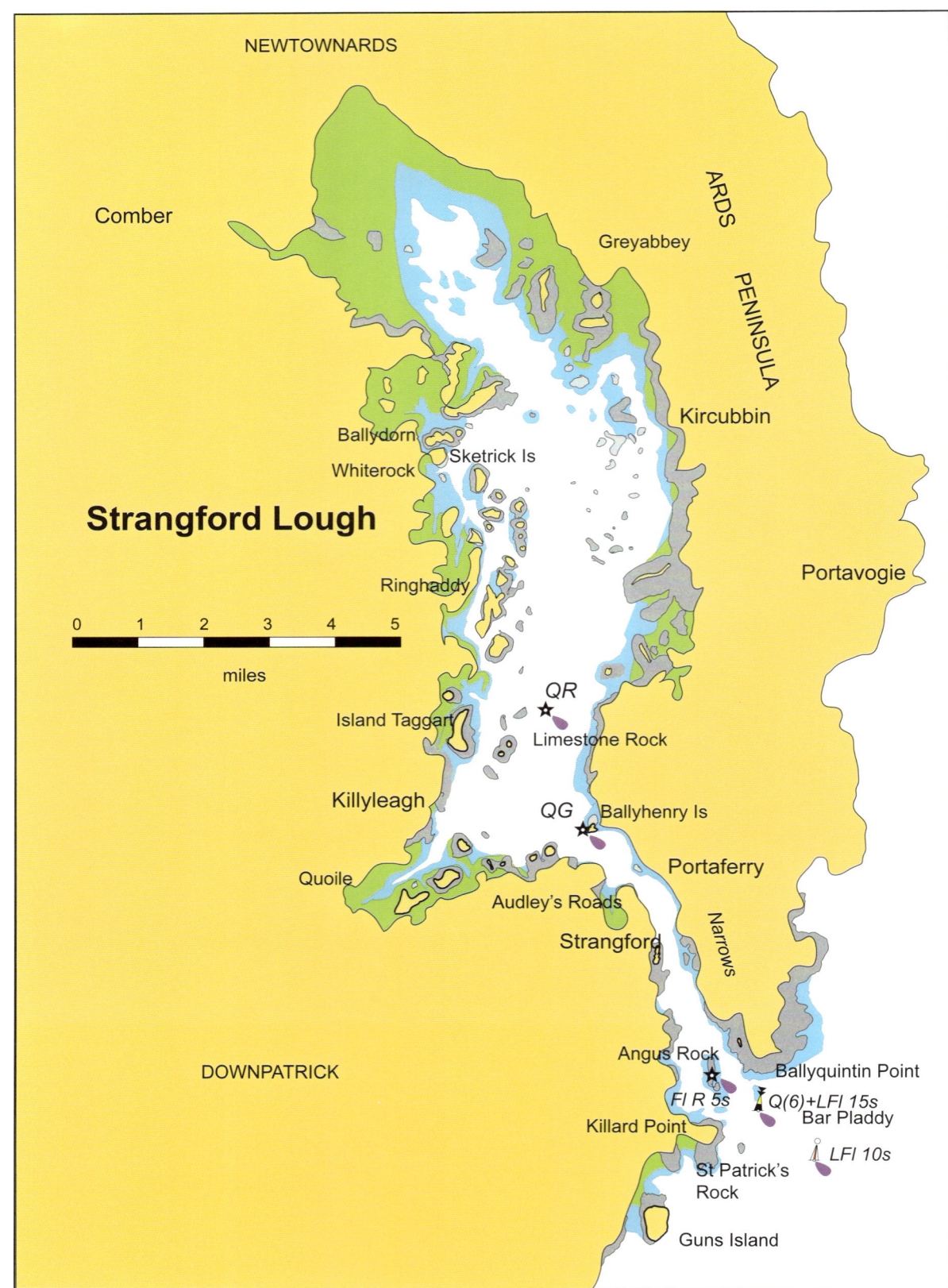

### Charts

SC5612 covers the whole coast described in this chapter. In terms of individual charts, AC2156 is indispensable for Strangford Lough and the Ards coast. AC2159, Strangford Narrows, is optional. AC1753 is essential for Belfast Lough or if exploring the Copelands. AC 1752 is optional. AC2198 and 2199 cover the North Channel coast, and AC1237 is needed only if spending time in Larne Lough.

*St Patrick's Rock and its perch, at the S side of the entrance to Strangford Lough*

## Tidal Streams – Strangford Lough and Approaches

Offshore, SE of the fairway buoy, the tide turns NE at HW Belfast +0200 and SW at HW Belfast –0600, running SW for almost 8 hours. In the Narrows, the in-going stream begins at HW Belfast –0400 and the outgoing at HW Belfast +0200, reaching a maximum rate of 8 knots at springs. There is only a 15-minute period of slack water at the turn, and the streams run at 3 knots within an hour either side of this. Rates W of Angus Rock and N of Bar Pladdy are less. Close N of Gowland Point on the E side there is a large circular eddy called the Routen Wheel, which can be dangerous for small craft at times. The streams begin to slacken above Strangford and Portaferry, and quickly dissipate once the Lough opens up. Noticeable streams run through some of the channels in the Lough, notably Ringhaddy Sound and in the approaches to Ballydorn.

## Dangers

*Strangford Entrance and Narrows:*

**St Patrick's Rock** (dries), 2 cables E of Killard Point

**Bar Pladdy** (0·6m), 5 cables SSW of Ballyquintin Point

**Angus Rock,** in mid-channel 1M N of Killard Point. The summit of the rock is above-water but drying reefs extend for 5 cables S and 1 cable N of the light tower

**Pladdy Lug,** drying rock 4 cables WSW of Ballyquintin Point

The shores from the entrance to Rue Point at the narrows are foul with rocks and drying reefs on both sides, extending out to **Salt Rock** on the W side and **Gowland Rocks** on the E.

**Walter Rocks,** dry 3·4m, 4 cables NW of Portaferry

*Strangford Lough:*

The drying and below-water hazards in Strangford Lough easily number over a hundred, and no attempt is made here to list them all. The most significant ones, on account of their position close to the main fairway, include:

**Skate Rock** (dries 0·9m), **Barrel Rock** (dries 0·6m) and the **Rigg** (0·3m), near the channel to Killyleagh and Quoile

**Verde Rocks** (locally Rathgorman Pladdy), drying, SE of Ringhaddy Sound

**Long Sheelah** (dries 3·5m), **Hadd Rock** (dries), **Blackdog Rock** (dries 0·9m) and **Dead Man's Rock** (dries 0·9m) on the W side of the main fairway to White Rock Bay and Ballydorn, with **Tip Reef** (dries 0·6m) on the E side of this fairway, and at the entrance to the channel to Kircubbin.

**Rig Pladdy** and **Downey Pladdy**, drying, on either side of the fairway E of Mahee Island.

## Lights and Marks

*Strangford Lough – entrance:*

**Strangford Fairway** buoy, RWVS L Fl 10s, AIS

**St Patrick's Rock**, 9m red stayed perch, unlit

**Bar Pladdy** buoy, S Card Q(6)+LFl 15s

**Pladdy Lug,** white stone beacon, unlit

**Tail of Angus,** black stone beacon, unlit

**Angus Rock,** white tower with red top, Fl R 5s 15m 6M

**Dogtail Point,** green perch Oc(4) G 10s 2m 5M

**Salt Rock,** white tower with red top Fl R 3s 8m 3M

**Gowland Rocks,** white pillar with green top, Oc(2) 10s 6m 5M

*Strangford and Portaferry harbours and approaches:*

**Swan Island,** white pillar with red top Fl(2) WR 6s 5m, W115°–334° R334°–115°. Shows white over the Narrows channel to SE and NW, red inshore

**South Pladdy,** white pole beacon Fl(3) 10s

**Watch House Point Rock,** red pole QR 3m 3M

*Strangford entrance from the SE; St Patrick's Rock lower R centre, Killard Point centre with Angus Rock beyond, Ballyquintin Point R*

**Strangford East,** leading lights 256°, front Oc WRG 5s 6m W9M, R6M, G6M, R190°–244° G244°-252° W252°–260° R260°–294°. Rear Oc R 5s 10m 6M

**North Pladdy,** white pole beacon, N Card Q

**Portaferry Marina breakwater,** Iso WRG 4s G320°–021° W021°–097° R097°–140°. Shows white over the approach from the W, green over the shallows to the S and red over the breakwater to the N

**Portaferry Marina** entrance buoys, 2×SHM, unlit

**Portaferry Pier,** orange mast OcWR 10s 9m W9M R6M, W335°–005° R005°–017° W017°–026°.

*Strangford Lough:*

**Church Point,** white pyramid beacon with red top, Fl(4) R 10s

**Ballyhenry Point,** white pillar with green top, QG 3M

**Killyleagh Town Rock** beacon, brown brick tower, unlit

**Limestone Rock,** red pole beacon, QR 3m 3M There are slim poles, unlit, as follows (this is not necessarily an exhaustive list):

*South of Limestone Rock:*

on Walter Rock, Skate Rock, Barrel Rock, the Rigg, the Bradley shoal, the Toad Stone and the gravel spit E of Gibbs Island in the Quoile; and on Long Rock (E end), on the spit W of Don O'Neill Island, on Selk Rock (NW and SE ends), Limestone Pladdy and the W end of Limestone Rock. At Mill Rock, N of Killyleagh, a line of 4 poles extends E from the shore.

*In the approaches to Ringhaddy Sound:*

on Brownrock Pladdy, Brown Rock and Verde Rocks.

*Between Pawle Island and Rainey Island:*

on Long Sheelah (W and E ends), Jane's Rock, Sand Rock, Sand Rock Pladdy, Hadd Rock, the 0·3m shoal between Greenisland Rock and Roe Island, Dead Man's Rock, Bradock Rock and on the SE side of the narrow N entrance to Ballydorn.

*On the E side of the Lough and on the channel to Kircubbin:*

on Tip Reef, Sand Rock Pladdy, Michael's Rock, Round Skart Rock and Newtown Rock.

*NE of Rainey Island:*

on Rig Pladdy.

In addition, spar buoys, usually black, are placed to mark some of the other dangers. These pole beacons and buoys are maintained by the sailing clubs around the Lough and are generally reliable, but a beacon can easily go missing. When covered, the pladdies often betray their positions by a change in the colour of the water, a smooth slick or a patch of weed. Note that there are two distinct Sand Rocks and two Sand Rock Pladdies. McLaughlin Rock, 1M S of Don O'Neill Island, is unmarked, as are all the rocks in the Lough with more than 2m of water.

There are also many racing marks moored around the Lough. Consult (for example) www.slyc.org.uk for details.

*Typical Strangford Lough pladdy and marks; Long Sheelah from the W*

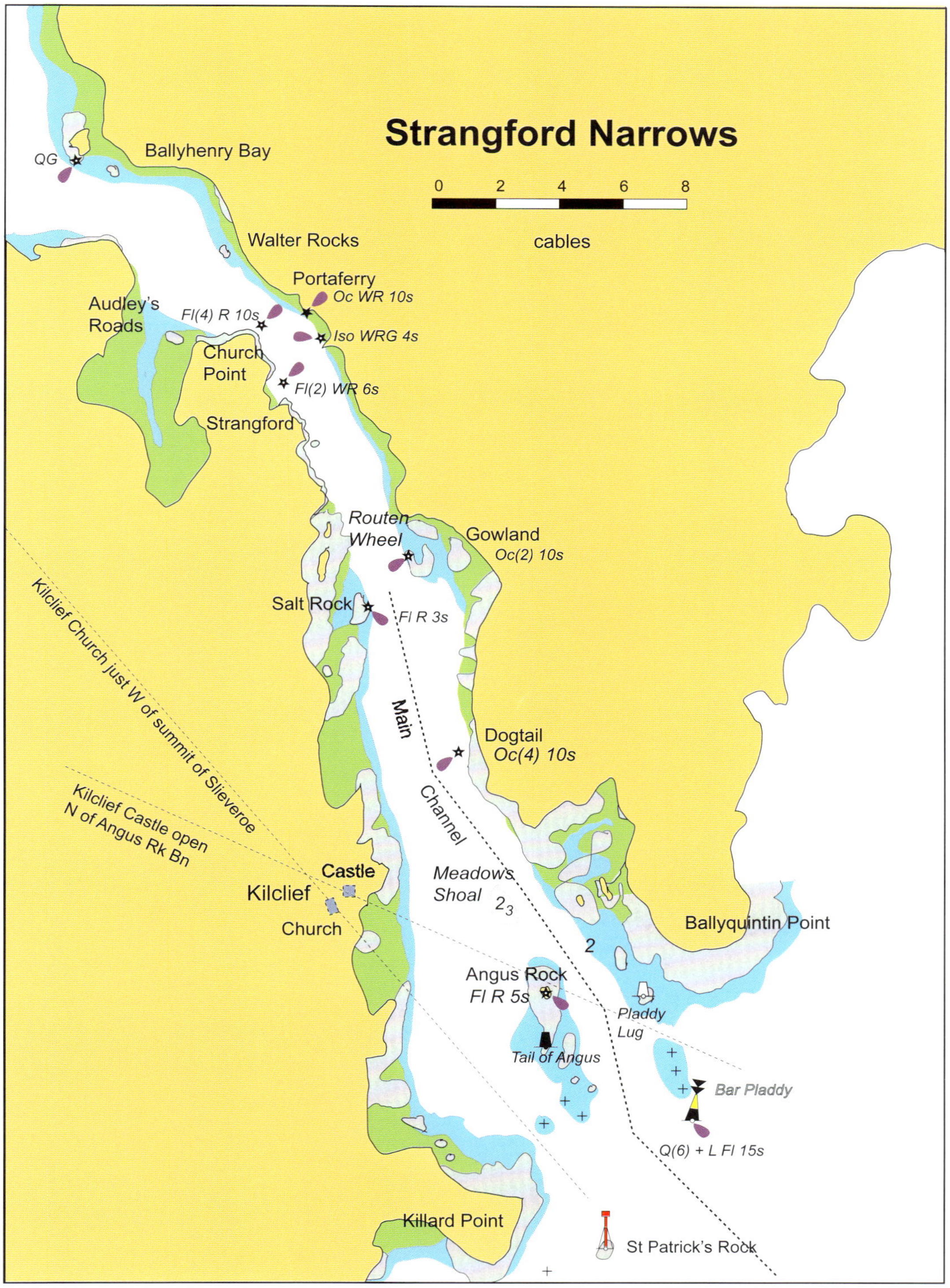

**Strangford Narrows**

0   2   4   6   8

cables

QG

Ballyhenry Bay

Walter Rocks

Audley's
Roads

Portaferry
*Oc WR 10s*

Fl(4) R 10s

*Iso WRG 4s*

Church
Point

Fl(2) WR 6s

Strangford

*Routen
Wheel*

Gowland
*Oc(2) 10s*

Salt Rock

*Fl R 3s*

Kilclief Church just W of summit of Slieveroe

Main

Dogtail
*Oc(4) 10s*

Channel

Kilclief Castle open
N of Angus Rk Bn

**Castle**

Kilclief

Church

*Meadows
Shoal*  2 3

2

Ballyquintin Point

Angus Rock
*Fl R 5s*

*Pladdy
Lug*

*Tail of Angus*

+

+

+   *Bar Pladdy*

*Q(6) + L Fl 15s*

Killard Point

St Patrick's Rock

+

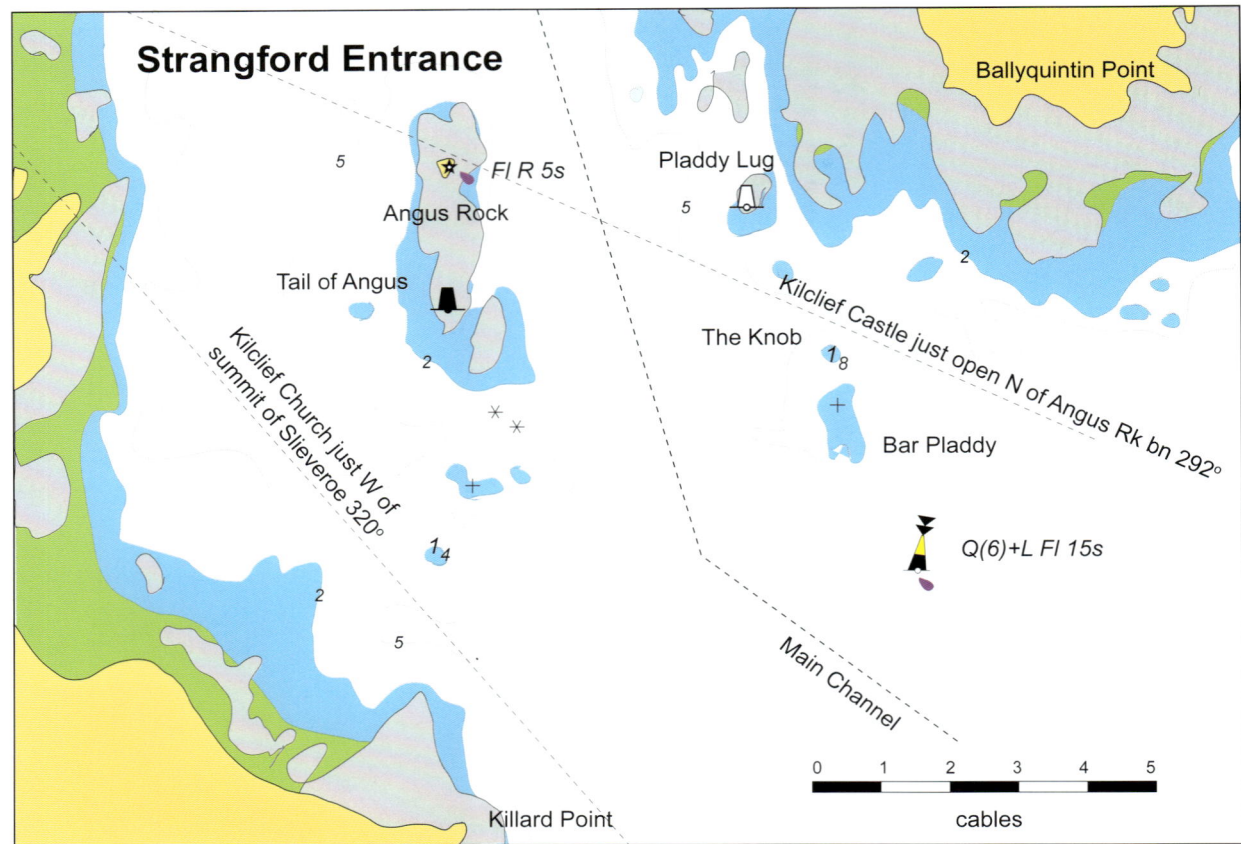

Strangford Entrance

- 5
- Fl R 5s
- Angus Rock
- Pladdy Lug
- Ballyquintin Point
- 5
- Tail of Angus
- *Kilclief Castle just open N of Angus Rk bn 292°*
- The Knob
- 1 8
- 2
- *Kilclief Church just W of summit of Slieveroe 320°*
- Bar Pladdy
- 2
- 1 4
- Q(6)+L Fl 15s
- 2
- 5
- Main Channel
- Killard Point

| 0 | 1 | 2 | 3 | 4 | 5 |

cables

## STRANGFORD LOUGH
### Caution

In Strangford Lough it is particularly necessary to be constantly aware of the vessel's exact position and of the positions of the nearest hazards, and to be able to relate what is seen to what is on the chart. AC2156 or SC5612, based on a survey carried out in 1953, gives a remarkably accurate representation of the present hydrography, and should be kept to hand at all times and constantly referred to, bearing in mind also the offset between the chart and WGS84 (GPS) datum. The seabed is extremely irregular, rocky shoals rise steeply from deep water, and most of the islands are very similar in profile and appearance. Black Rock, 5 cables NE of Island Taggart, is described on the chart as 5m high, but is only about 1·5m.

At the time of writing (2007) there are works in progress to install tidal generators in the Narrows abreast of Salt and Gowland Rocks. Consult www.irishcruisingclub.com for the latest information on the progress of these works and any associated changes to navigational aids.

### Environmental protection

The ecosystem in Strangford Lough is unique

*Kilclief Church (L) just W of Slieveroe summit leads through the west channel. Kilclief Castle, R*

*Strangford entrance, seen from the shore at Kilclief, with a strong southerly wind blowing against the ebb tide. Angus Rock beacon, upper L, and Tail of Angus beacon R. Note how relatively calm the West Channel is*

and valuable, and visiting yachts are requested to take every precaution to avoid damaging it. On no account should any waste be dropped overboard or any fuel spilt. Many of the islands are bird sanctuaries (terns being the main species), and landing on them is prohibited during the breeding season, which extends from March to August. The list includes but is not confined to Don O'Neill, Swan, Roe, Jackdaw, Green, Bird and Round Islands.

## Strangford Entrance
54°19'N 5°30'W, *AC2156, 2159, SC5612*
The ebb tide against an onshore wind raises steep and dangerous seas at the entrance and for at least a mile out to sea. Even in calm conditions, the meeting of the ebb stream with the main body of water outside raises a confused sea. The optimum time to enter and leave is within 15 minutes of slack HW; at this stage, the flood tide having run for six hours, the sea state at the mouth is at its calmest and there is the maximum depth in the minor channels. At this state of the tide, it is always safe to enter, and it is safe also to leave in any reasonable weather. A yacht capable of 6 knots should take her departure from Audley's Roads at HW Belfast +0100 against the last of the flood stream.

**Entering from the S,** St Patrick's Rock may be left on either hand, but beware of the rock with 2·4m, close SE of Killard Point. **From the N,** the transit of St Patrick's Rock perch with the beacon on Guns Island leads S of Quintin Rock. The main channel is well marked and lit, but there are also navigable channels N of Bar Pladdy and W of Angus Rock. The key landmarks for these channels are the castle and

church at Kilclief, on the W shore. The castle is a tall, grey, stone building made up of four castellated towers, while the church, close W of the castle, is a tall, plain, grey barn-like building with a small bell-tower at one end *(see photographs)*.

## Main Channel
The main channel is bounded by Angus Rock to the W and by Bar Pladdy buoy and Pladdy Lug beacon to the E. From the S, do not turn in until Portaferry waterfront is visible E of Angus Rock. From Portavogie and the N, leave the Bar Pladdy buoy to starboard after rounding Ballyquintin Point. Give Pladdy Lug beacon a berth of half a cable. To avoid the Meadows shoal, keep Dogtail and Gowlands beacons in line 341°. Mid-channel is free of dangers from here until the Lough opens up.

## West Channel
The passage W of the Angus Rock is less subject to the tide and tends to be much calmer in onshore winds against the tidal stream. It has a least depth of 2·4m; however it is narrow, a rock with 1·4m lies close E of mid-channel, and rocks with 0·8m lie on either hand. From the S, approach on a course of 320° with Kilclief Church just W of the 85m-summit of Slieveroe on the skyline. There is a radio mast on this summit *(see photograph)*. This transit leads W of the 1·4m rock. When the Tail of Angus beacon is abeam, turn N and leave Angus Rock tower well to starboard.

## Channel N of Bar Pladdy
This channel between Bar Pladdy and Ballyquintin Point has 2·1m but The Knob, with

*Kilclief Castle just visible
N of Angus Rock beacon
leads through the channel
N of Bar Pladdy*

1·8m, lies a cable N of Bar Pladdy. Keep
Kilclief Castle just visible N of the Angus
Rock tower 292° and pass half a cable ■ off
the Pladdy Lug beacon *(see photograph)*.

**Caution**
When using these passages (particularly N
of Bar Pladdy) take particular care to avoid
being set off the transit line by the strong
tidal stream.

*Pladdy Lug beacon*

*Strangford from the SE; Swan Island, centre R, the pier and ferry slip centre; Audley's Roads, top. The ferry's
track runs S of Swan Island; the spare ferry (R) is on her mooring.*

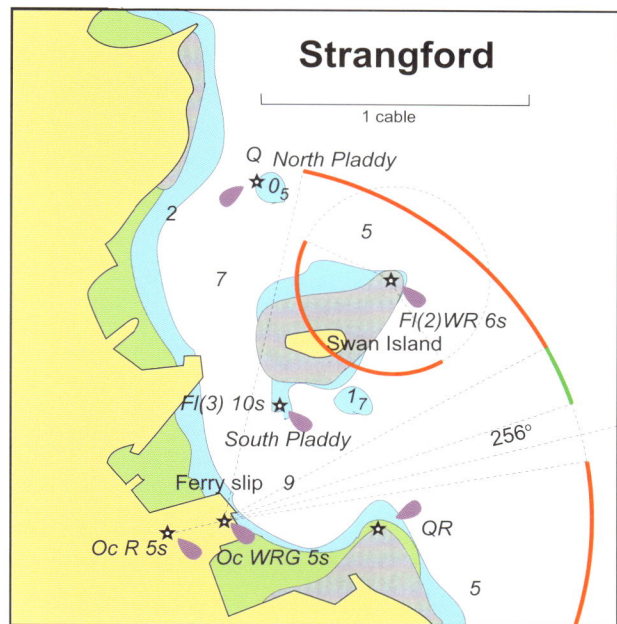

**Strangford**

54°22'·4N 5°33'W, *AC2156, 2159, SC5612·7*

The picturesque village of Strangford, on its bay on the W side of the Narrows, is sheltered by Swan Island and is the W terminus of the car ferry. Its pier can offer a temporary alongside berth on its face, or on its SE side with sufficient rise of tide, but the pools N and S of Swan Island have no room to anchor out of the tide and the ferry's track. The pier has 5m and is the ferry's overnight berth. There is 0·4m at the steps on the SE side. The bay is just out of the main tidal stream and is subject to eddies which result in a N-going drift except for an hour either side of HW. Do not obstruct the ferry, and when manoeuvring take note of the way the moored boats are lying.

Shops, PO, pubs, restaurants, ATM. Water on the pier. Slip suitable for trailer sailers.

**PORTAFERRY**

54°22'·7N 5°33'W

Portaferry is one of only two significant towns situated directly on the shores of the Lough. It is the E terminus of the ferry and has a 30-berth marina with a floating breakwater. The marina has 2·5m and the entrance faces S. Two unlit green buoys mark the limit of the dredged basin S of the breakwater. Approach steering between E and NE (or at night, in the white sector of

*Portaferry from the NW*

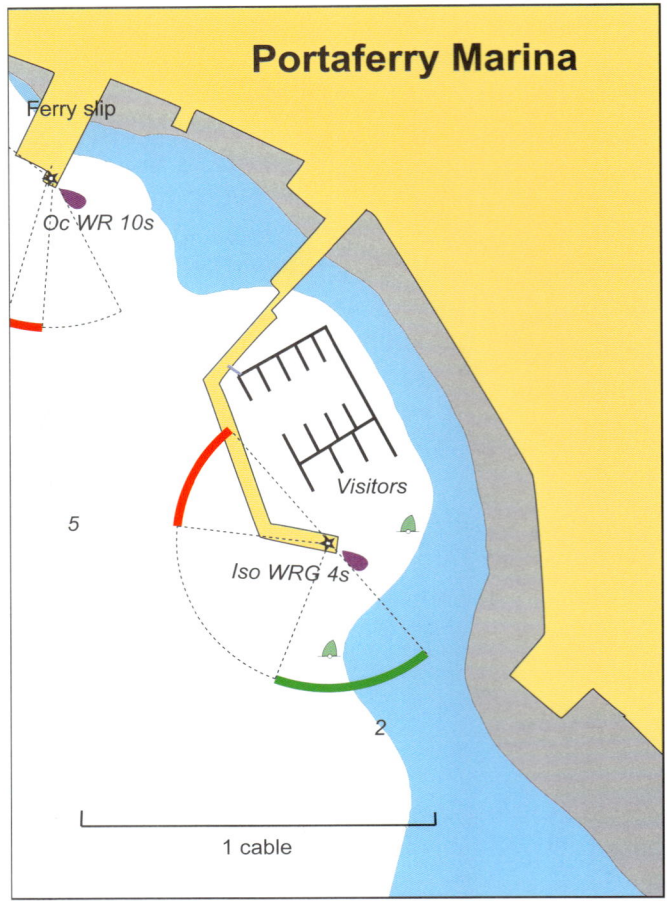

**Portaferry Marina**

Ferry slip

Oc WR 10s

Visitors

Iso WRG 4s

5

2

1 cable

Showers at the marina or at Barholm Apartments, 200m; laundry facilities at Barholm. Water and shore power on the pontoons. Portaferry has shops, PO, pubs, restaurants, banks, ATMs, filling station. RNLI inshore lifeboat station.

**Anchorages – S end of Strangford Lough**

- **Audley's Roads**, the bay 5 cables NW of Strangford, is a delightful, safe and popular anchorage. Anchor in 4 to 5m between the ruined pier below Audley's Castle and the pole opposite, which marks the shoal extending from the SE shore. The tide runs strongly across the mouth of the bay.

- **Ballyhenry Bay**, on the NE shore 7 cables from Portaferry, is sheltered from NW to E. The tide runs strongly across the mouth of the bay. Beware Walter Rocks on the S side and a wreck, which seldom covers, 2 cables SE of Ballyhenry beacon. From the NW, approach with the small wind turbine bearing 054°, to clear the wreck and John's Rock, inside it.

- The bay between Jackdaw and Chapel Islands has anchorage in 2 to 3m, no further in than a line joining the S sides of the islands.

Strangford (and all of Strangford Lough) Constant +0145 Belfast, MHWS 3·8m, MHWN 3·1m.

the breakwater light) and leave the buoys to starboard. Beware of the strong cross tides; the depths decrease sharply, SE of the buoys. The stream runs strongly through the marina during the top half of the tide. Marina manager 028 4272 9598.

*Audley's Roads from the S; Audley's Castle centre R with Ballyhenry Island beyond; Don O'Neill Island top L*

*The wreck in Ballyhenry Bay; Ballyhenry Point beacon, centre R*

## Directions – Killyleagh and Quoile

With Ballyhenry beacon directly astern, steer 275° for Killyleagh Town Rock beacon, leaving the slim pole markers on Skate Rock and the Rigg to port. The Rigg, with 0·3m, is particularly hazardous because of its position, and its perch may not be dependable. Entering the Quoile between Green Island and the Bradley shoal, favour the port hand and leave the Toad Stone and Gibbs Island perches to starboard. There is deep water all the way to the Yacht Club pontoon but stay close to the moorings when E of Gore's Island.

## QUOILE RIVER

54°23'N 5°38'·5W, *see Plan*

The Quoile River was dammed in 1962 by a tidal barrier designed to protect the town of Downpatrick from flooding. Quoile YC, on Castle Island immediately below the barrier, has a 50m-long pontoon with 3m alongside, and visitors' moorings. There is a drying rock about 30m NNW of the end of the pontoon, marked by a pole and a small buoy with an E Card topmark. The Club welcomes visitors and has bar and showers. There is anchorage on the NW

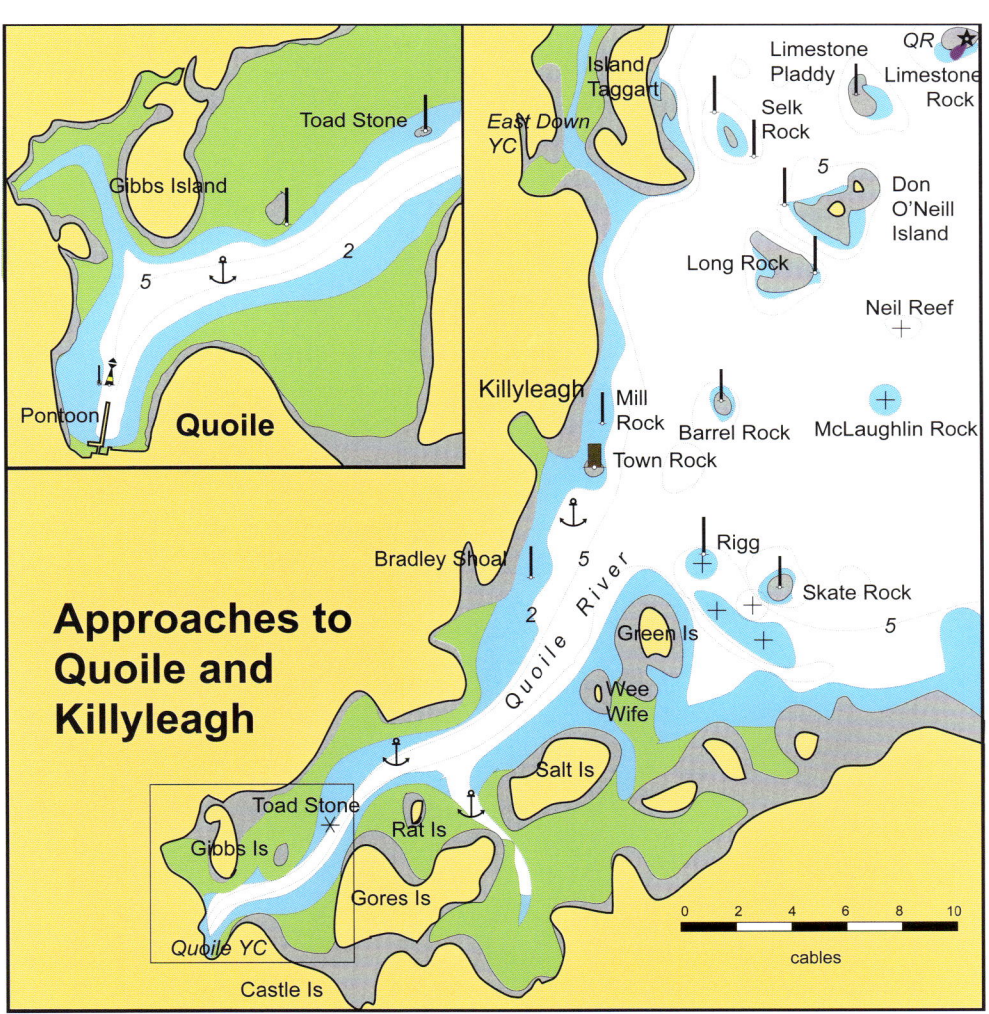

*Quoile from the SE; the YC and pontoon, bottom L, the tidal barrier L and Gibbs Island top R*

side of the channel, N of Rat Island, and in the channel between Salt Island and Gore's Island. The latter is said to be the site of St Patrick's first landing in Ireland.

## KILLYLEAGH
54°23'·5N 5°38'·6W, *see Plan*
Anchor in 2 to 3m, S of the Town Rock beacon. In summer, Killyleagh YC maintains a 25m-long pontoon, with 2m at its outer end; the YC may also be able to provide a visitor's mooring, and has bar and showers. The channel to the old Town Dock is shallow and the bay dries out. The Town Dock itself has been refurbished as part of a housing development and is no longer suitable for berthing, but offers convenient dinghy landing except at LW. Water and shore power on the YC pontoon. Killyleagh has shops, PO, pubs, restaurants, banks, ATMs, Internet access, doctors. Buses to Downpatrick and Belfast. Irish Spars & Rigging (028 4482 8882, www.irishspars.com) is based in Killyleagh. The town's impressive castle was originally built by the de Courcy family in the 12th century,

and Killyleagh was the birthplace in 1660 of the naturalist Sir Hans Sloane, after whom Sloane Square in London was named.

**Directions – Ballyhenry and Killyleagh to Whiterock and Ballydorn**
Most of the navigable channels are clearly depicted on AC2156. The main routes are:
- E of McLaughlin Rock (which is unmarked and hazardous) and Limestone Rock, or
- W of Long Rock and Don O'Neill (locally Dunnyneill) Island and between Selk Rock

*Quoile YC pontoon (Ed Wheeler)*

*Killyleagh from the S; the YC pontoon and anchorage, foreground, with the Town Dock beyond, and Town Rock with its beacon tower, to the R. Island Taggart, upper centre, Pawle Island and Islandmore at top. Selk Rock, Black Rock and Brown Rock are visible upper R, beyond Island Taggart*

and Limestone Pladdy, then either

- E of Long Sheelah, Hadd, Blackdog and Dead Man's Rocks, or
- between Long Sheelah and Jane's Rock, then between Sand and Dunsy Rocks, then SW of Sand Rock Pladdy and Green Island, then close NE of Darragh Island, then leaving Conly Island and Bradock Rock to port (beware the spit E of Parton Island) and Veagh and Trasnagh Islands to starboard, or
- between Long Sheelah and Jane's Rock,

then between Sand and Hadd Rocks, then NE of Sand Rock Pladdy, then between Green and Great Minnis Islands, then leaving Little Minnis, Drummond and Inishanier Islands to starboard and Roe and Inisharoan Islands to port. Beware the 1·5m shoal W of Great Minnis.

Don O'Neill Island is distinctively different from the others in the Lough in being relatively high, humpbacked and tree-clad, and it makes a very useful and conspicuous reference point.

## Island Taggart

54°24'·5N 5°38'W, *see Plan*

The channel W of Island Taggart is the home of East Down YC. There are moorings in Holme Bay, to the SE, and the club has a pontoon, with 2m alongside, in the Inner Pool W of Island Taggart. This is accessible above half flood. Entering from Holme Bay, favour the island side (there are poles on either side of the entrance). The club welcomes visitors and has bar and showers. The channel N of the YC pontoon is navigable right through on a high and rising tide, the shallowest point being just S of the small Dodd's Island. Great care is required, with continuous monitoring of the echosounder.

There is a pleasant anchorage in the bay at the N end of the channel, between Island Taggart and Castle Island, and a deep channel W of Black Rock and Brown Rock; stay within 50m of Black Rock and the Brown Rock pole, and beware Long Point spit SW of Castle Island.

## RINGHADDY SOUND

54°26'N 5°37'·4W, *see Plan*

Ringhaddy Sound, W of Pawle Island, Islandmore and Dunsy Island, is splendidly sheltered and very attractive. Ringhaddy Cruising Club has its clubhouse and pontoon facility opposite Islandmore. The leading line shown on AC2156 is no longer of value since the windmill at

*Ringhaddy Sound from the SW; Islandmore R, with Dunsy, Green, Great Minnis, Little Minnis and Drummond Islands beyond; Gull Rock and Sand Rock Pladdy top R; Greenisland Rock, Darragh, Parton, Roe and Inishanier Islands top L.*

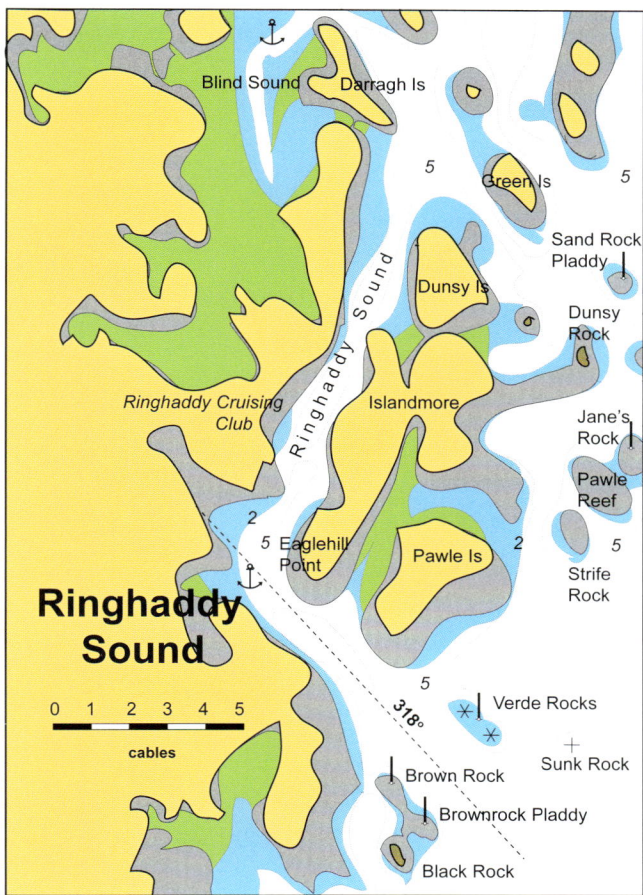

The position of the moorings generally indicates the deep water. The tide runs through the Sound at up to 2 knots.

The yacht club pontoon is available as a temporary berth and has 1·8m. Water on the pontoon.

Anchorage is available in 4m in the channel W of Eaglehill Point.

**Blind Sound**
54°28'·3N 5°37'·9W, *see Plan of Ringhaddy Sound*
There is good anchorage in this bay between Darragh and Conly Islands. Anchor in 3m, with Parton Island just closed behind the N end of Darragh Island.

**WHITE ROCK BAY**
54°29'N 5°38'·1W, *see Plan*
This bay S of Sketrick Island is the home of Strangford Lough YC. The bay has many moorings and one can usually be made available to a visitor. Give the tiny Bradock Island (tree-clad, with a single house) a berth of 1·5 cables to clear Bradock Rock (normally marked) and enter the bay steering W. The Yacht Club welcomes visitors and has a pontoon with 1·2m at its outer end, water and shore power. The Club (028 9754 1883) is staffed during office hours, has bar and showers and can advise on all local facilities. Whiterock Boatyard, 0778 878 2481, all repairs; mechanical repairs, Marine

Killinchy is not now visible, but the Sound can easily be identified from the SE by the forest of masts in the anchorage. Hold mid-channel in the approach but beware the spit which extends E from the W side, just S of the club pontoon. This is well illustrated in the aerial photograph.

*Ringhaddy Sound from the E; Ringhaddy CC pontoons*

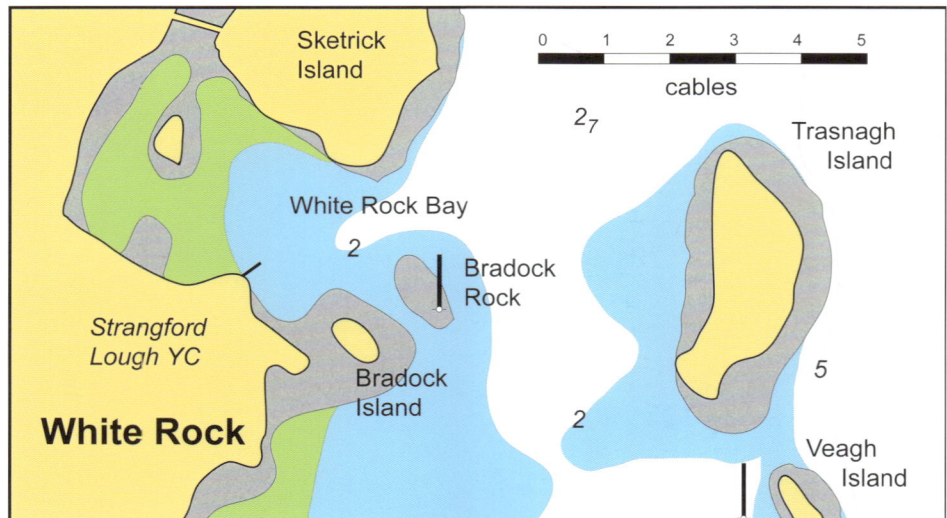

*White Rock Bay from the SW; Sketrick Island, centre, Rainey and Mahee islands beyond. Ballydorn, upper L,*
*Calf Island and Lythe Rock, top R*

**BALLYDORN**

54°29'·4N 5°38'·2W, *see Plan*

The channel between Rainey Island and the shore is the home of Down Cruising Club, whose clubhouse is the former lightship *Petrel,* built in 1917 and acquired by the club in 1968. A pontoon with 2·5m is moored alongside the lightship. The channels N and S of Rainey Island drain the extensive drying bay to the NW, and the tidal streams reach 3 knots in the narrow entrances at Ballydorn. A stranger is advised to enter and leave near slack water. Enter close S of Rainey Island. There is a small drying patch (shown on AC2156) in mid-

Engine Services, Killinchy (agent for Nanni-diesel), 0783 131 1412. Sketrick Sailmakers, 028 9754 1400 or 0771 206 7731; pub/restaurant on Sketrick Island, 1 km; nearest shop at Balloo, 3 km.

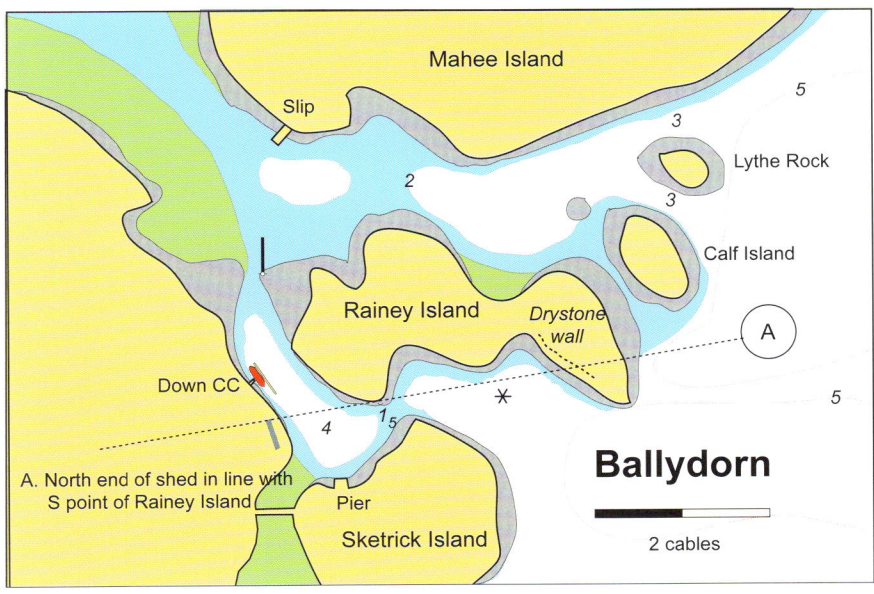

*Ballydorn from the E*

Ballydorn

A. North end of shed in line with S point of Rainey Island

2 cables

bring the wooded SW tip of the island in transit with the N end of a long black shed on the shore to the W *(see photographs)*. Take the narrows in mid-channel and then hold to the mainland side approaching the lightship. The narrows has 1·5m and the pool 3 to 4m.

The exit N of Rainey Island has less than 0·5m and is very narrow, but is navigable with great care at slack HW. There is a pole beacon marking the end of the spit stretching NW from Rainey Island. Approach from the pool steering NNW and leave the pole very close to starboard, then steer for the slipway on Mahee Island opposite, until in deeper water. Lythe Rock and Calf Island lie in the E entrance to the channel between Rainey and Mahee Islands; there is 3m on either side of

channel between Rainey and Sketrick Islands; the moorings in the channel are mostly S of this patch but the deeper channel lies N of it. Keep the S side of Rainey Island close aboard until abreast the W end of a drystone wall along the shore and at the low waist of the island, then

*Ballydorn entrance; the S tip of Rainey Island in line with the N end of the long black shed*

*N exit from Ballydorn; the channel (L centre) is directly above the mooring buoy*

Lythe Rock but the channel between Calf and Rainey Islands is foul.

The club welcomes visitors and has bar and showers. Water, shore power and diesel on the pontoon (diesel available to members and to visitors from outside the Lough); pub/restaurant on Sketrick Island, 400m.

### Channels to Kircubbin
54°27'·3N 5°34'·5W
Kircubbin is the only accessible village on the E shore of the Lough N of Portaferry, and lies behind a maze of drying rocks and shoals; but there are several navigable channels to it. The most straightforward of these is entered between Tip Reef, marked by a pole, and Gransha Point. From a position 2 cables E of Long Sheelah, steer 041° for 1·5M. This leads between Hoskyn's Shoal (2·4m) and a 0·3m patch 2 cables E of it; err nothing to the E. Then steer 003° for 1·5M; Sand Rock Pladdy, which should be left on the port hand at the turn, has a pole beacon. Monaghan Bank, the promontory S of Kircubbin Bay, is a conspicuous steep escarpment facing seaward.

Other channels include Bird Island Passage (marked on AC2156); the passage E of the S and N Buckley Rocks; and the passage N of the Sheelahs Islands between Bullock Pladdies and Downeys Pladdy. These channels are navigable with care and with judicious use of well-chosen GPS waypoints, but no useful transits can be described.

## BALLYQUINTIN POINT TO BELFAST LOUGH
This low-lying and rock-strewn coast has many hazards, on one of which, the South Rock, Ireland's first rock lighthouse was built in 1797. The tower still stands, but was abandoned in 1877, and the light was replaced by a lightship moored two miles out to sea. The South Rock is now the only remaining light vessel in Ireland, and while its future is for the time being assured, reinstatement of the old lighthouse has been among the future options considered.

### Tidal Streams
At the South Rock light float the S-going flood starts at LW Belfast and the N-going ebb at HW Belfast +0015, spring rate 1·4 knots. The streams run SW-NE between South Rock and the North Rocks. The flood runs S across The Ridge and close E of South Rock; the ebb runs ENE past the S side of South Rock and turns N outside The Ridge. At the Skulmartin buoy the flood starts SSE at +0540 Belfast and the ebb NNW at –0035 Belfast, spring rate 2·3 knots. For details of streams around the Copeland Islands and in Belfast Lough, see below.

### Dangers
The coast is generally foul for 5 cables offshore. The following dangers are further out or are particularly hazardous:
**Kearney Pladdy,** 2·1m, 5 cables SE of Kearney Point

*South Rock; Ireland's first rock lighthouse, and Ireland's last lightship*

**Butter Pladdy**, 1·8m, 1M SE of Kearney Point

**Crooked Pladdy,** 2·1m, 1·5M E of Kearney Point

**South Rock**, dries 2·7m, 1·8M NE of Kearney Point, with drying and underwater rocks extending 1M ENE to The Ridge (2·4m).

**The Breast**, 2·1m, 8 cables N by W of South Rock

**North Rocks,** two islets 1m high surrounded by drying rocks and connected to the shore by a drying reef, the whole extending 2M ESE from Ringboy Point, S of Portavogie

**Skulmartin Rock,** dries 1·2m, 1·2M ESE of Ballywalter

**Nelson Rock,** 1·2m, 5 cables ENE of Ballywalter pier

**The Reef,** dries 0·1m, 6 cables E of Ballyferris Point

**Wee Scotchman Rock** (less than 2m), reef extending 1·3 cables E by N from Donaghadee S Pierhead

**Deputy Reefs** (less than 2m), 5 cables NE of Foreland Point

**Foreland Spit** (less than 2m), 3 cables N by E of Foreland Point

**Rid Rock** (awash), 2 cables S of Carn Point, Copeland Island

**The Platters** (less than 2m), extending 2·5 cables E of Copeland Island

**Ninion Bushes** (less than 2m), 5 cables NE of Copeland Island

**Gillet Spit,** (less than 2m), extending 2·5 cables S from Mew Island

**South Briggs**, dries 0·6m, 6 cables NW of Orlock Point

## Lights and Marks

*Strangford Lough to Donaghadee:*

**Strangford Fairway** buoy, safe water mark RWVS, L Fl 10s, AIS

**Butter Pladdy** buoy, E Card Q(3) 10s

**South Rock,** disused lighthouse tower on the rock, 18m, unlit

**South Rock** light float, red hull and tower, Fl(3) R 30s 12m 20M, Horn (3) 45s, Racon (T) 13M, AIS

**North Rocks,** red conical beacon, 12m, unlit

**Plough Rock** buoy, PHM Fl R 3s

**Portavogie South Pier,** grey pillar Iso WRG 5s 9m 9M, G shore–258° W258°–275° R275°–348°. Shows white over the approach channel to the E, red to the SE over Plough Rock and green to the NE over McCammon and Selk Rocks

**Portavogie North Pier,** green pole beacon, Fl G

**Skulmartin Rock,** red stayed perch with cage topmark, unlit

**Skulmartin** buoy, safe water mark RWVS, L Fl 10s

**Ballywalter Pier,** pole beacon Fl WRG 1·5s 5m 9M, G240°–267° W267°–277° R277°–314°. Shows white over the approach channel to the E, red to the SE over Skulmartin Rock and green to the NE over Nelson Rock

**Donaghadee Harbour,** S Pier, white tower Iso WR 4s 17m W18M R14M, W shore–326° R326°–shore. Shows red over the reefs inshore to the SE, white elsewhere. Siren 12s

*Donaghadee Sound*

**Governor Rocks** buoy, PHM Fl R 3s

**Foreland Point,** red stayed perch beacon, unlit

**Foreland Spit** buoy, PHM Fl R 6s

**Deputy Reefs** buoy, SHM Fl G 2s

*North Rocks beacon*

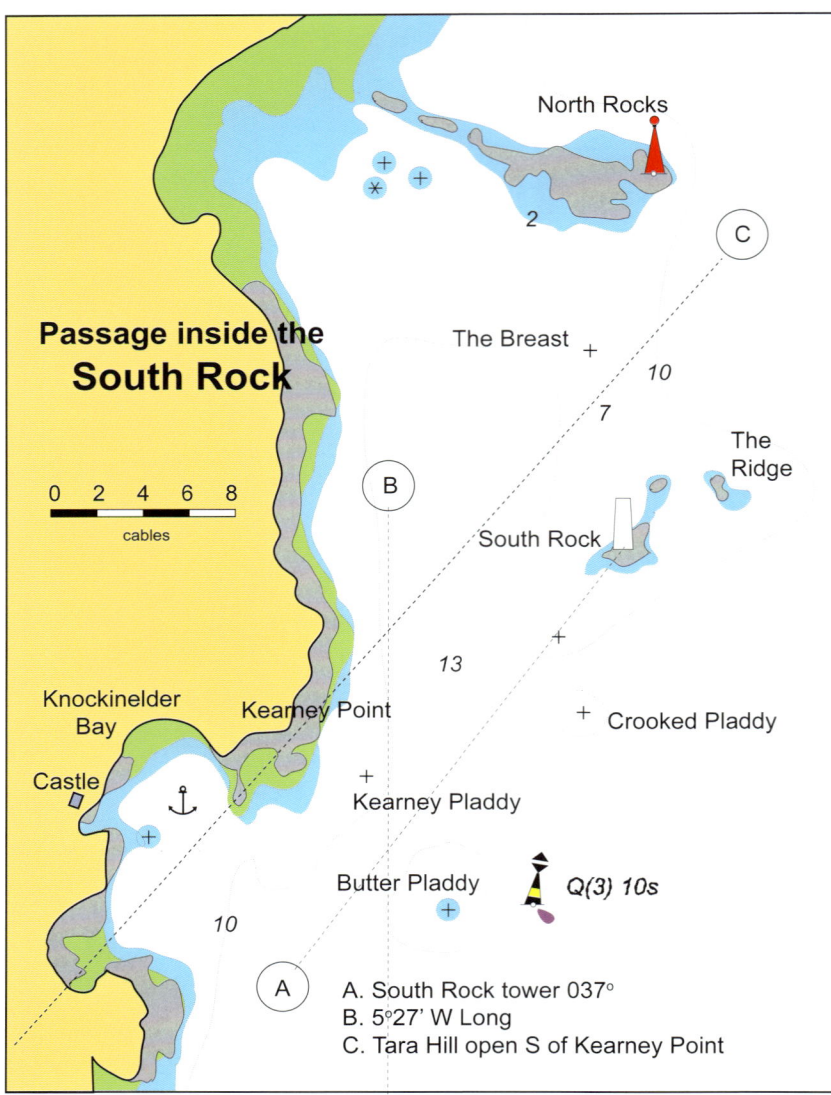

**Passage inside the South Rock**

0  2  4  6  8
cables

North Rocks

The Breast

The Ridge

South Rock

Knockinelder Bay

Kearney Point

Castle

Crooked Pladdy

Kearney Pladdy

Butter Pladdy    Q(3) 10s

A. South Rock tower 037°
B. 5°27' W Long
C. Tara Hill open S of Kearney Point

**Coast – Ballyquintin Point to Donaghadee**

St Patrick's Rock perch in line with the beacon on Guns Island clears all the rocks SE of Ballyquintin Point. There is a clear passage, with least depth 7m, W of the South Rock and Butter Pladdy *(see Plan)*. A bearing of 037° on the South Rock tower leads between But-

ter Pladdy and Kearney Pladdy; alternatively, make good due N along longitude 5°27'W until Tara Hill is open S of the long, low Kearney Point 221° *(see photograph)*, then stay on this transit to pass between South Rock and North Rocks and SE of The Breast. Give North Rocks a berth of a cable and steer to leave the Plough Rock buoy to port. From there to Donaghadee the coast has rocks and reefs extending up to 7 cables offshore; give it a berth of a mile.

**Caution**

A steep and dangerous sea can build up in the vicinity of The Ridge, and can extend out to the South Rock light float in a strong wind over the tide. In such conditions either pass E of the light float, or use the inside passage, W of South Rock and E or W of Butter Pladdy.

**Knockinelder Bay**

54°22'·2N   5°28'W,   *SC5612, AC2156 and Plan*

The bay SW of Kearney Point is sheltered in winds between SW and NNE and offers good anchorage in 3 to 4m, sand. Approach with the conspicuous castle bearing W to NW to avoid the rocks off either headland.

*Tara Hill open S of Kearney Point clears The Breast and leads between South Rock and North Rocks*

*Portavogie from the NW; Green Island and Bird Island at top*

## PORTAVOGIE

54°27'·5N 5°25'·3W, *SC5612·9, AC2156 and Plan*

Situated at the easternmost point of Ireland, Portavogie is one of Northern Ireland's principal fishing ports. The fishery, traditionally for white fish but now almost entirely for shellfish, is not what it was; yachts are welcome, but must take it as they find it, and the fishing boats must still be accorded priority in the harbour. The entrance should not be attempted in E winds of F5 or greater. The harbour has a maintained depth of 3m.

### Directions

The entrance channel faces due E and lies between Plough Rock to the S and McCammon Rocks to the N. The highest point of McCammon Rocks never covers, and Plough Rock shows at half tide, but there are patches with 1·2 and 1·8m close N and S of the channel. From the S, keep the North Rocks beacon open W of the South Rock tower to clear all dangers until the Plough Rock buoy is identified. If Plough Rock is showing, it is safe to pass a cable SW of the buoy; otherwise leave the buoy close to port. Identify the pierhead and steer to leave it close to port. From the N, after passing outside Burial Island, identify the Plough Rock buoy and leave it close to port.

The pierhead should be approached on a course between 258° and 275°, the white sector of the pierhead light. The entrance faces NNE and is 24m wide, but the entrance to the main harbour basins is only 10m. Yachts should proceed into the outer basin (see Plan) and follow directions from the harbour staff. Keep a sharp lookout for traffic coming out. A fenderboard is recommended to cope with the sheet piling of the harbour walls. Constant +0005 Belfast, MHWS 4·7m, MHWN 3·9m, MLWN 1·4m, MLWS 0·6m.

### Facilities

Shops, pub/restaurant, ATM, filling station. Chandlery (NI Fish Producers' Organisation), on the quay.

McCammon Rocks (0.3m high)

Portavogie

0   1   2

cables

2FG
Iso WRG 5s

$1_8$

$1_2$

6   W

8

5

3   3   $2_4$

$1_8$

2

$0_6$

$2_1$

Plough Rock (dries 3m)

*Portavogie entrance from the E*

*Portavogie entrance; Plough Rock buoy, top L*

**Burial Island**

54°29'·4N 5°25'W, *AC2156, SC5612·9*

The tiny Burial Island, 8m high, is Ireland's easternmost land. It is surrounded by reefs which seldom cover and extend 3 cables N, and 2 cables E and S, from the island. The channel between Burial Island and the shore is navigable with care in settled weather. On a course of 350° with Plough Rock buoy directly astern, and staying one-third of the channel's width

from the island, there is a least depth of 3m. Otherwise give the E side of the island a berth of at least 3 cables.

**Ballyhalbert Bay**

54°30'N 5°26'·5W, *AC2156, SC5612·9*

The bay is clean and offers good temporary anchorage in W or SW winds, a cable N of the pier in 5m. The pier, just inside Burr Point, dries. Shop and pub.

**Skulmartin Rock**

54°32'·3N 5°26'·5W, *AC2156, SC5612·9*

The dangerous Skulmartin Rock is the furthest-offshore hazard between South Rock and Donaghadee. There is no passage inside it, and shallows extend 2 cables S, and a cable N and E, from the rock. Give the perch a berth of at least 2 cables.

**Ballywalter**

54°32'·7N 5°27'·5W, *AC2156, SC5612·9*

Ballywalter, 1M WNW of the Skulmartin Rock, offers temporary anchorage in winds between S and NW, and has a drying pier. Approach with the church spire in line with the pierhead, 272°, and anchor in 4 to 5m, sand. Shop and pub.

*Ballyhalbert Pier*

*Skulmartin Rock from the SE; Ballywalter beyond*

*Ballywalter from the S*

*Ballywalter Pier*

## DONAGHADEE

54°38'·8N 5°31'·2W, *AC2198, 1753, SC5612·10 and Plan*

The first harbour at Donaghadee was built in the 1660s as a terminal for the earliest packet boats to Portpatrick in Scotland, and the present harbour, with its massive walls, was designed by the great Scottish engineer John Rennie in the early 1800's. It was overtaken by the development of the steamboat and the emergence of Larne and Stranraer as the premier short-sea steamer ports. Donaghadee harbour is open to the NE and its inner part is badly silted up, but in most winds it offers good shelter. There is a visitors' berth, with deep water, immediately inside the S pier. Constant +0005 Belfast, MHWS 4·0m, MHWN 3·4 m, MLWN 1·1m, MLWS 0·5m.

*Donaghadee*

## Directions

From the S, give the shore a berth of 3 cables until the harbour entrance is well open, and approach steering SW. From the N, do not err to the W of a direct course from the Governor and Deputy buoys.

## Facilities

Water on the S pier. Supermarkets, shops, PO, pubs, restaurants, banks, ATMs, doctors. Filling station; Internet access at the library. HM phone 028 9188 2377. Electronic repairs, Marine Services Ireland (Raymarine agents), 0780 390 3460. Buses to Belfast. RNLI all-weather lifeboat station.

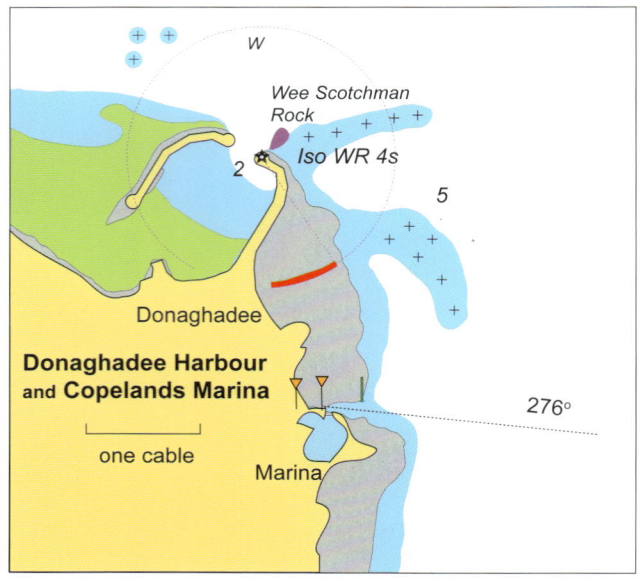

*Donaghadee Harbour entrance*

*Donaghadee Harbour; visitors' berth*

## Copelands Marina

The marina occupies a small basin 3 cables S of Donaghadee harbour, and is enclosed by a sill which dries 1m. The approach is between drying reefs and the entrance has a sharp turn to port through a 6m-wide gap between the walls. Leading marks, orange triangles on poles, lead in 276°, the rocks on the N side are marked by a green pole, and the entrance can be identified from seaward by the word "Marina" and an arrow, prominently painted on the sea wall. It is possible to borrow a little to the N of the leading line, but the marks lead very close to the rocks on the S side. The marina is accessible to vessels up to 11m in length. Diesel; 20t travelhoist.

## COPELAND ISLANDS

54°39'·6N 5°31'·6W, *SC5612·10, AC1753 and Plan*

The Copeland Islands – Copeland itself, Lighthouse Island and Mew Island – lie one to three miles off Donaghadee, and mark the S entrance to Belfast Lough. Copeland Island is privately owned, with seasonal residents, and tourist boats bring visitors from Donaghadee in summer. The first light was built on Lighthouse Island in the early eighteenth century, and upgraded with a new tower in 1815. In 1882 the lighthouse was rebuilt on Mew Island. Lighthouse Island is now a bird sanctuary. Copeland Sound, between Copeland and Lighthouse Islands, and Donaghadee Sound, between Copeland Island and the mainland shore, are navigable, but only the latter is marked.

## Tidal Streams

Inshore S of Donaghadee the S-going flood stream starts at HW Belfast +0540 and runs strongly for three hours. It then slackens and turns N, and for 5M between Ballyferris Point and Foreland Point it runs N for nine hours and S for three. Off Ballyferris Point the eddy is narrow but at its N end it eventually extends out to the E side of the Copelands. By HW Belfast –0200 this N-going eddy is meeting the stream coming SE past Deputy Reefs, and the combined stream then runs E and N between the islands, meeting the main stream and forming the Ram Race. This starts SE of Mew Island and runs strongly NNE until shortly after HW Belfast, at rates up to 5 knots, the race extending 5 cables to N and S. In Donaghadee and

*Copelands Marina approach from the E; leading marks, centre. RNLB* Sir Samuel Kelly, *veteran of the 1953* Princess Victoria *disaster, undergoing restoration in the adjacent yard, R*

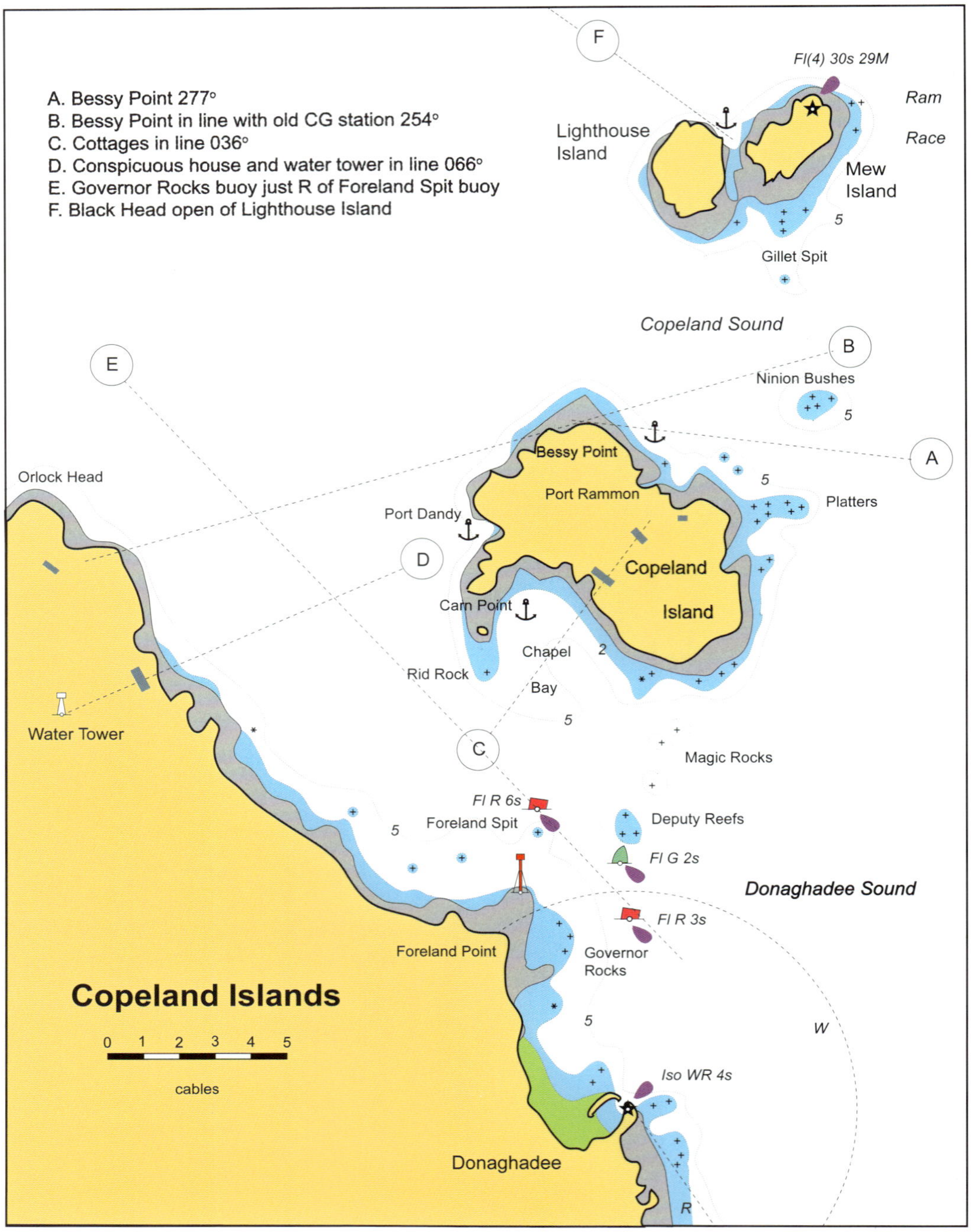

A. Bessy Point 277°
B. Bessy Point in line with old CG station 254°
C. Cottages in line 036°
D. Conspicuous house and water tower in line 066°
E. Governor Rocks buoy just R of Foreland Spit buoy
F. Black Head open of Lighthouse Island

Fl(4) 30s 29M

*Ram*

*Race*

Lighthouse
Island

Mew
Island

Gillet Spit

*Copeland Sound*

Ninion Bushes

Orlock Head

Bessy Point

Port Rammon

Port Dandy

Platters

Carn Point

Copeland

Island

Chapel

Rid Rock

Bay

Water Tower

Magic Rocks

Fl R 6s

Foreland Spit

Deputy Reefs

Fl G 2s

*Donaghadee Sound*

Fl R 3s

Foreland Point

Governor
Rocks

**Copeland Islands**

0   1   2   3   4   5

cables

*W*

Iso WR 4s

Donaghadee

*R*

Copeland Sounds the tide turns a little earlier; SE at +0420 Belfast and NW at –0115 Belfast, and reaching 3 to 4 knots at springs. Along the N side of Lighthouse Island on the N-going ebb, the stream is imperceptible.

**Directions**
The conventional direction of buoyage is north-

*Bessy Point in line with the old CG station on Orlock Head (centre) leads N of the Ninion Bushes*

*Donaghadee Sound from the S; Copelands Marina bottom R, Foreland Point upper L, Copeland Island top R with Lighthouse Island and Mew Island beyond*

wards. **From the S**, identify the Governor Rocks and Foreland Spit buoys and leave them close to port, then give the coast S of Orlock Head a berth of 2 cables, keeping the Governor buoy in line with, or right of, the Foreland buoy. For Copeland Sound, a bearing of 277° on Bessy Point (the N point of Copeland Island) leads between the Ninion Bushes and the rocks E of the island, but it is safer to pass N of the Ninion Bushes, keeping Bessy Point in line 254° with

the old coastguard station and mast above Orlock Head *(see photograph)*. In heavy weather, steer to pass at least 2M E of Mew Island.

**Anchorages**

There are four practicable anchorages around the islands.

* Chapel Bay is sheltered in winds between W and NE. From the S, approach the bay with Donaghadee harbour lighthouse mid-

*Chapel Bay, Copeland Island; the grey-roofed cottage (centre) in line with the cottage on the skyline. The boat at the jetty is Quinton Nelson's* The Brothers, *which was built by James Laird of Bangor in 1935 and still provides excursions from Donaghadee*

*Water tower and white house in line leads into Port Dandy*

way between the two port-hand buoys astern. From the N, keep these two buoys in transit ahead until a low, long grey-roofed cottage on the island comes in transit 036° with a white cottage on the skyline, then turn on to this transit and steer into the bay. This avoids the hazardous Rid Rock. The low cottage is hard to pick out but there is a conspicuous blue-painted cottage close NW of it *(see photograph)*. Anchor in the W half of the bay, a cable E of Carn Point in 3m, mud. Note that there is a drying rock 0·5 cable SW of the jetty at the head of the bay, and there are other hazardous rocks close to the shores.

- Port Dandy, on the W side of Copeland Island, is sheltered in winds between NE and SE. The transit of the water tower behind Orlock Head with a conspicuous solitary white house on the mainland shore *(see photograph)* leads in. The rocky shore on the N side of the inlet is steep-to. Anchor out of the tide in 4m, mud, just inside the bay.

- Off the N side of Copeland Island, between Bessy Point and Port Rammon, is a pleasant anchorage in light S winds. Beware of the rocks E of Port Rammon; the beach at the head of this little inlet should not be open of its N point. The green hut and flagstaff are at the head of the next bay SE of Port Rammon.

- There is good anchorage in the N end of the channel between Lighthouse Island and Mew Island. The N and W shores of Lighthouse Island are clean, provided Black Head, on the Antrim coast to the NW, is kept open of the N point of Lighthouse Island. The channel almost dries at the narrows.

## BELFAST LOUGH
*AC2198, 1753, SC5612, Imray C64*

Belfast Lough was a strategic harbour from the earliest times. The castle of Carrickfergus was the seat of Norman power in Ulster in the 13th century, but it was only with the Industrial Revolution that the port city of Belfast came into its own. The great shipyard of Harland & Wolff was for many years the world's largest, and built all of the famous White Star Liners including *Titanic* and her two sister-ships, and also the 1946 *Ark Royal* and P & O's *Canberra*. With the decline of its shipbuilding industry, Belfast has turned to celebrating its maritime heritage. The cruiser *Caroline*, built in 1914 and the last surviving veteran of the Battle of Jutland, is moored at Alexandra Wharf on the SE side of the river, as the Royal Naval Reserve clubhouse, and the tender *Nomadic,* built in 1911 by Harland and Wolff to serve the *Titanic* in Cherbourg, is moored at Queen's Quay in the city centre. For trivia enthusiasts, the world record for riveting was established by James Moir at Workman Clark's shipyard in Belfast in 1911, when he set 11,000 in a shift, an average rate of one rivet every 3·6 seconds.

    Belfast is a down-to-earth, practical

HMS Caroline *at her berth in Belfast; ironically the shipyard cranes, as listed structures, have more legal protection than the ship. She has however some experience in defending herself*

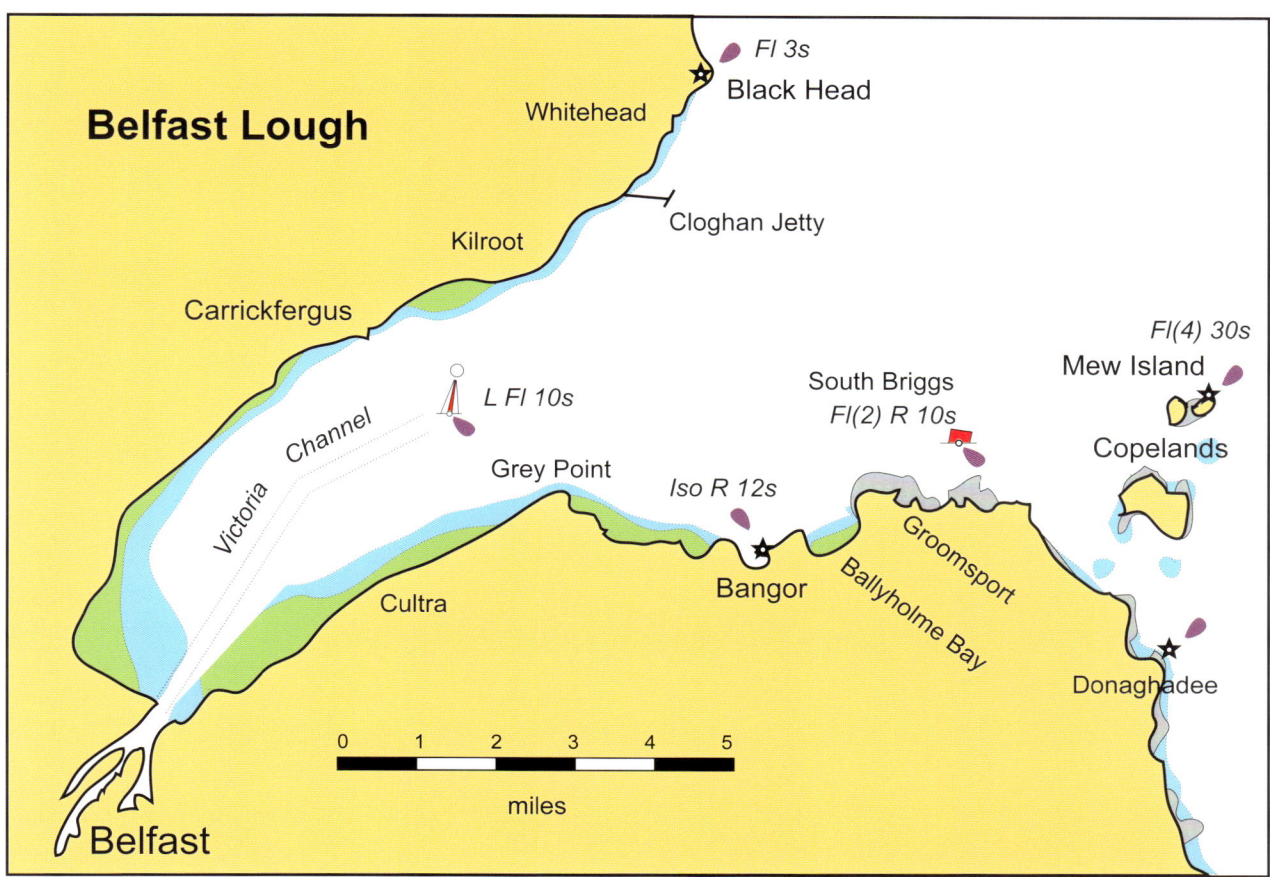

and no-nonsense place with some of the most helpful people in Ireland. Years of sectarian strife and hard-won peace have only added to the city's admirable ability to solve day-to-day problems and keep the world turning. Here were born J.B. Dunlop, inventor of the pneumatic tyre, and William Thomson, Lord Kelvin, eminent physicist and inventor of marine instruments and the Kelvin scale of temperature.

Bangor (52,000) grew from fishing village to seaside resort in the 19th century, and is today a prosperous town within the commuter belt of greater Belfast. Carrickfergus (20,000) has the oldest and best-preserved Norman castle in Ireland, dating from 1177. The parents of the 7th American president Andrew Jackson emigrated from the town.

## Tidal Streams
The streams within the Lough are mostly less than 1 knot but are well characterised; see the tidal charts below. The set is coastwise except in mid-channel between Bangor and Cloghan Jetty, where the streams are rotatory clockwise.

## Dangers
**South Briggs**, dries 0·6m, 6 cables NW of Orlock Point
**Drying banks** extending up to 5 cables offshore at Cultra (SE of the Victoria Channel) and between Carrickfergus and Kilroot
**Cooling water outfall** 4 cables S of Kilroot power station
**Hailcock Rock,** dries 0·9m, 1·5 cables offshore at Whitehead.

## Lights and marks
*Belfast Lough – S side:*
**Mew Island,** black tower, white band Fl(4) 30s 37m 29M. Racon (O) 14M
**South Briggs** buoy, PHM Fl(2) R 10s
**Groomsport** ldg lts 202°, 2 Oc G
**Groomsport E Entrance,** 2 perches SHM, 1 perch PHM, unlit
**Groomsport W Entrance,** 1 perch SHM, 1 perch PHM, unlit
*Bangor:*
**Eisenhower Pier**, red tower Iso R 12s 9m 14M
**Bangor Harbour** Dir Oc WRG 10s 1M, G093°-104·8° W104·8°-105·2° R105·2°-117°,

shows white through the entrance, red to N, green to S of approach line

**Pickie Breakwater**, green pole on piled dolphin 2FG vert

**Marina entrance**, green pile beacon Fl G 3s

**Central Pier Head**, pole beacon Q

*Belfast Lough – N side:*

**Black Head**, white tower Fl 3s 45m 27M, AIS

**Cloghan Jetty** buoy, SHM QG

**Kilroot** intake, Oc G 4s

*Carrickfergus:*

**East Pier**, green column Fl G 7·5s 5m 4M

**Marina E breakwater**, QG 8m 3M

**Marina W breakwater**, QR 7m 3M

**Marina entrance**, Dir Oc WRG 3s 5m 3M, G308°–317·5° W317·5°–322·5° R322·5°–332°

*Belfast:*

**Fairway** buoy, safe water mark RWVS, L Fl 10s, Horn 16s, Racon (G), AIS

The channel to Belfast Harbour is marked by lateral buoys and pile beacons Fl R and Fl G.

**Caution**

Commercial traffic in Belfast Lough is constant and heavy, and includes large high-speed ferries. Skippers of small vessels are reminded that IRPCS Rule 9 specifies that a vessel under 20m in length or a sailing vessel shall not impede larger vessels confined by a narrow channel. The Victoria Channel SW of the fairway buoy is a "narrow channel" within the terms of this rule, and in the rest of the Lough yachts should give way to commercial shipping as a matter of courtesy and good seamanship.

**Directions**

From the S, leave the South Briggs buoy to port and give Ballymaccormick Point, at the W side of Ballyholme Bay, a berth of 2 cables. The S shore is clean from there to Grey Point; between there and Cultra there are rocks and shoals extending up to 3 cables offshore. From the N, note the conspicuous Cloghan Jetty; a berth of 2 cables clears all dangers between Black Head and the jetty. Steer to pass 5 cables S of the

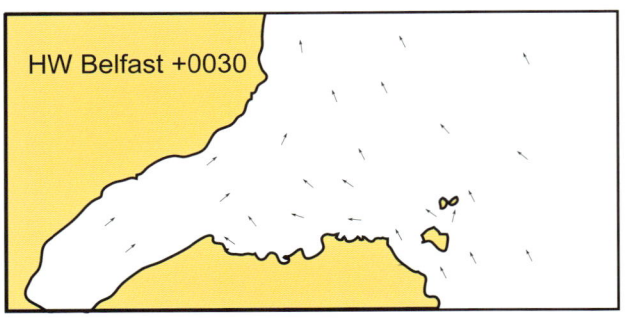

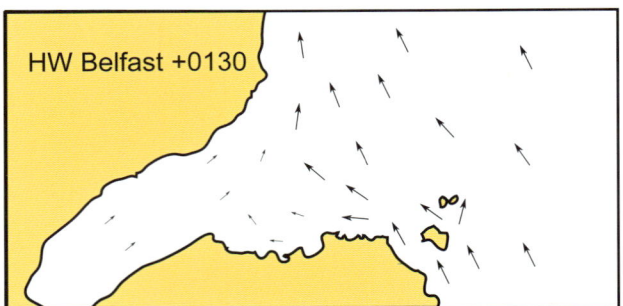

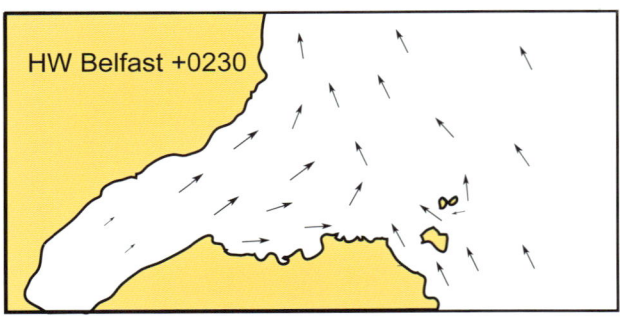

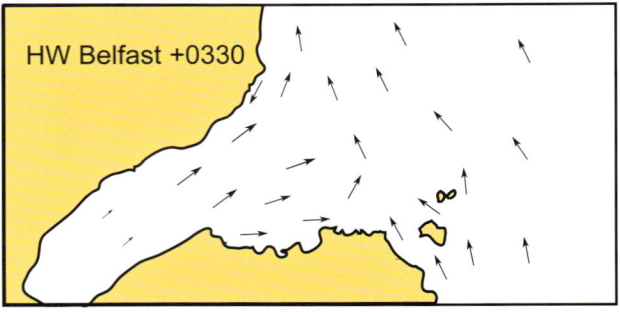

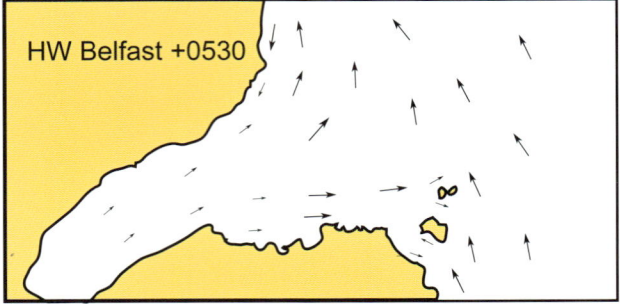

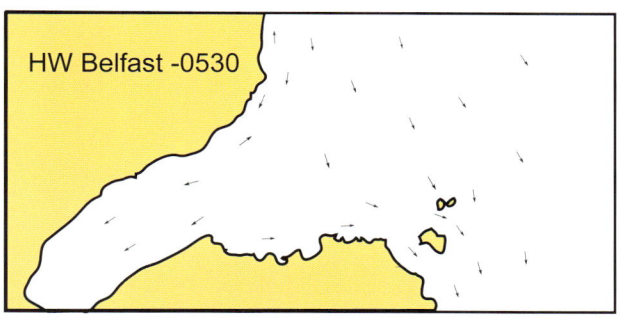

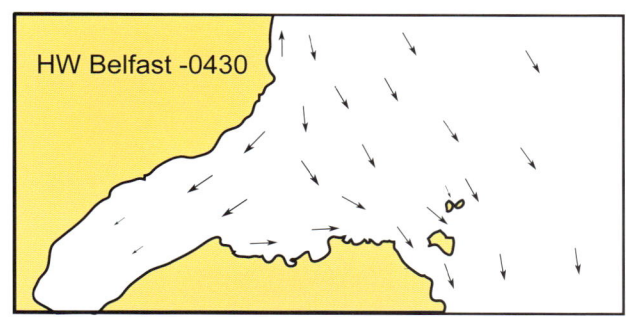

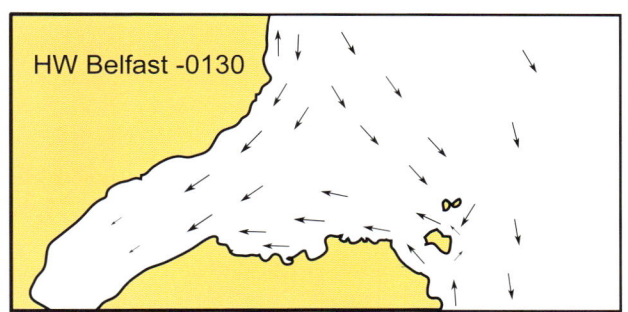

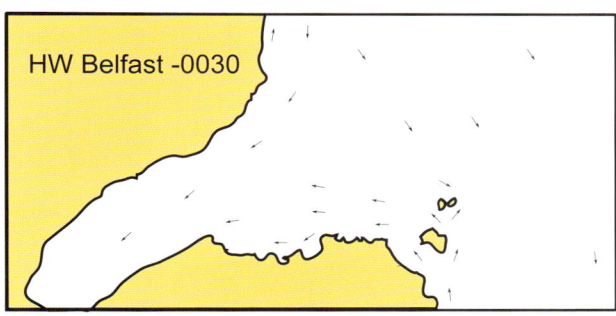

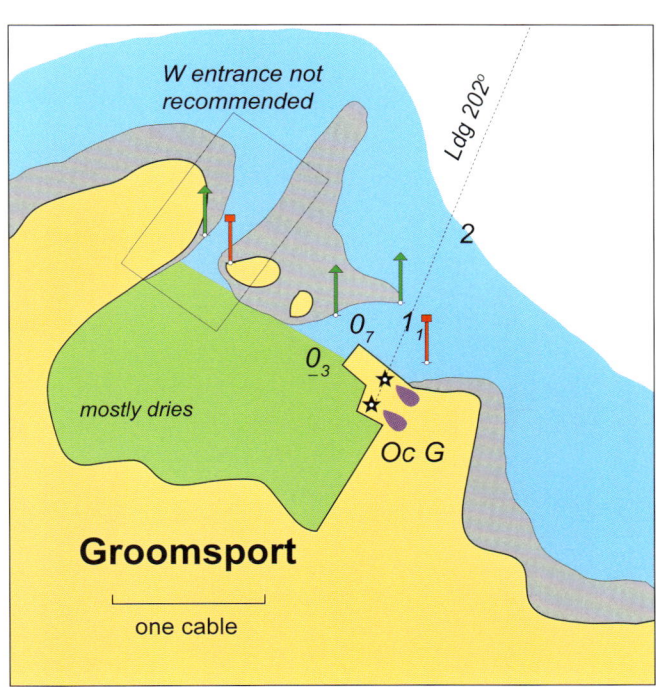

**Groomsport**

conspicuous Kilroot power station to avoid the shallows E of Carrickfergus. The fairway buoy is 1·5M SE of Carrickfergus, and the Victoria Channel, with maintained depth and marked by buoys and pile beacons, runs WSW from there to Belfast Harbour.

**Groomsport**

54°40'·7N 5°36'·8W, *AC1753, SC5612·12 and Plan*

Groomsport Bay, W of the South Briggs, provides temporary anchorage in offshore winds. The small natural harbour, protected from the NE by two small islets and a drying reef, mostly dries, and the pier also dries. There are E and W entrances; the E entrance has leading lights, but a stranger should not attempt entry by night. The pier nevertheless offers a possible alongside berth for a small yacht above half tide. Approach on the leading line 202° between one port- and two starboard-hand perches. The front

*Groomsport entrance from the NE; the leading marks are visible L of the flagstaff. The port-hand perch, centre*

leading mark is a slim red pole, the rear a slim wooden pole *(see photograph)*. There is 1·1m inside the first starboard-hand perch, and 0·7m at the pier head.

The W entrance is marked by port- and starboard-hand perches but is not recommended to a stranger. Groomsport is the home of Cockle Island Boat Club, phone 028 9146 4431.

### Ballyholme Bay
54°40'·6N 5°38'·7W, *AC1753, SC5612·10*
The bay offers anchorage in 3 to 5m, sheltered from E through S to W but exposed from NE to NW. Ballyholme YC welcomes visitors.

### BANGOR
54°40'·2N 5°40'·4W, *SC5612·10, AC1753 and Plan*
Bangor Harbour was (until the construction of the North Breakwater, now the Eisenhower Pier, in 1984) critically exposed to the north, and so never really achieved commercial success as a port, but it accommodated a wide variety of excursion steamers and small coasters. The last cargo was loaded in 1990. The fine new harbour encloses a 550-berth marina, and

*Bangor Harbour and Marina from the E; Grey Point upper L and the Long Hole bottom R*

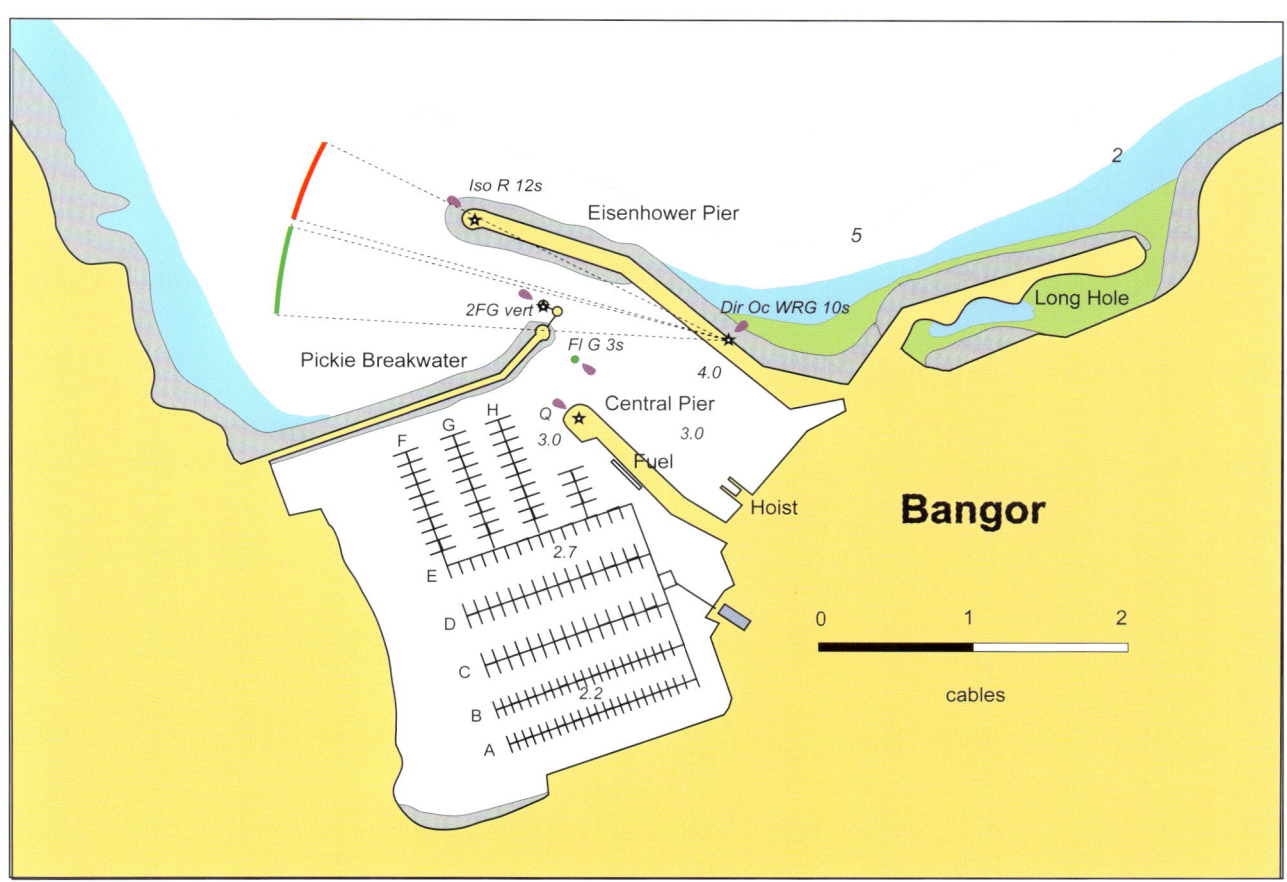

fishing and naval vessels, training ships and replica craft such as the *Golden Hinde* and the *Mathew* use the piers. The name of Eisenhower Pier commemorates the major role played by Bangor as a naval anchorage during World War II, and a visit by the General in the run-up to D-Day. East of the harbour and overlooking Ballyholme Bay is the clubhouse of the Royal Ulster Yacht Club. From offshore to the N, the two church spires in Bangor are conspicuous. From E or W, identify the pierhead, approach the entrance on the leading line 105° and leave the piled dolphins and the green pile beacon to starboard.

## Marina

The marina monitors VHF Ch 80. Water and shore power on the pontoons; diesel on the Central Pier. Showers and laundry, Wi-fi. RUYC welcomes visitors; its Sir Thomas Lipton Room has fascinating memorabilia of Lipton and his five *Shamrocks*. Chandlery, BJ Marine 028 9127 1434. GRP and timber repairs, Bangor Yacht Services 028 9188 8600 or 0771 172 5947. Electrical repairs, Billy Harrison 028 9146 9027, Crowhill Marine 0788 449 8624. Chandlery, and principal Admiralty Chart agents for Northern Ireland, Todd Chart Agency 028 9146 6640. Supermarkets, shops, restaurants, pubs, PO, banks, ATMs. RNLI inshore lifeboat sta-

*Bangor Harbour entrance from the WNW (Ed Wheeler)*

*Cultra from the NW; RNIYC slip and clubhouse*

tion. Belfast Coastguard MRCC is situated at the marina. Trains and buses to Belfast.

## Harbour

The harbour walls are normally reserved for commercial, naval and fishing vessels but a berth can be made available for a yacht taking fuel from a tanker. The Long Hole, a one-time quarry long flooded, lies close E of the harbour; it has some moorings (and was once used for wintering paddle steamers!) but it is shallow and rocky.

## Cultra

54°39'·5N 5°49'·3W, *AC1753*
The Royal North of Ireland YC has its clubhouse and slip at Cultra, 3M SW of Grey Point, and welcomes visitors. Anchor 4 cables offshore, clear of the moorings. Bar and dining room at the YC.

## BELFAST HARBOUR

Fairway buoy 54°41'·7N 5°46'·4W, *AC1753, 1752, SC5612·13 and Plan*
The city's busy commercial port area occupies the navigable portion of the

River Lagan, with docks to N and S, and extends 2·5M from the head of the Lough to the Queen Elizabeth Bridge. Above the bridge, which has limited headroom, are pontoons at the Lagan Weir, accessible to small power craft, and immediately below the bridge in the Abercorn Basin on the S side is the Laganside pontoon. Lagan Weir is a tidal barrage designed to retain navigable water in the Lagan at low tide and to protect the city from flooding by exceptionally high tides. It has five

*Belfast Harbour approaches; the Victoria Channel from the NE*

*Laganside Pontoon*

hydraulic flap gates which are lowered between HW±0230 to allow boats which can pass under the bridges to reach the upper stretch of the river. The channel as far as Abercorn Basin has no tidal or headroom restrictions. The pontoons are managed by the Dept of Social Development of the Northern Ireland government.

The passage through the Harbour to the Laganside pontoon requires advance planning but is well worth making. First contact Lagan Weir on VHF Ch 71 or by phone on 028 9027 7624 or 0786 095 4814 to ascertain that a berth is available, and before entering the Victoria Channel contact the Port Control tower on VHF Ch 12 to request permission to transit the port. It is essential to maintain a listening watch on Ch 12 for updates on shipping movements, and

yachts must keep close to the sides of the navigable channel. Inform Port Control on arrival, on departure and when leaving the Victoria Channel.

Traffic signals are displayed at Lagan Weir to indicate the status of the gates; a red cross means no passage and a green arrow means that the gates are lowered to allow passage. Going upriver, use gate 2, and downriver gate 4. The gates number from the W bank.

Above the Lagan Weir the river is navigable for 3M to the weir at Stranmillis, with an available depth of 1·5m but limited headroom below the bridges.

Belfast is a Tidal Standard Port; MHWS 3·5m, MHWN 3·0 m, MLWN 1·1m, MLWS 0·4m.

**Facilities**
All the facilities of a seaport city. Chandlery, Jamison & Green, Ann Street, 028 9032 2444, www.jamisonandgreen.co.uk, and McCready's, Corporation Street, 028 9023 2842. Rigging and sail repairs, Tedfords, Ormeau Road, 028 9032 6763. Engine repairs, Robert Craig & Sons (Volvo Marine and Yanmar agents) 028 9023 2971, Massey Marine 0796 768 8869. Two airports; train connections to Dublin, Londonderry, Bangor and Larne; bus services to all parts of Ireland. Ferries to Stranraer, and Douglas, Isle of Man.

*Lagan Weir, looking up-river*

*Carrickfergus from the E; marina L, the harbour R*

# CARRICKFERGUS

54°42'·4N 5°48'·5W, *AC1753, SC5612·12 and Plan*

Carrickfergus marina and harbour lie on the N side of the Lough 5·5M SW of Black Head and 5·5M NW of Bangor. The entrances are W of the prominent castle, and the conspicuous green and red beacons on the marina breakwaters stand out clearly against the four-storey white apartment buildings behind the marina itself. Approach the marina on a course of 320° towards the rather inconspicuous triangular leading marks and the directional light, both on the W breakwater, and turn to starboard round the E breakwater head. There is no commercial traffic at the harbour, whose entrance is 1·5 cables to the E.

## Marina

The marina has 280 berths and a minimum depth of 2m at the outer pontoons. The office monitors VHF Ch M and 80, phone 028 9336 6666. Water and shore power on the pontoons, pumpout station, laundry, Wi-fi.

## Harbour

The S half of the harbour has 2·9m; the N half is shallow. The entrance has 2·3m. A reef extends SE from the root of the E pier. The harbour has a few pontoons, a travelhoist dock and fuel berth, and a slipway accessible HW±0300. There are isolated piles in the harbour, several of which are painted as lateral marks. These should be left on the proper hand.

*Carrickfergus from the SE; marina entrance L, and the castle R*

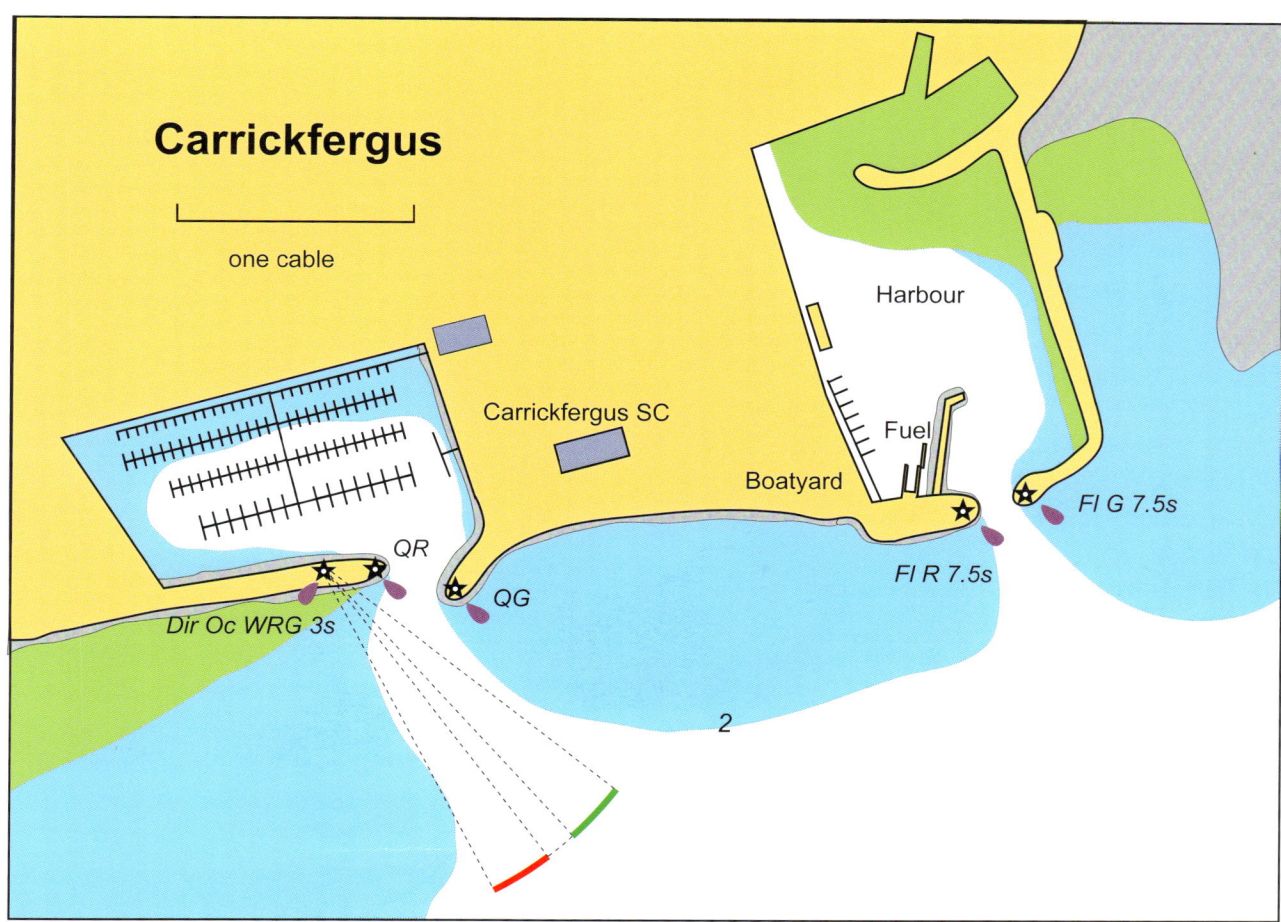

## Facilities
Carrick Marine Services (028 9335 5884, 0783 211 8576), hull, mechanical and electrical repairs, canvaswork and sail repairs, diesel, 45t travelhoist, hardstanding. Modest chandlery (Caters, 028 9335 1919). Supermarkets, shops, pubs, restaurants, PO, banks, ATMs, doctors. Filling station 400m from the marina. Bus and train service to Belfast. Taxis, 028 9336 2727 and 3666. Carrickfergus Sailing Club (028 9335 1402 or 9302) has its clubhouse between the harbour and marina, with bar and dining room, and welcomes visitors.

Constant +0005 Belfast, MHWS 2·9m, MHWN 1·8m.

## Whitehead
54°45'N 5°42'W, *AC1753, SC5612·12*
The bay at Whitehead, a mile NE of Cloghan Jetty, offers anchorage in offshore winds but is exposed from NE to SW. Beware Hailcock Rock and rocks drying 0·3m and 0·9m S and N of it. The anchorage off the County Antrim YC slipway should be approached steering W to NW. Anchor in 3 to 4m, good holding in sand and stones. A tripping line is recommended. The YC (028 9337 2322) welcomes visitors and has bar and showers.

*Carrickfergus Marina entrance*

*Cloghan Jetty from the E*

## BELFAST LOUGH TO FAIR HEAD
*AC2198, 2199, SC5612, Imray C64*

North of Belfast Lough, the Antrim coast slopes steeply to the sea, with some impressive stretches of cliff scenery including The Gobbins, 80m high and almost vertical, on the coast of Islandmagee. In 1641, in reprisal for what would nowadays be termed a "terrorist incident", the garrison at Carrickfergus threw the entire population of Islandmagee – 300 people – off the cliffs. The busy port of Larne lies at the entrance to Larne Lough, an otherwise shallow inlet three miles long which is also an important sailing centre. Between Larne and Fair Head, the picturesque villages of Glenarm, Carnlough, Cushendall and Cushendun nestle at the foot of the Glens of Antrim. This area was once very remote; there was never a railway line here, and the road along the steep and cliffbound coast dates from relatively recent times. As a result these communities relied heavily on communication by sea. Glenarm  has a charter dating from the 12th century, and its castle, open to the public, is the seat of the Earls of Antrim. The harbour has a fine new marina. Carnlough's old harbour was originally built for the shipment of limestone from the local quarries, and a mineral tramway ran from the quarries to the harbour; the bridges across the village streets still exist. Offshore lie The Maidens, with their important lighthouse.

### Tides
This coast has strong tidal streams, and they are a first consideration in passage planning. In the middle of the North Channel the NW-going ebb stream begins at HW Belfast and reaches 3·5 knots at springs. The SE-going flood begins at +0600 Belfast and reaches 4 knots. Off Islandmagee the ebb does not begin until +0115 Belfast, and may reach 6 knots at springs close to the Isle of Muck. Close inshore between Larne and the Isle of Muck there is a S-going eddy from +0300 Belfast; this eddy gradually widens, and at -0600 Belfast generates a N-going counter-eddy close inshore. This continues during the S-going flood, which begins here at –0445 Belfast. At –0300 Belfast a N-going eddy begins between Black Head and the Isle of Muck, extending about 1·5M out to sea and causing a race off the island and overfalls where it meets the main stream. This continues until the main stream here turns N at +0115 Belfast.

N of Larne, the main NW-going ebb also begins at HW Belfast.

HW Belfast: the main NW-going ebb begins in the middle of the North Channel between Belfast Lough and Fair Head, and also inshore N of Larne.

+0115 Belfast: the N-going ebb begins off Islandmagee

+0300 Belfast: a S-going eddy starts close inshore

*The Gobbins*

*The Maidens from the S; the old (L) and present (R) lighthouses. Kintyre in the distance*

between Islandmagee and Larne, and gradually widens, running until –0445 Belfast. S-going eddies also begin inshore N and S of Garron Point, running from Cushendun to Cushendall and then across Red Bay and E to Garron Point, and extending up to 5 cables offshore between Garron Point and Ballygalley Head.

+0540 Belfast: a strong S-going local eddy starts 7 cables NE of Tornamoney Point, N of Cushendun, and runs for 4 hours, reaching 3 knots at springs.

+0600 Belfast: the main SE-going flood begins in the middle of the North Channel between Belfast Lough and Fair Head, and also inshore N of Larne.

–0600 Belfast: a new N-going counter-eddy starts close inshore between Islandmagee and Larne

–0445 Belfast: the S-going ebb begins off Islandmagee

–0400 Belfast: a N-going eddy starts inshore between Torr Head and Fair Head, and runs until the main NW-going ebb stream begins 4 hours later, extending across the E entrance to Rathlin Sound by –0200 Belfast. There is no corresponding eddy on the ebb so at this point the tide runs SE for 2·5 hours and NW for 10.

–0300 Belfast: a N-going eddy starts between Black Head and the Isle of Muck, extending about 1·5M out to sea and causing a race off the island

and overfalls where it meets the main stream. This continues until the main stream here turns N at +0115 Belfast.

*The Isle of Muck*

–0240 Belfast: a strong N-going local eddy starts 7 cables NE of Tornamoney Point, and runs for 8 hours, reaching 4 knots at springs.

## Dangers

**Hunter Rock**, 0·8m, 1·8M NE of Barr's Point
**The Maidens**, two groups of islets and rocks, the main group 4M ENE of Ballygalley Head including **East** and **West Maiden**, **The Saddle**, and **Sheafing Rock**, 1m high, with **The Bushes** and **The Griddle** (dries 1·8m). A second group, 1·3M N of West Maiden, includes **Russell's Rock**, 1m high, **Allen's Rock** (dries 1·5m) and **Highland Rock** (dries 1·5m)

## Lights and Marks

*Larne and Approaches*
**North Hunter Rock** buoy, N Card Q
**South Hunter Rock** buoy, S Card VQ(6)+L Fl 10s, AIS
**Chaine Tower**, grey tower Iso WR 5s 23m 16M, W230°-240°, R240°-shore
**Larne** leading lights 184° Oc 4s 12M, front white with red stripe on red piled structure 6m, rear white with red stripe on red tower 14m
**No 1** buoy, SHM QG
**No 3** buoy, SHM Fl(2) G 6s
**Ferris Point,** white tower, AIS
**No 2** beacon, PHM Fl R 3s
**Continental Quay,** 2 FG vert
**Islandmagee Harbour,** 2 FR vert
**No 4** beacon, PHM Fl(2) R 6s
**Ballylumford B Jetty,** 4×2 FR vert
**Ballylumford A Jetty,** 2×2 FR vert
**No 5** buoy, SHM QG
**No 7** buoy, SHM QG
**No 6** Buoy PHM Fl R
**No 9** Buoy SHM Fl G

*Coast from Larne Lough to Fair Head:*
**East Maiden,** white tower, black band, Fl(3) 20s 29m 24M, Racon (M) 11–21M
**West Maiden,** conspicuous disused lighthouse,
unlit
**Carnlough Harbour**, N pier, white tower, black bands Fl G 3s 4m 5M
**Carnlough Harbour**, S pier, white tower, black bands Fl R 3s 6m 5M
**Glenarm Marina, E breakwater**, Iso R 6s 3M
**Glenarm Marina, W breakwater**, Fl G 3s 3M
**Red Bay Pier**, Fl 3s 10m 5M
*Scottish coast:*
**Corsewall Point**, white tower Fl(5) 30s 34m 22M
**Mull of Kintyre**, white tower Fl(2) 20s 91m 24M, Horn Mo(N) 90s

## Directions – Belfast Lough to Larne

Black Head and the coast to the N are steep-to, and a berth of 0·5 cable clears all dangers. The Isle of Muck is connected to the shore by a boulder spit which was originally a man-made causeway, and now barely dries. There is a deep spot near mid-channel which is navigable near HW with local knowledge, but no reliable directions can be given for a stranger. The N-facing bay at Portmuck, on the mainland immediately N of the island, provides a temporary anchorage in settled weather. There are rocks within 0·5 cable of the shore N of Portmuck, and Skernaghan Point, further N, should be given a berth of 1·5 cables to avoid a drying reef and a rock with 0·8m, extending N of the point.

## Isle of Muck

The island is a bird sanctuary, home to many species but noted for its puffins and roseate terns. Anchorage in suitable weather is available W of the island, either S or N of the drying boulder spit in 3·5m (on the S side) or 6m (on the N side).

*Portmuck; view S from the anchorage, with the slip open W of the pier*

## Portmuck

54°51'N 5°43'·7W, *AC1237*

A drying reef extends 0·75 cable NE from the point N of the pier. **From the S**, leaving the N point of the Isle of Muck close to port, give the point a berth of 2 cables and approach the bay on a course of 160°. **From the N**, the same course clears all dangers. Anchor in the bay in 5m with the slip open W of the pier and the N point of the Isle of Muck bearing 065°.

## Brown's Bay

54°51'·5N 5°46'W, *AC2198, 1237*

This is a useful passage anchorage in offshore winds, although prone to swell. Anchor as convenient in 2 to 4m. Landing in the SW corner.

## LARNE

54°51'·5N 5°47'·5W, *AC2198, 1237, SC5612 and Plan*

Larne is Northern Ireland's principal RoRo port, and conventional and fast ferries, and cargo ships, arrive and leave around the clock on services to Troon, Cairnryan and Fleetwood. The port is on the W side of the entrance to Larne Lough. On the Islandmagee shore opposite is the Ballylumford power station complex, with two jetties and two cooling-water outfalls. East Antrim Boat Club has its clubhouse and slip at Wymer's Jetty, between the port area and Curran Point. The inner part of the Lough is generally shallow with wide drying sandbanks, but lies amid pleasant rural surroundings, offers attractive anchorages and is used by the Boat Club for its race events. There is a disused cement works at Magheramorne on the S shore, and the channel to its derelict pier, though it has not been dredged for many years, remains navigable. The SE corner of the lough largely dries, and a power cable with a clearance of 16m crosses the channel.

The gas interconnector pipeline between Scotland and Ireland, which makes landfall on Islandmagee, crosses Larne Lough, running 105° from Curran Point. It is marked by four yellow buoys and by yellow diamond signs on shore. Yachts should cross the pipeline only in deep water, and should avoid anchoring near it. The outfalls from the power station are situated on the E side of the channel 1·6 cables NNW of Ballylumford "B" Jetty and close SE of Ballylumford "A" jetty. These areas should be avoided.

### Tidal Streams

The flood stream divides NW of Barr Point, flowing SSW into Larne Lough and SE down the coast. In the entrance the tide turns at HW

*Larne Harbour from the N; Chaine Tower R centre, Ballylumford power station chimneys L centre*

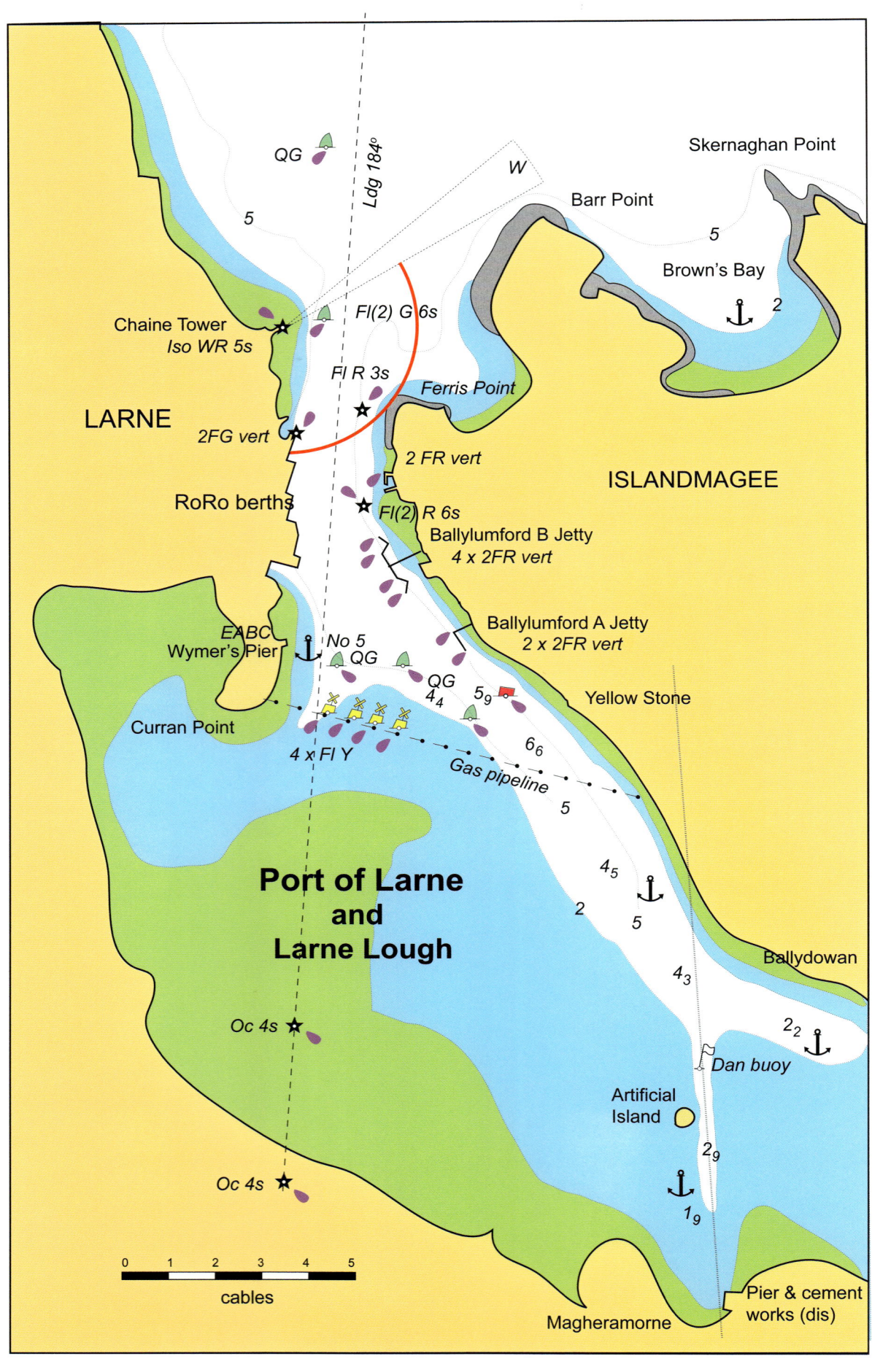

QG

Ldg 184°

W

Skernaghan Point

Barr Point

5

Brown's Bay

2

Chaine Tower
*Iso WR 5s*

Fl(2) G 6s

Fl R 3s

Ferris Point

LARNE

*2FG vert*

2 FR vert

ISLANDMAGEE

RoRo berths

Fl(2) R 6s

Ballylumford B Jetty
*4 x 2FR vert*

*EABC*
Wymer's Pier

No 5
QG

Ballylumford A Jetty
*2 x 2FR vert*

QG
4₄

5₉

Yellow Stone

Curran Point

6₆

4 x Fl Y

Gas pipeline

5

4₅

**Port of Larne
and
Larne Lough**

2

5

Ballydowan

Oc 4s

4₃

2₂

*Dan buoy*

Artificial
Island

2₉

Oc 4s

1₉

0   1   2   3   4   5

cables

Pier & cement
works (dis)

Magheramorne

*Larne Harbour from the S; Curran Point, bottom L, East Antrim BC and Wymer's pier centre and the commercial port beyond. Ballylumford B jetty, R; Ferris Point and Barr point top R*

and LW by the shore, maximum rate 1·5 knots. Off Ballylumford "A" Jetty the flood starts at –0545 Belfast, but at –0215 Belfast a weak eddy starts running N, maximum rate 1·1 knots, and continues until the main stream turns NW. Further S, the streams are weak. Constant +0005 Belfast, MHWS 2·8m, MHWN 2·5m, MLWN 0·8m, MLWS 0·4m.

## Directions
From the E, give Skernaghan Point a berth of 2 cables and Barr and Ferris Points a berth of a cable. From the N, leave No 1 and No 3 buoys to starboard. Before entering, call Larne Port Control on VHF Ch 14 or 028 2887 2179 for permission to transit the port area and to check on impending traffic movements. Keep a sharp lookout for shipping approaching or leaving. The Port Control Office is the conspicuous tower, with radar scanner, on Ferris Point. Yachts should keep to the E side, close to No 2 and No 4 beacons. Beyond the power station jetties the channel runs SW, 1 to 2 cables off the shore, and is unmarked.

## Anchorages
- Off the EABC clubhouse and slip, in 2 to 7m, NW of the No 5 buoy. The Club can often arrange a mooring for a visiting yacht.
- Off the E shore, 2 cables S of the pipeline

*Wymer's Pier, Larne, and the East Antrim BC clubhouse and slip*

marker, in 2 to 4m
- Close W of the ruined pier at Ballydowan, 1M SW of Ballylumford "A" jetty, in 2m.

Wymer's Pier, at the Boat Club, has 0·3m at its head. There are no alongside berths for a yacht in Larne. Note also that the construction of the Ballylumford "A" outfall and the gas pipeline have made the former anchorage at the Yellow Stone unavailable. There is a boat harbour on the Islandmagee side N of the power station, which is used by the small passenger ferry to Larne, but the harbour is shallow and of little use to yachts.

## Facilities

Water hose at Wymer's Pier. Diesel and petrol from filling station, 300m. Supermarkets, shops, PO, pubs, restaurants, banks, ATMs, Internet access, doctors, hospital in Larne, 1 km from Wymer's Pier. East Antrim BC (028 2827 7204) welcomes visitors, has bar and showers, and can advise on repair facilities in Larne. Taxis, phone 028 2826 0007. Train and bus services to Belfast; ferries to Cairnryan, Troon and Fleetwood. RNLI all-weather lifeboat station.

## Magheramorne

54°49'·2N 5°46'·1W, *AC1237, SC5612·16 and Plan*

There is a pleasant anchorage in Magheramorne Bay on the S side of the Lough, between the disused cement works and the small artificial island to the N. It is reached through the formerly dredged channel to the cement-works pier, which still has at least 2·5m of water but is only 50m wide and marked only by a privately-maintained dan buoy at its N end. The buoy is 2·5 cables N by E of the artificial island, and the channel runs 175° from there to the conspicuous remains of the pier, passing 0·5 cable E of the island. Anchor in 2m, halfway between the island and the pier.

## LARNE to FAIR HEAD

The coast is steep-to, and a berth of 2 cables clears all dangers. If working against the tide, the streams are weaker inshore and there are useful counter-eddies in the bays. Ballygalley Bay is clean, and offers possible anchorage in offshore winds, in 4 to 5m.

*Magheramorne; the disused cement-works pier, L*

*Glenarm Marina from the NW*

## GLENARM

54°58'·5N 5°57'W, *AC2198, 2199, SC5612·14 and Plan*

Glenarm, 7 cables W of Path Head, has a 70-berth marina with 4m throughout. The breakwaters are conspicuous from seaward and are lit. Enter steering SE. The basin has plenty of room to round up. The marina is owned by Larne Borough Council. Marina manager, phone 028 2884 1285 or 0770 360 6763. Water

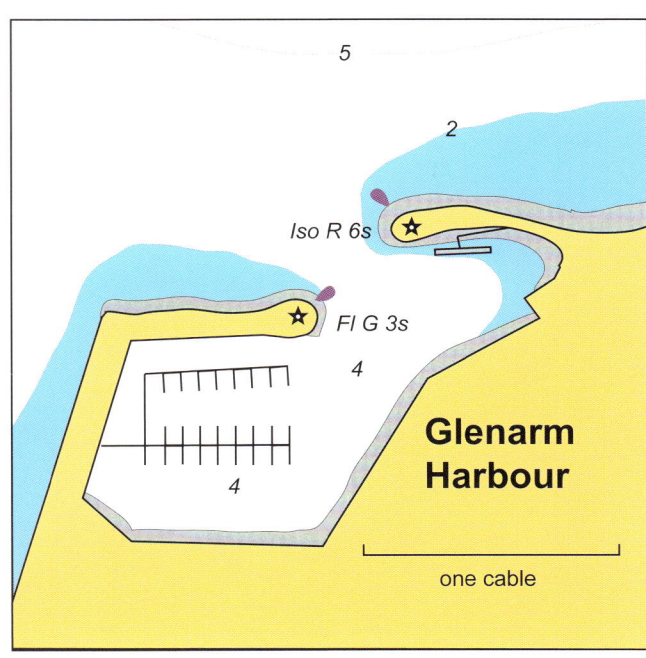

*Glenarm Harbour*

and shore power on the pontoons; diesel available at the marina but must be carried aboard in cans. Shops, PO, pubs in Glenarm village.

There is a fish farm E of Glenarm Bay. Black Rock, off Straidkilly Point between Glenarm and Carnlough, never covers.

## Carnlough

54°59'·5N 5°58'·5W, *AC2198, 2199, SC5612·14 and Plan*

Carnlough harbour has 1m in the entrance and 1·3 to 1·5m everywhere inside, except in its N corner. The entrance is 18m wide between breakwaters marked by black-and-white striped beacons, and is hazardous in onshore winds of more than F5. Approach steering 310° on the line of the leading marks, red triangles with white stripe. Berth alongside the NW wall below the leading mark, or on the outer half of the NE pier. The inner harbour is entirely taken up by local boats on moorings. The slip is not suitable for trailer sailers. Shops, PO, pubs, hotel, restaurants, bank/ATM, Internet access. HM phone 028 2884 1285 or 0770 360 6763.

Anchorage is available a cable to seaward of the harbour entrance in 5m. Constant –0015 Belfast, MHWS 1·8m, MHWN 1·5m.

*Carnlough harbour from the E*

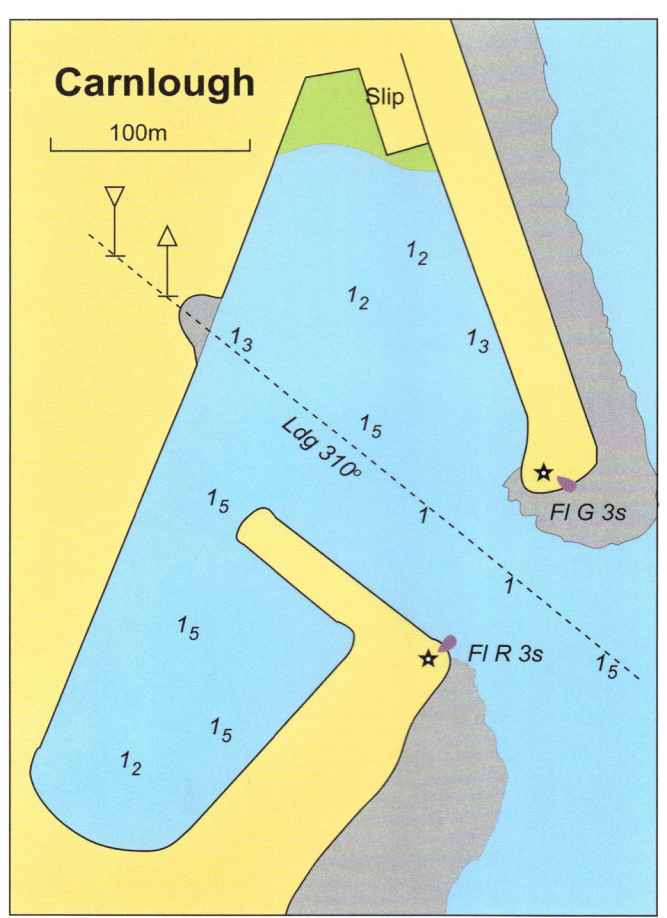

## Red Bay

55°04'N 6°02'·8W, *AC2199, SC5612·14*

This bay provides safe anchorage in winds between SE and NW, with good holding, although even in moderate S or SW winds there can be fierce squalls off the hills. From the S, give the coast W of Garron Point a berth of 2 cables to avoid the remains of a ruined pier 5 cables E of the head of the bay. Red Bay pier, NE of Glenariff village, has 2·9m at its head and offers a temporary alongside berth, but a fenderboard is necessary. Anchorage, on sand, is available either in the S corner of the bay, or SW of the pier head in 2·5m. Shop at Glenariff village.

Cushendall, 1M N of Glenariff in Red Bay, has a slip at its lifeboat station and offers anchorage off the slip in 3 to 6m. There are visitors' moorings. Cushendall Sailing Club (028 2177 1673) has showers and bar. The village has shops, hotel and filling station. RNLI inshore lifeboat station. Const +0020 Belfast, MHWS 1·6m, MHWN 1·5m, MLWN 0·3m, MLWS 0·2m

There is a fish farm between Red Bay and Garron Point.

## Anchorages between Red Bay and Fair Head

- **Cushendun Bay** – anchorage in offshore

*Carnlough harbour entrance, from the SE*

winds at the S end of the bay in 4 to 9m.

- **Torr Head** – on the bay close S of Torr Head is a house with a jetty and slip. Temporary anchorage out of the tide is available in the bay in moderate offshore winds. It is also possible to anchor in the bay close N of Torr Head.

- **Murlough Bay** – this bay 1·4M SE of Fair Head has a long white cottage on the shore, and a boat slip and boathouse. Above-water rocks afford the slip some shelter from the NE. Temporary anchorage out of the tide, in moderate offshore winds, in 2·5m, clean sand, close SE of the outermost of the rocks. Approach steering 220° towards the slip.

*Red Bay from the SE; Cushendall village, top R*

*Red Bay pier*

# Chapter 4

## Ballycastle to Lough Swilly

*Malin Head from the W; the Garvan Islands, centre, Inishtrahull upper L. On the horizon are visible Islay, the Mull of Kintyre (56M distant), Rathlin Island and Fair Head.*

The north coast of Ireland is rugged and beautiful. The part described in this chapter consists of cliffs and sandy bays; the large inlets of Lough Foyle and Lough Swilly are the only ports with all-weather access, but many other harbours and anchorages make this a wonderful cruising ground. The islands of Rathlin and Inishtrahull, the former now a thriving community and a magnet for birdwatchers, the latter spectacular in its lonely isolation, lie across tide-swept sounds.

### Charts

SC5612 covers the coast as far west as Culdaff, and includes Lough Foyle as far as Londonderry. AC2798 Lough Foyle to Sanda and AC2811 Sheep Haven to Lough Foyle cover the whole of this section, with the exception of Lough Foyle itself. AC2494 Plans on the North Coast of Ireland has detail charts of Rathlin Sound and Rathlin Harbour, Ballycastle, Portrush and the River Bann to Coleraine; it is excellent, and either this chart or SC5612 is essential for detailed exploration. West of Lough Foyle, there is no coverage in the form of a Small Craft Folio, and the individual charts must be carried. AC2697 Lough Swilly is necessary if entering the Lough; it also extends as far E as Trawbreaga Bay and has a plan of Culdaff Bay. AC2511 Approaches to Londonderry is needed if going beyond Greencastle, but AC2510 is optional. There are, unfortunately, no large-scale charts of Inishtrahull or Garvan Sounds.

### FAIR HEAD to PORTRUSH

This beautiful 20-mile coast has some of Ireland's most remarkable history, geology and wildlife. It was from the clifftop castle of

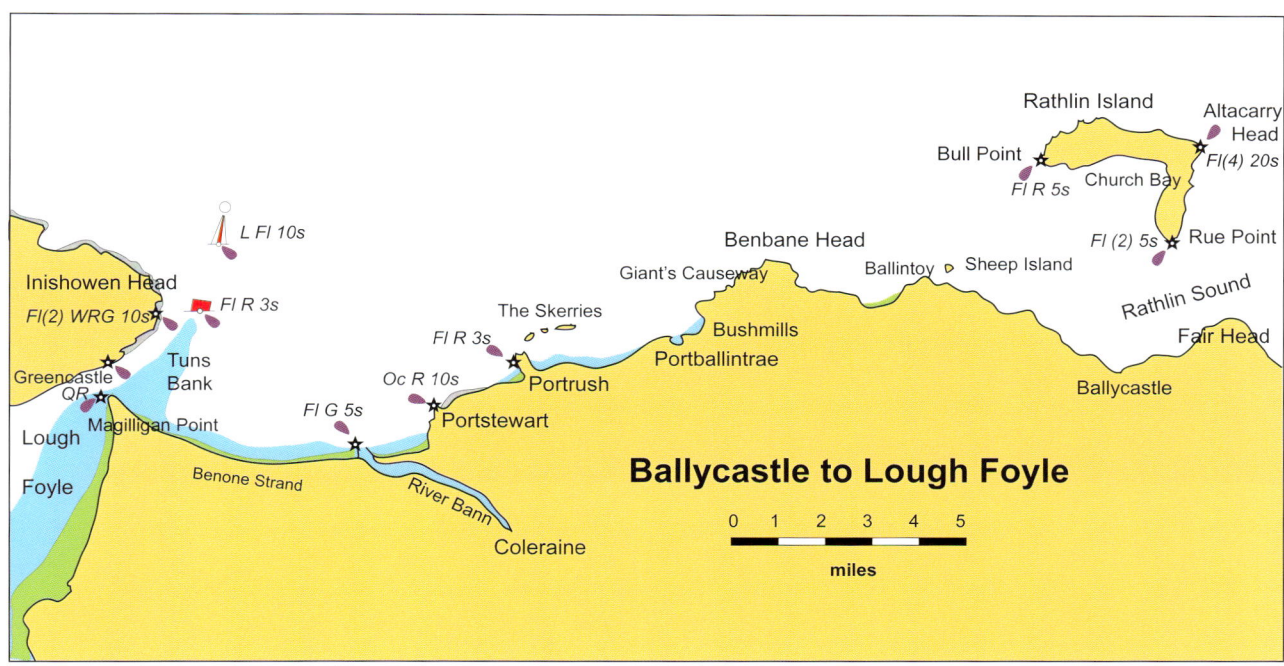

Dunluce that the MacDonnells ruled their 16th-century fiefdom spanning Ireland and Scotland, and it was against the cliffs of Benbane Head, four miles to the NE, that the Armada galleon *Girona* met her end in 1588. Between the two lies the Giant's Causeway, and the cliff scenery here, with its columnar basalt, is spectacular. Along the coast and on Rathlin Island, dazzling white veins of limestone contrast with the black of the basalt, and close east and west of Fair Head there were once coal mines in the cliff face. The tiny islet of Carrickarede, with its famous rope bridge, is just east of Ballintoy. In a cave on Rathlin in 1306 the fugitive Scottish king Robert Bruce was inspired (by an indefatigable web-building spider) to make one more effort to fight the English occupation of Scotland, an effort which was to be resoundingly successful at Bannockburn eight years later. Rathlin is a magnet for birdwatchers, puffins being among the island's most numerous birds. The charming town of Ballycastle (4,000) is renowned for its annual Lammas Fair, which takes place each year at the end of August. Portrush (5,700), once a remote fishing port, developed in Victorian times into Ulster's premier seaside resort, and has still the relaxed ambience of a holiday town.

**Tides**

The rise and fall along this coast is small, due to the proximity of the Port Ellen (Islay) amphidrome; spring range is a metre at Ballycastle and 1·7m at Portrush. At Ballycastle and Rathlin the rise of tide is irregular and the tidal curves are quite asymmetric; the constant at Ballycastle is –0445 Belfast at springs but –0200 Belfast at neaps.

The waters around Rathlin Island have some of the strongest tidal streams in Ireland, reaching 6 knots at springs, and rates are significant all along this coast, diminishing to 2 knots or so off Portrush. Broadly speaking the tide turns W at HW Belfast and E at LW Belfast, but the patterns in Rathlin Sound are complex, and the Sound has a named whirlpool, Slough-na-more. Tidal charts for this area are reproduced below.

Slough-na-more is hazardous from HW Belfast +0130 to +0230. Strong to gale force W and NW winds blowing against the tide cause steep and dangerous seas in Rathlin Sound and close N and E of the island in the MacDonnell Race. In such conditions either pass 2M NE of the

*The Storks*

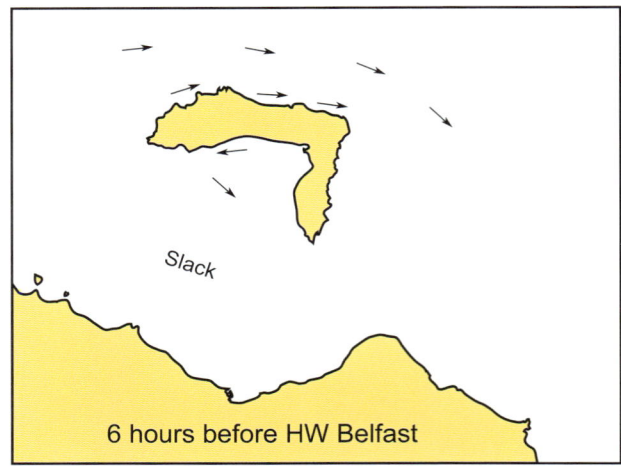

6 hours before HW Belfast

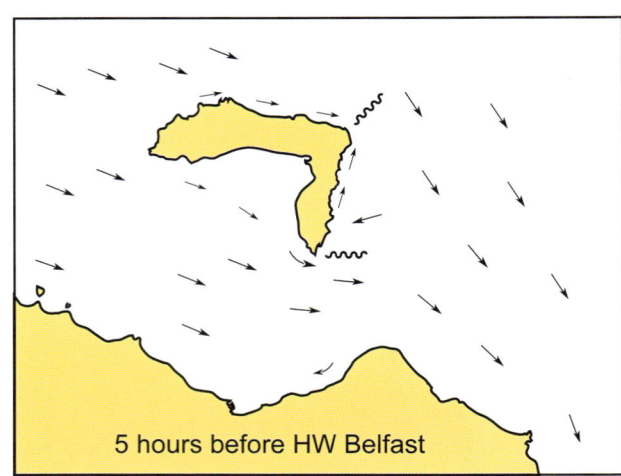

5 hours before HW Belfast

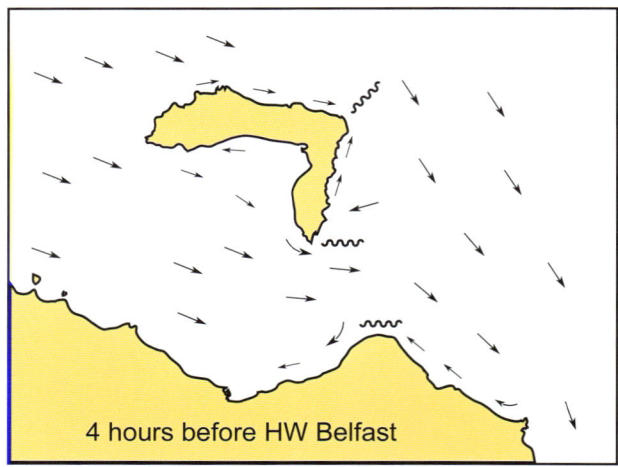

4 hours before HW Belfast

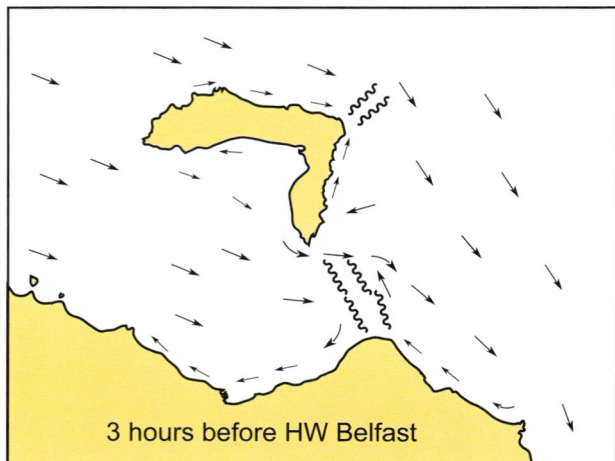

3 hours before HW Belfast

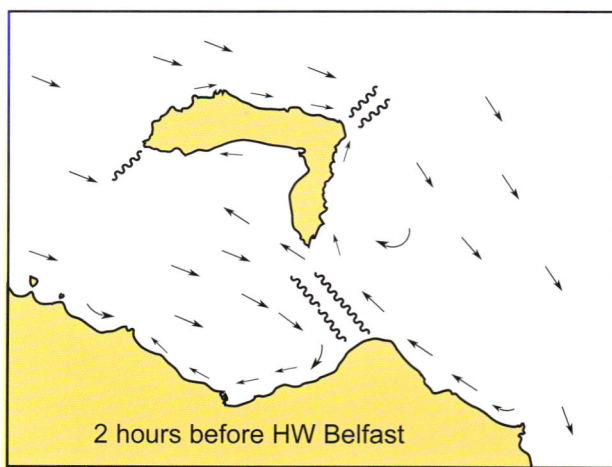

2 hours before HW Belfast

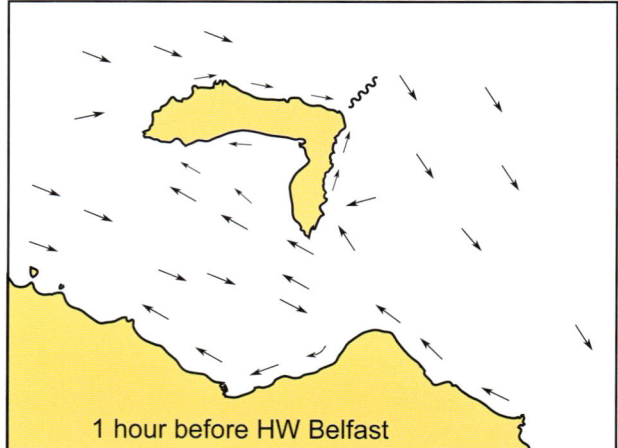

1 hour before HW Belfast

island (also avoiding the TSS) or preferably wait for slack water. Winds up to F5 against the tide should not cause a well-found yacht any problems in the Sound.

The ideal time to pass W through Rathlin Sound is at HW Belfast +0330, when the most turbulent two hours of tide are over. This coincides with the likely ETA in the Sound during a fair-tide passage from Larne or Glenarm to Portrush. Heading E and S from Portrush, leave at HW Belfast +0500 (HW Portrush -0300), staying close inshore to avoid the last of the W-going stream. This enables a yacht to arrive in Rathlin Sound at the turn of the tide and to benefit from a full 6 hours of S-going tide in the North Channel.

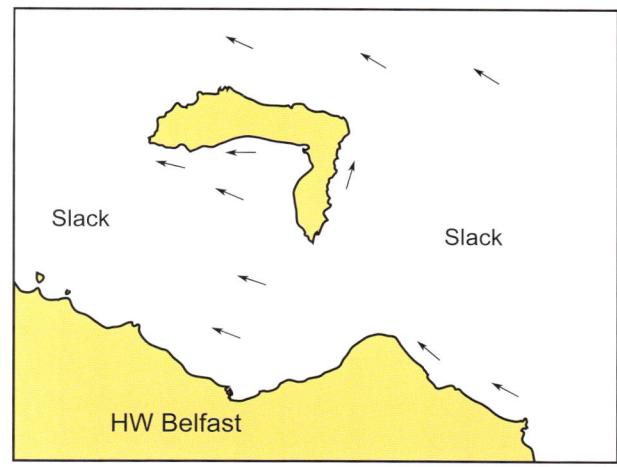

HW Belfast

Slack          Slack

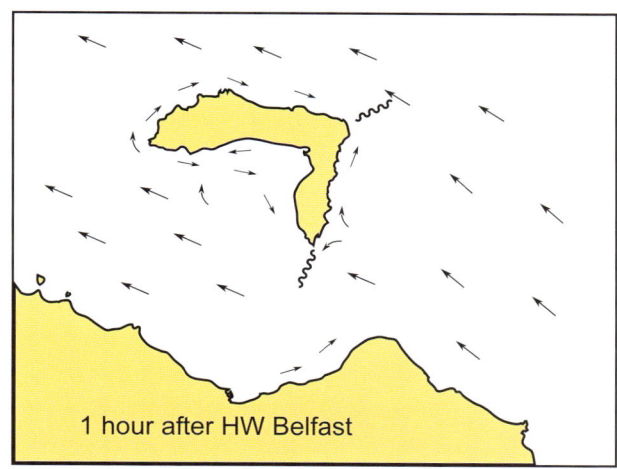

1 hour after HW Belfast

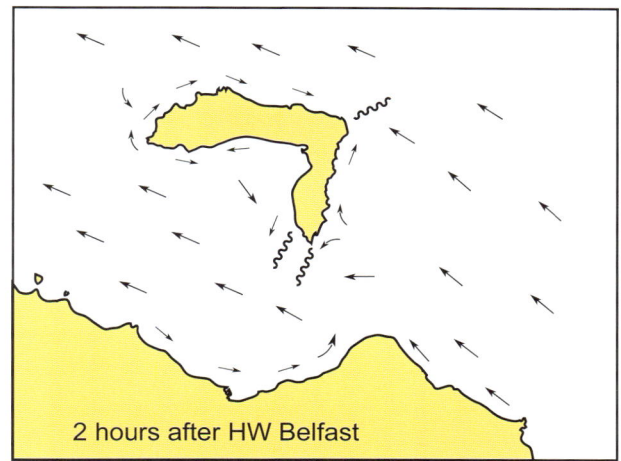

2 hours after HW Belfast

Slough-na-more is hazardous for half an hour either side of this time

3 and 4 hours after HW Belfast

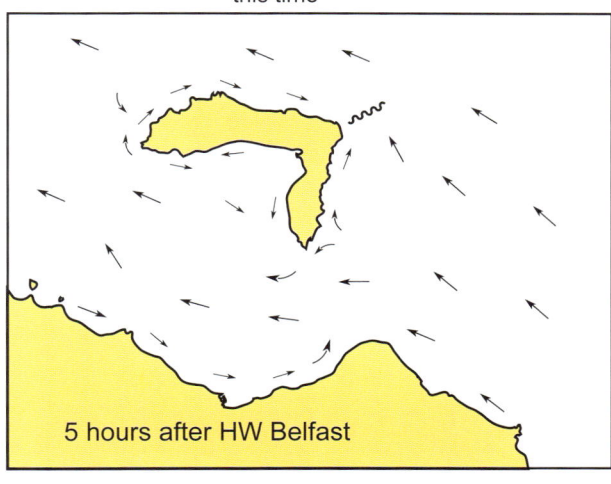

5 hours after HW Belfast

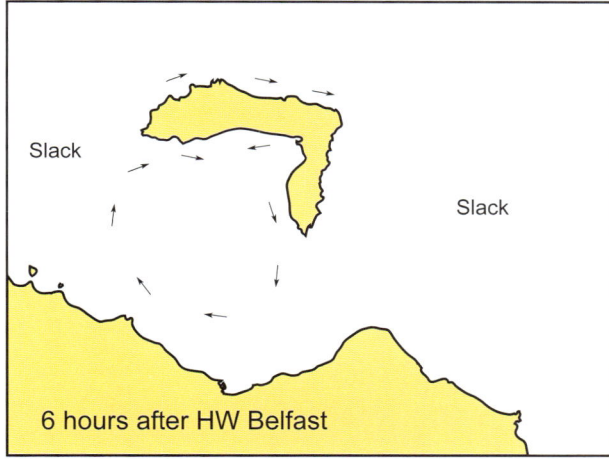

6 hours after HW Belfast

Slack

Slack

## Dangers

**Carrickmannanon,** dries 0·3m, 5 cables NE of Kinbane Head

**The Storks,** drying 2·1m, 7 cables offshore 2·5M E of Ramore Head

**The Skerries,** group of islets and rocks extending for 1·5M ENE of Ramore Head

**Carr Rocks,** drying 0·6m and 0·9m, at the SW extremity of the Skerries chain

## Lights and Marks

**Mull of Kintyre,** white tower Fl(2) 20s 91m 24M, Horn Mo(N) 90s

**Altacarry Head,** white tower, black band Fl(4) 20s 74m 26M, Racon (G) 15–27M

**Rue Point,** white tower, black bands Fl(2) 5s 16m 14M

**Drake** buoy, S Card Q(6)+L Fl 15s

**Manor House,** Port Entry Light Oc WRG 4s

*Ballycastle from the E. The pontoon on the N breakwater is not in position*

5M, G020°–023° W023°–026° R026°–029°, shows white over Rathlin Harbour entrance, green to S, red to W of approach

**Rathlin Harbour** S breakwater Fl(2) G 6s 3·5m 3M

**Rathlin Harbour** N breakwater Fl R 2s 5m 3M

**Ballycastle** N breakwater Fl(3) G 6s 6m 6M

**Ballycastle** S breakwater Fl(2) R 4s 5m 1M

**Rathlin West**, white tower Fl R 5s 62m 22M

**The Storks**, red conical beacon, unlit

**Portrush N Pier,** Fl R 3s 6m 3M

**Portrush S Pier,** Fl G 3s

**Portrush** leading lights 028° FR (occas)

*Rhinns of Islay:*

**Orsay**, white tower Fl 5s 46m 24M

**Traffic Separation Scheme**

There is a TSS E and N of Rathlin Island. The lanes are each 2M wide; the middle of the E- and SE-bound lane runs from a point 3M N of Bull Point, to 3M NE of Altacarry Head, to 4M NE of Torr Head, and the middle of the NW- and N-bound lane is 4M further to the N and NE. The inshore traffic zone on the Irish side is 2 to 3M wide.

The lanes should be crossed at right angles, or as nearly as possible.

**Directions – Rathlin Sound and approaches to Ballycastle**

Fair Head is clean, but from there to Ballycastle the shore should be given a berth of 2 cables. The E-going eddy in Ballycastle Bay on

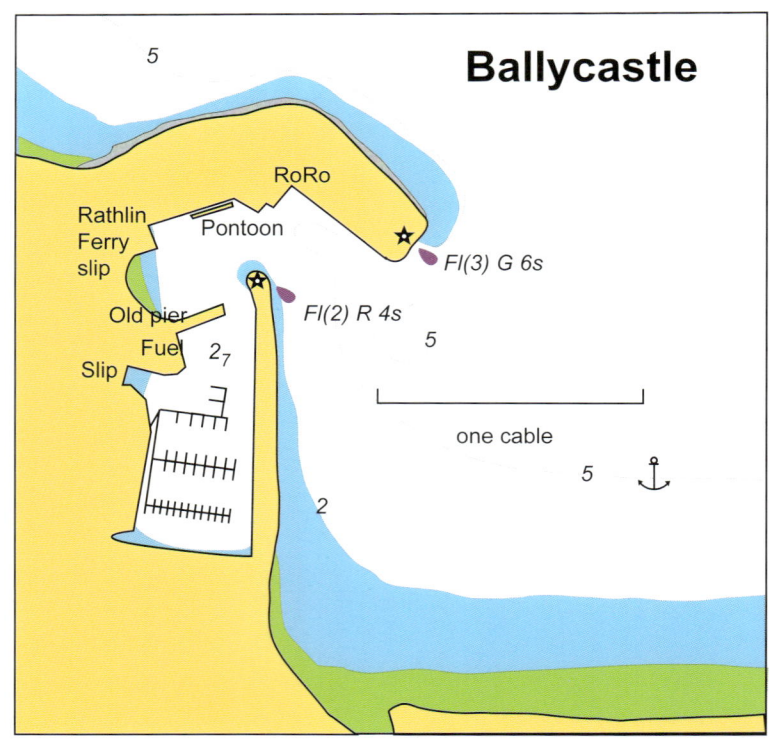

the W-going tide is very pronounced, and in strong SE'lies the wind funnels down over the bay from the high ground S of Fair Head. Rue Point, the S point of Rathlin, is also clean, and a berth of a cable clears all dangers from there to Rathlin Harbour in Church Bay. The World War I wreck of the armoured cruiser *Drake*, once a hazard to navigation, now has 8m over it, but the S Card buoy is still on station.

## BALLYCASTLE

55°13'N 6°14'W, *AC2494, SC5612·19 and Plan*

The S tip of the N breakwater is clean but the N and NE-facing sides have rock armouring which should be given a berth of at least 50m on approach. Be alert for vessels leaving, particularly large RIBs, of which there are many in this area. These provide diving, birdwatching and ferry excursions to and around Rathlin Island. At the time of writing (2007) there is no regular service using the link span inside the N breakwater at Ballycastle. The inner harbour and marina have little room for manoeuvre and yachts longer than 12m or so may prefer to berth on the pontoon W of the link span. The Rathlin Island ferry uses the slip at the root of the N breakwater. The inside of the old pier is reserved for fishing vessels. The marina is well-sheltered but the outer harbour is somewhat subject to swell, particularly in strong NW to N winds. Visitors are requested to contact the marina office in advance of arrival on VHF Ch 80 or by phone 028 2076 8525, mobile 0780 350

5084 (office hours). The marina is owned by Moyle District Council.

### Facilities

Water and shore power on the pontoons. Diesel by hose. Slip suitable for trailer sailers. Showers and laundry at the marina office building. The town has supermarket, shops, restaurants, pubs, banks, ATMs, Internet access, doctors. Taxis. Buses to Belfast. Ferry to Rathlin Island.

### Anchorage

Anchor SE of the harbour in 5m, sand. Sheltered from W to ENE but liable to sudden swell.

Constant (springs) –0440 Belfast, (neaps) –0155 Belfast, MHWS 1·2m, MHWN 1·1m, MLWN 0·7m, MLWS 0·2m.

*Church Bay, Rathlin, from the W. The pontoon has been built since the photograph was taken.*

*Rathlin Harbour from the SW; Manor House Pier, centre L*

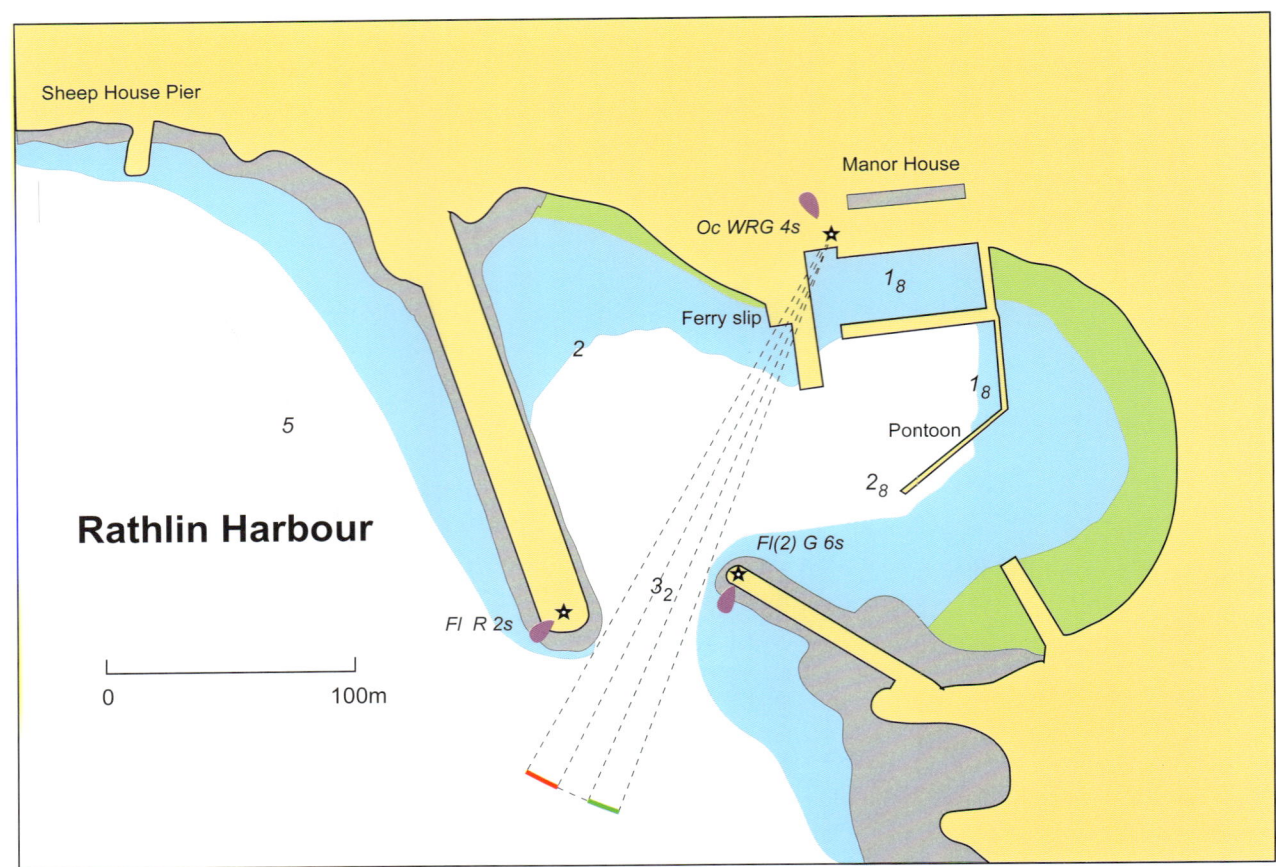

## RATHLIN ISLAND

55°17'N 6°13'W, *AC2798, 2494, SC5612 and Plan*

Tidal streams in the crook of the island, NE of the direct line between Bull and Rue Points, are relatively weak and often run counter to the main stream in the sound. The strong tides in the Sound can have the effect of reducing the swell felt at the harbour, but strong winds from W or NW may make the harbour entrance hazardous, particularly during the last two hours of the E-going tide.

The entrance to the harbour in Church Bay lies between rock-armoured breakwaters projecting SSE and NW from the shores, and is dredged to 3·5m at LAT. **From the W**, identify the Drake buoy (S Card) and leave it a cable to starboard. **From the E**, steer to pass midway

*Rathlin Harbour*

between the buoy and the shore to the E. Approach the harbour entrance on a course of 024° (at night, the white sector of the directional light leads in) and pass midway between the breakwater ends.

## Harbour

The pontoon has 2.8m at its outer end, decreasing to 1.8m at the elbow. On its SE side the deep water extends only 20m from the

*Ushet Port, Rathlin Island; Fair Head across the Sound*

pontoon. The inner harbour offers a sheltered alongside berth in 1.8m, although when the ferry is in her overnight berth there is a gap of only 6m between her starboard side and the E wall of the inner harbour entrance.

Anchorage is possible in 1·2m inside the W breakwater, N of the ferry's track. The old S pier, within the harbour, dries, as does the small Sheep House Pier, 0·5 cable W of the W breakwater.

## Facilities

Water and shore power on the pontoon. Small shops, PO, pubs, restaurant. Ferry to Ballycastle.

## Anchorages around Rathlin

- Anchorage is available in 5 to 8m, close W of the harbour. Sheltered from NW to SSE but exposed to swell in W to NW winds.
- **Ushet Port** *(see photograph)* is a narrow rocky gut 2 cables NNE of Rue Point. It used to be considered as emergency shelter for small vessels in offshore winds but the improved harbours at Church Bay and Ballycastle now fulfil that role. It is possible to anchor at Ushet Port, about 20m within the

entrance, by taking warps to the boulders on either side.
- **Arkill Bay**, 8 cables N of Ushet Port, is sheltered from winds between SW and NW. Anchor close to shore in 5m.
- **Cooraghy Bay**, 7 cables E of Bull Point, provides shelter in moderate N winds. Anchor in 4m, SE of the boat quay. Convenient for landing to visit the birdwatching centre at Bull Point.

## Directions – Rathlin and Ballycastle to Portrush

Most of the dangers on this passage are above-water or well marked, but Carrickmannanon, 5 cables offshore NW of Ballycastle, is an exception. Bengore Head open of Ballintoy Point clears the rock to seaward. There is a clear passage inshore of the rock, on the transit of the N point of Carrickarede and the S point of Sheep Island *(see photograph)*. The channel between Sheep Island and the shore is foul. A berth of 2 cables clears all dangers from Sheep Island to Skerries Roads. Leave the Storks beacon at least a cable on either hand. The S side of the main Skerries islands is steep-to, but beware of the Carr Rocks at the W end of the group. They

*Carrickmannanon (breaking) from the E; Sheep Island, L. Carrickarede is just out of the picture to the L*

*Carrickarede*

*Ballintoy from he SW; Sheep Island upper R, Rathlin in the distance*

may be avoided by keeping Reviggerly reef and Ramore Head close aboard. The coast is dotted with former salmon-fishing stations, several of them with barely room to turn a small boat round between the rocks.

### Carrickarede *(Carrickarade on the charts)*
55°14'·3N 6°19'·5W, *AC2494*

Carrickarede, 3·5M WNW of Ballycastle, is best known for its rope bridge, now a major tourist attraction but designed originally to provide access to the islet's salmon-fishing station. The old landing and ruined cottage are on the SE side, overlooking a bay with 5 to 10m of water and sheltered from S to W. The bay is subject to swell but provides an intriguing temporary anchorage (usually with a large crowd of spectators) in favourable weather.

### BALLINTOY HARBOUR
55°15'N 6°21'·6W, *AC2494, SC5612·21 and Plan*

This small harbour lies immediately W of Sheep Island. Temporary anchorage in the approach to the harbour is available in settled weather, and with sufficient rise of tide the harbour provides a temporary alongside berth for a small yacht. The harbour is sheltered from the NW by a chain of rocky islets terminating in **Rock-on-Stewart** (dries 0·8m) and a rock with 1·8m, close NE of it. **From the E**, leave Sheep

Island a cable to port and steer for the entrance. **From the W**, keep the N end of Carrickarede closed behind Sheep Island until the entrance opens up. The transit of Ballintoy church tower with the prominent lookout house *(see photograph)* leads SE of Rock-on-Stewart. Note that the church tower is not visible from close inshore. The islets on the starboard hand are clean and steep-to on their SE sides, and the S shore of the bay is reported also clean but has not been exhaustively surveyed recently. The outer quay has 1·3m; the inner harbour is shallow and full of small-craft moorings. Anchorage is available in 4 to 5m in the approach to the harbour. Sub-

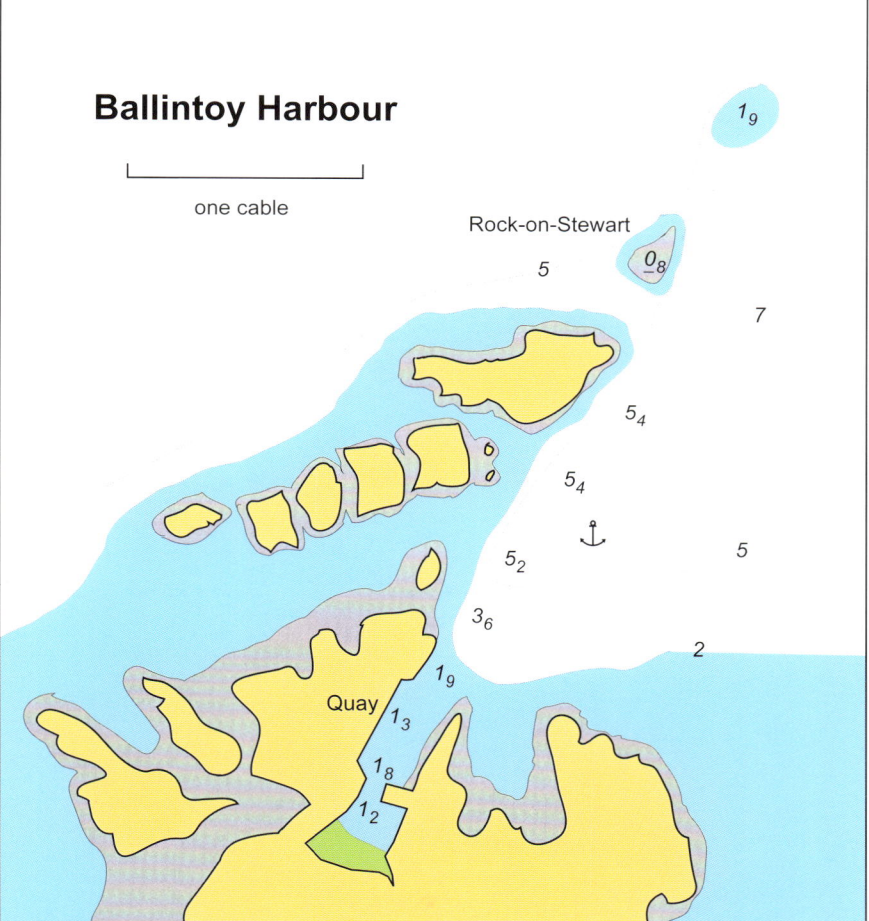

*Ballintoy approach; the lookout house and church, top L*

*Ballintoy*

*Portbradden*

*Dunseverick*

### Dunseverick

55°14'·5N    6°26'·3W,
*AC2798, SC5612·18*
Dunseverick, recognisable by the cluster of buildings and caravans near the shore, has a boat slip and a small pier with 0·5m at its head and a pole beacon with triangular topmark. Approach only in settled weather with no swell, on a course of 220°, leaving the rocky islet close N of the pier to starboard.

ject to swell. There is a tearoom at the harbour.

### Portbradden

55°14'·1N 6°24'·5W, *AC2798, SC5612·18*
Portbradden, at the W end of the splendid Whitepark Bay, provides a landing at its jetty but shelter only in moderate offshore winds.

### Portballintrae

55°13'·5N 6°32'·9W, *AC2798, SC5612·18 and Plan*
The village of Portballintrae lies around a horseshoe bay 3·2M SW of Bengore Head, and is the

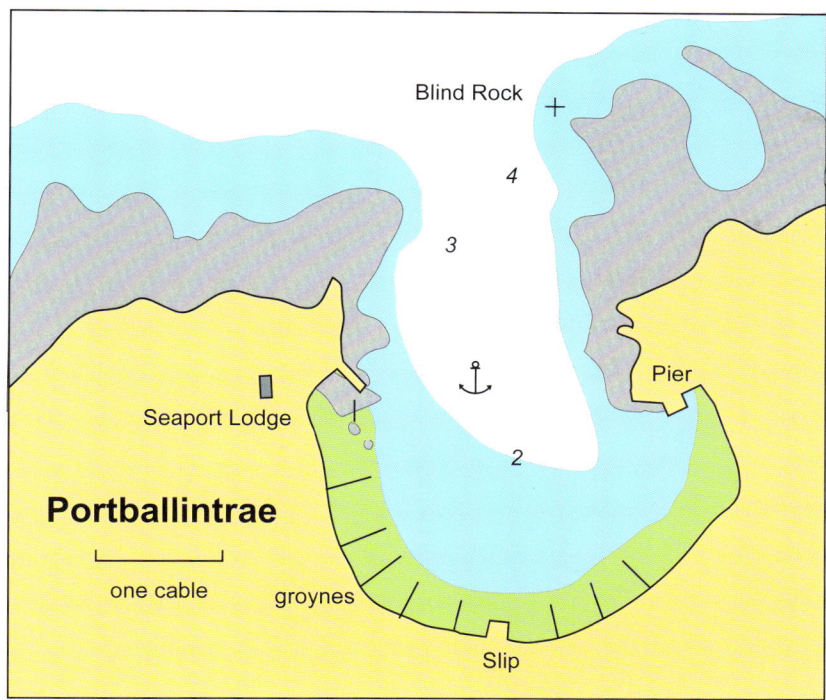

only significant built-up area on the coast between Ballycastle and Portrush. The bay is subject to swell but provides reasonable anchorage in offshore winds. A heavy swell from the N breaks right across the mouth and makes the anchorage hazardous. Enter steering S for the conspicuous slipway on the beach, taking particular care to avoid **Blind Rock** on the E side of the entrance, and anchor in 2·5m when the head of the W pier comes in line with the distinctive classical Seaport Lodge. The pier on the E side of the bay has 0·9m at the steps and is used by diving and sea-angling boats. The slip is not suitable for trailer sailers. Boat club, pubs and hotels.

*Portballintrae from the SE; Seaport Lodge, centre. The Storks, upper centre with the Skerries beyond, and Ramore Head top L. Inishowen Head and Glengad Head in the distance.*

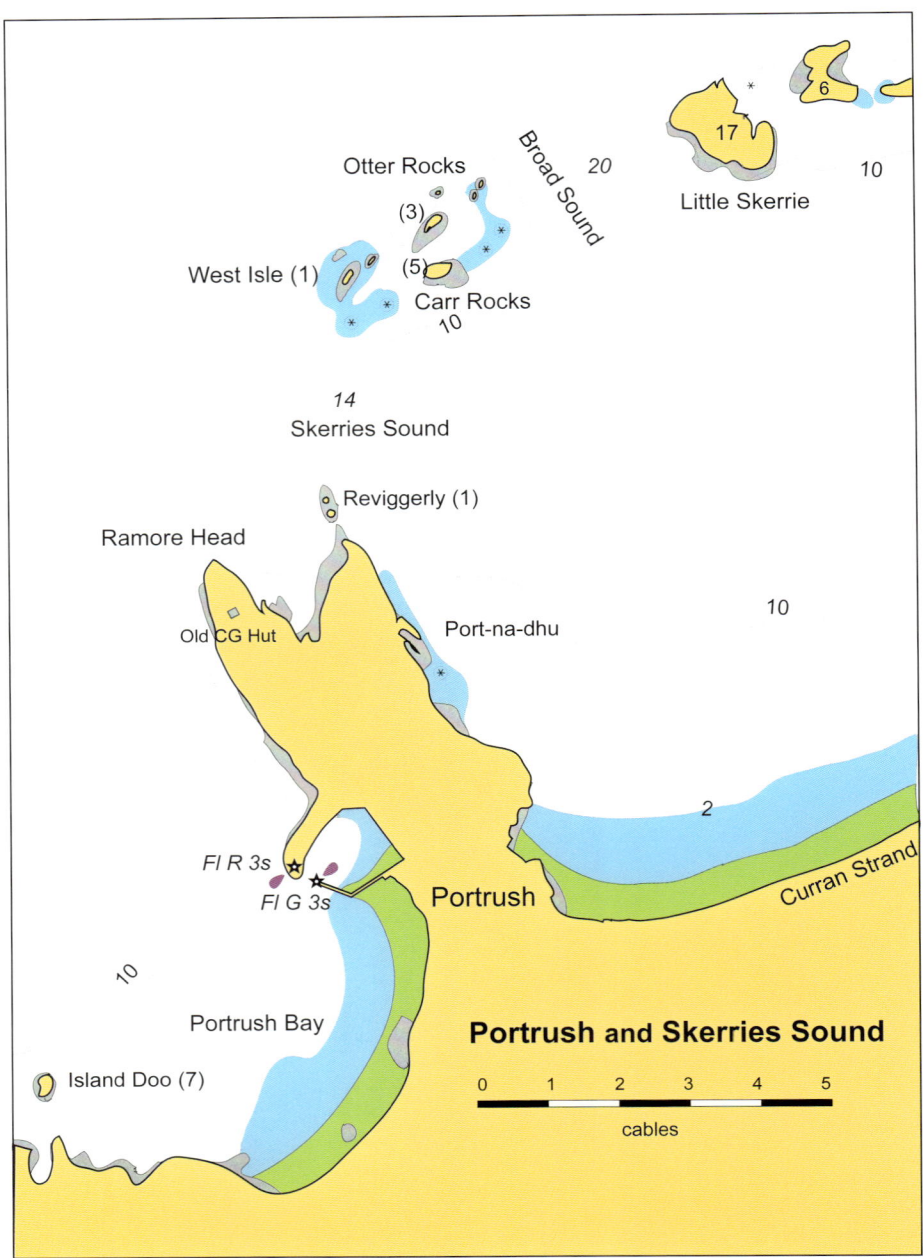

Otter Rocks

(3)

Broad Sound

20

17

6

10

Little Skerrie

West Isle (1)

(5)

Carr Rocks

10

*

*

*

14

Skerries Sound

Reviggerly (1)

Ramore Head

10

Old CG Hut

Port-na-dhu

*

2

Fl R 3s

Fl G 3s

Portrush

Curran Strand

10

Portrush Bay

**Portrush and Skerries Sound**

Island Doo (7)

| 0 | 1 | 2 | 3 | 4 | 5 |

cables

## Skerries Roads

55°13'·2N 6°37'·5W, *AC2494, SC5612·21*

Skerries Roads provide an attractive anchorage in moderate winds between W and NE. The best spot is close inshore abreast the notch in the Large Skerrie, in 5 to 7m.

## PORTRUSH

55°12'·3N 6°39'·8W, *AC2494, SC5612·21, Imray C64, C53 and Plan*

The busy holiday resort of Portrush, flanked by splendid beaches on either side, has perhaps the most convenient harbour on the north coast. The town sits astride the promontory of Ramore Head, and its man-made harbour, a cable each way, faces SW into Portrush Bay. It of-fers secure shelter in all summer weather although in strong to gale force W to NW winds the entrance can be hazardous and the swell can penetrate into the harbour. In heavy onshore weather even the lifeboat is occasionally unable to return to base and must wait in the Foyle for conditions to moderate. A 1989 photograph of the Arun class *Richard Evans* leaving Portrush harbour into a F11 NW wind, and waves 14m high, is acknowledged by the RNLI to be the best picture ever taken of a lifeboat on service.

## Directions

From the E, Ramore Head and the cliffs S of it are steep-to and may be approached to within half a cable. Leave Reviggerly close to port

*Portrush entrance from the NW. Note the boulders exposed off the N breakwater*

to avoid the Carr Rocks at the SW end of the Skerries group. Identify the W breakwater, and do not turn in until the entrance is well open, to avoid sunken boulders extending 20m SW from the breakwater end. At night, the red light on the W breakwater head is an excellent mark but may be hard to distinguish among the town lights from a position well out to sea.

**Harbour**

There is a 40m-long pontoon along the NW wall of the harbour. When approaching the pontoon, note that there is sufficient deep water to round up beyond the lifeboat. Berth alongside the pontoon or the NW wall itself and contact the HM, whose office is on the quay. HM phone 028 7082 2307, VHF Ch 12 (office hours). There is no commercial traffic in the harbour. The SE half of the harbour is taken up by trots of moorings *(see photograph)*.

*Portrush from the SW; Ramore Head, L, with Reviggerly off the point at L centre, and West Isle and the Carr Rocks beyond; the Little Skerrie, top, and the Large Skerrie, top R*

## Facilities

Diesel and water by hose on the quay. Supermarket, shops, restaurants, pubs, banks, ATMs, laundry, Internet access, doctors. Portrush Yacht Club (established in 1894) has its clubhouse on the quay and extends a warm welcome to visitors. Showers at the YC or by arrangement with the HM. Bus and train connections to Coleraine and Belfast. RNLI all-weather lifeboat station.

Constant –0435 Belfast, MHWS 2·1m, MHWN 1·4m, MLWN 1·1m, MLWS 0·4m.

## PORTRUSH to LOUGH FOYLE

The coast west of Portrush continues rocky and steep-to as far as the holiday town of Portstewart (6,500) and then gives way to the most glorious sweep of golden beach in Ireland, extending 10M by way of Portstewart, Castlerock, Downhill and Benone Strands to Magilligan Point at the entrance to Lough Foyle. The beaches deepen into navigable water two cables offshore. Two miles west of Portstewart, the River Bann reaches the sea between stone breakwaters, marking the entrance to the port and university town of Coleraine (20,700), four miles upriver. On the cliffs of Downhill, overlooking the beach, stands the Mussenden Temple, a classical-Roman-style memorial dating from 1780 and a conspicuous landmark from seaward. The distinctive 350m-high scarp of Binevenagh then stands above the low sandy promontory of Magilligan, with its prison (brightly lit and visible at night well out to sea!) and its military firing range. Firing trials seldom, if ever, impinge on freedom of coastwise navigation here.

The narrows between Magilligan Point and Greencastle afford entrance to Lough Foyle, a teardrop-shaped shallow tidal basin 20M in length with a maintained channel along its NW side leading to the historic city and port of Londonderry. Derry, as it is commonly referred to, is the second city of Northern Ireland and has a population of 110,000. It was from Derry in 563 AD that Columkille, or Columba, sailed to establish his monastery of Iona. The city has played a key role in almost every political upheaval in Ireland's long and chequered history, and its celebrated siege, successfully defended in 1689, was pivotal in securing Ireland for the British crown. Derry today is vibrant, energetic and independent-minded, and retains a keen sense of its history. The old city walls, predating the siege, still stand intact.

Lough Foyle marks the border between the two jurisdictions; the SE shore, Magilligan Point and Londonderry are in Northern Ireland, the border meets the Lough shore N of Culmore Point, and most of the NW shore, and Moville and Greencastle, are in the Republic.

## Tidal Streams

The coastwise streams here are relatively weak, seldom exceeding 1·5 knots. Between Ramore Head and the Bann there is an eddy along the shore during the second half of both the ebb and flood. The streams in the entrance to Lough Foyle run at 3·5 knots at springs, the ebb in mid-channel commencing at HW Belfast –0300 (HW Galway +0330) and the flood at HW Belfast +0300 (HW Galway –0300). Around Magilligan Point the tide turns an hour earlier. On the NW side of the entrance between Warren Point and Moville there is a useful eddy on both ebb and flood, extending 50 to 100m offshore. Between Moville and Culmore the streams reach 2·5 knots. The ebb stream continues out to sea on the NW side of the Tuns Bank, steadily slackening but still able to raise a steep and confused sea in strong NW to NE winds. Refer to the tidal diagrams under *Lough Foyle to Malin Head*, below.

## Dangers

**Tuns Bank,** sandbank occasionally drying in places, extending 3M NE from Magilligan Point

## Lights and Marks

**Outfall** buoy, Fl(2) Y 10s, 1.5M W of Portrush Harbour
**Portstewart Point,** red hut, Oc R 10s 21m 5M
*River Bann entrance:*
**East Mole,** Fl R 5s 6m 2M
**West Mole,** Fl G 5s 4m 2M
**River Bann** leading lights 165° Oc 5s 2M, white pillars, front 6m rear 14m
*Lough Foyle entrance:*
**Foyle** buoy, safe water mark RWVS, L Fl 10s, AIS
**Tuns** buoy, PHM Fl R 3s

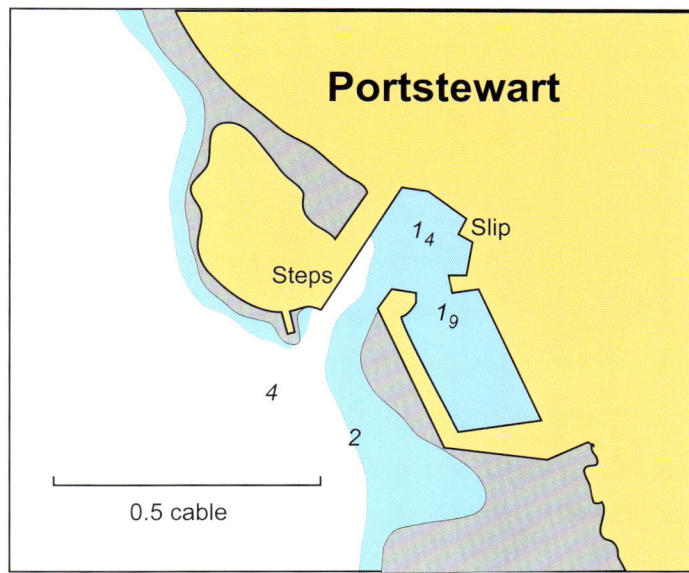

**Portstewart**

Slip

1₄

Steps

1₉

4

2

0.5 cable

**Inishowen Head (Dunagree Point)**, white tower, black bands, Fl(2) WRG 10s 28m, W18M R14M G14M, G197°–211° W211°–249° R249°–000°; Horn (2) 30s. Shows white over the approach from the NE and the fairway buoy, red over the Tuns Bank to the E, and green to the N.

**Metal Man,** green and white triangular metal beacon on Bluick Rock, unlit

**Warren Point,** white tower Fl 1·5s 11m 4M

**Greencastle S breakwater,** Dir Fl(2) WRG 3s 4m W11M R9M G9M, G307°–040° W040°–045° R045°–055°. Shows white over the channel to the SW, green over the banks to the S and SE, and red inshore to the W of the channel

**Magilligan,** red piled structure QR 7m 4M

**McKinney's Bank** buoy, PHM Fl R 5s

**Moville**, white hut on piles Fl WR 2·5s 11m 4M, W240°–064° R064°–240° Shows white over the channel and to the SE, red inshore to NE and SW.

The channel between Moville and Culmore Point is marked by three more buoys and 26 pile beacons, Fl R and Fl G

*Culmore Point to Londonderry:*

**Culmore Point**, Q 6m 3M

**Culmore Bay** buoy, SHM QG

**Ballynagard**, Fl 3s 6m 3M

**Otterbank**, Fl R 4s 6m 3M

**Brookhall**, QG 6m 3M

**Mountjoy**, QR 5m 3M

**Clooney**, Fl R 4s

**St Columbs**, PHM Fl R 5s

**Aberfoyle**, Fl R 2s

**Portstewart**

55°11'·3N 6°43'·4W, *AC2494, SC5612·21 and Plan*

This bustling holiday town has a small sheltered harbour which is the base for the River Bann pilot boat and sea angling vessels. The inner harbour has 1.9m with a 6m-wide entrance but is fully occupied by local moorings. Visiting yachts up to 11m or so in length may find a temporary berth on the NW wall just inside the breakwater, where there is 2m at the steps. Approach on a course of 030° and stay close to the NW breakwater on entry, since there is shallower water on the SE side. The slip is suitable for trailer sailers. Water tap at the slip; shops, pubs, restaurants, PO, banks, ATMs.

*Portstewart from the NW*

*Portstewart harbour entrance from the SW*

## COLERAINE
55°10'·6N 6°46'·4W, *AC2494, SC5612·19 and Plan*

The Barmouth, the entrance to the River Bann, lies between stone breakwaters projecting 2 cables N from the shore between Portstewart and Castlerock Strands. The entrance is dredged and the river channel to Coleraine is maintained at a depth of 3.4m at LAT, but the combination of a strong onshore wind or swell and the outflow from the river can cause steep and dangerous seas off the breakwaters. A stranger should not attempt to enter in N to NW winds of F6 or more, or if the swell is breaking over the east pierhead; Coleraine Harbour office monitors the Barmouth by CCTV and can advise on conditions, VHF Ch 12 or phone 028 7034 2012, office hours. The entrance is well marked and lit, and the channel to Coleraine is marked by pile beacons, Fl R and Fl G. In settled conditions, entry by day or night is straightforward. Coleraine receives about one cargo vessel a week, importing steel for construction and exporting scrap metal.

### Directions
From a position 3 cables NNW of the breakwaters, identify the leading marks and steer in on their line, then follow the marked channel. The first port hand mark is well over towards the W side, and it is easy to leave it on the wrong hand. The depths reduce suddenly outside the marked channel.

### Anchorage
There is a pleasant anchorage at Dougan's Bay, on the N side 1M within the entrance, where yachts lie on moorings. Anchor in 2 to 3m, mud.

### Marinas
**Seaton's (Drumslade) Marina**, on the N bank 2M upstream of Dougan's Bay, has 40 berths, and moorings. Phone 028 7083 2086 or mobile 0773 310 0915.

**Coleraine Marina**, on the NE bank 4M from the entrance, has 90 berths, with 3m at the outer pontoons. VHF Ch 16 and M1, phone 028 7034 4768. Water and shore power, diesel, 12t travelhoist, showers. Coleraine YC clubhouse is adjacent to the marina and welcomes visitors.

### Coleraine Harbour
The Harbour consists of a

*The Barmouth from the SE; Inishowen Head, upper L*

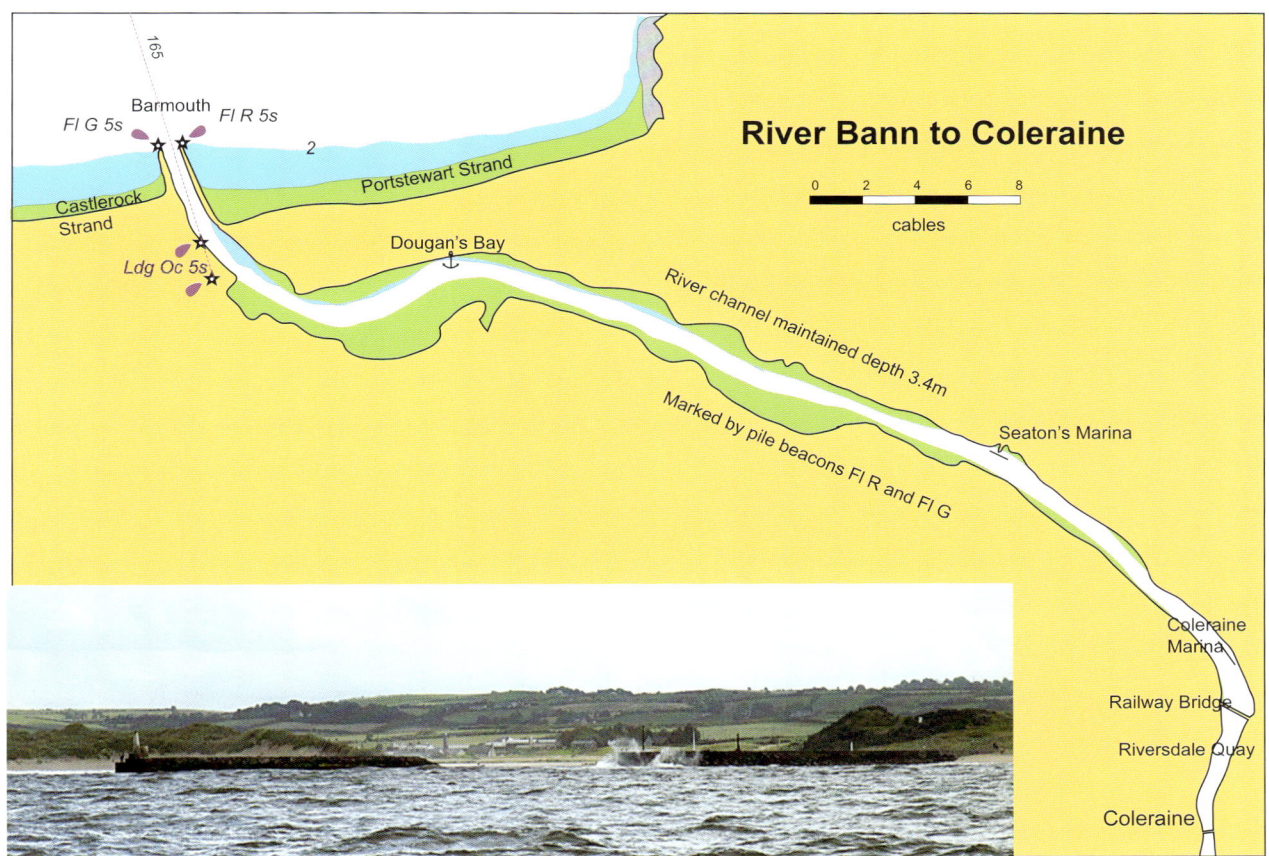

*River Bann entrance from the NW*

*Coleraine Marina from the S; Portrush on the coast, top. The Scottish island of Islay (31M distant) on the horizon*

quayside on the NE bank at Riversdale Quay immediately below the town but upstream of the (opening) railway bridge. The harbour offers winter storage for yachts (with excellent provision for covered storage) and boatyard facilities. To request bridge opening, phone the HM 028 7034 2012 during office hours with at least a few hours' notice. The harbour office monitors VHF Ch 12 (office hours) and visiting yachts are encouraged to listen on this channel for information on traffic movements.

### Facilities

Boatyard services and chandlery, Richard Connor 0771 211 5751. Coleraine has all the facilities of a large town; supermarkets, shops, pubs, restaurants, banks, ATMs, laundry, Internet access, doctors, hospital with full A&E. Train and bus connections to Belfast, Londonderry and Portrush.

Constant –0425 Belfast, MHWS 2·1m, MHWN 1·6m, MLWN 0·7m, MLWS 0·3m.

### River Bann above Coleraine

At Coleraine the Bann is crossed by a bridge with 1·8m headroom at MHWS, but the river is navigable for 32M to Lough Neagh, with five locks, by vessels of less than 1·3m draft and 3·3m air draft. Details of the passage are contained in "River Bann and Lough Neagh Pilot" by Michael Savage, published by the River Bann and Lough Neagh Association and available from Coleraine Marina.

### LOUGH FOYLE

55°15'N 6°54'W, *AC2798, 2511, SC5612, Imray C64*

Lough Foyle is accessible by day or night in any weather, but the tide runs strongly in the narrows between Greencastle and Magilligan Point, and the combination of a strong N to NE wind and the ebb tide raises a steep and confused sea for up to two miles to seaward of Inishowen Head. The Tuns Bank is a triangular area of sand extending for a mile NE of Magilligan Point, on the E side of the entrance. The NW side of the bank forms a ridge which in some years dries by up to a metre and in others is below water. Its NE tip is marked by a port-hand buoy, and the Foyle fairway buoy is 1M further out to sea.

**From the E,** the safest and most straightforward approach is N of the Tuns buoy,

*Lough Foyle from the NW; Dunagree Point and Inishowen Head lighthouse, lower R, Magilligan Point centre L*

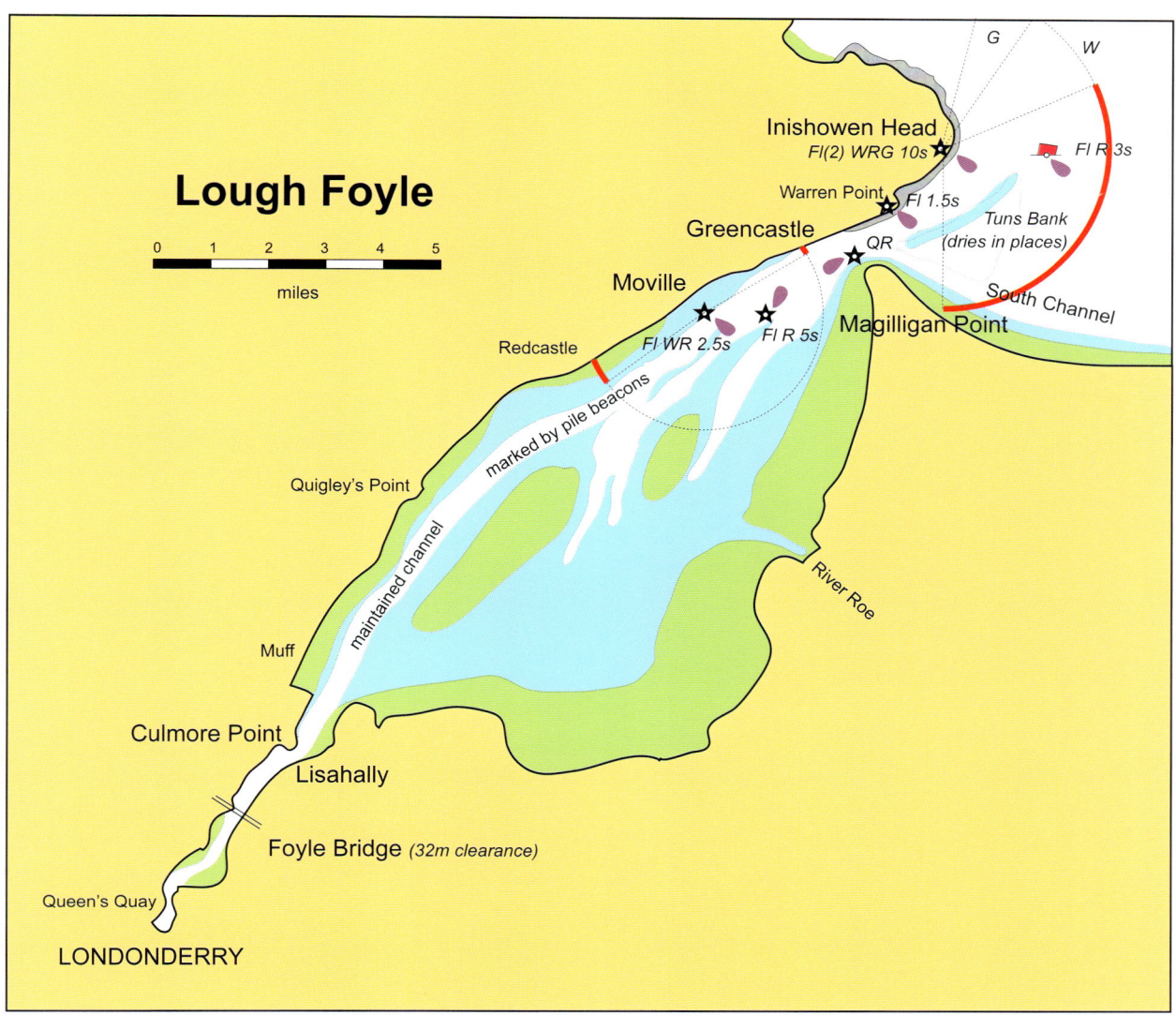

but there is a channel locally known as the South Channel or the Dorus, at least a cable wide and with 4·4m, between the bank and Benone Strand; this channel offers a convenient short cut in daylight and clear weather, and does not appear to be particularly prone to shifting of the sand.

**From the W,** give Inishowen Head a berth of 1 cable.

## Caution

The navigable channel in Lough Foyle and approaches is a "narrow channel" within the meaning of IRPCS Rule 9. A vessel under 20m, or a sailing vessel, must not impede any vessel which can navigate only within the channel.

## South Channel

55°11'N 6°55'W, *AC2511, SC5612·22*

**From the E,** head for the highest of the sand dunes behind Benone Strand (in approximately 6°54'W). When 5 cables off the beach, steer W until the radio mast on the summit of Crockaulin (325m) is in transit 304° above the castle ruins at Greencastle *(see photograph)*. The ruins are ivy-covered and may be difficult to pick out, but their vertical left-hand wall is slightly more conspicuous. The ruins are to the left of a new apartment building and to the right of the flat-roofed white building of the Fisheries School. This transit 304° leads through the South Channel in a least depth of 4·4m. When approaching Magilligan Point, borrow a little to the S of the line until in deeper water. **From the W,** steer to pass 2 cables N of Magilligan Point and pick up the transit line astern. In poor visibility, the outside passage NE of the Tuns Bank is safer, and the South Channel should not be attempted in heavy onshore weather.

*Crockaulin above Greencastle castle ruins leads through the South Channel at Magilligan*

### Magilligan Point

The HW mark at Magilligan Point is variable, and the shape of the point changes somewhat from year to year. The piled beacon W of the point has nevertheless remained a valid mark for many decades and the position of navigable water relative to the beach appears reasonably constant. While the high tide line advances and recedes by as much as two cables over a period of twenty to forty years, the current edition of AC2511, based on very recent data from the Ordnance Survey of Ireland and hydrographic surveys undertaken on behalf of Londonderry Port & Harbour Commissioners, can be trusted implicitly.

### White Bay

55°13'·6N 6°55'·5W, *AC2511, SC5612·22*
Immediately N of Inishowen lighthouse on Dunagree Point, this bay offers a feasible passage anchorage in offshore winds. Anchor in 2m, sand.

### GREENCASTLE

55°12'N 6°59'W, *AC2511, SC5612·22 and Plan*
The village of Greencastle is the premier fishing port of east Donegal and the site of Ireland's Sea Fisheries School. Its harbour is strategically located just within Lough Foyle and offers all-weather access, excellent shelter and good facilities. At the time of writing (late 2007) works are under way to build a new breakwater to the SW in order to extend the harbour and provide additional protection. With the decline of the fishing industry, the once-

*Inishowen Head lighthouse, centre, on Dunagree Point; White Bay beyond*

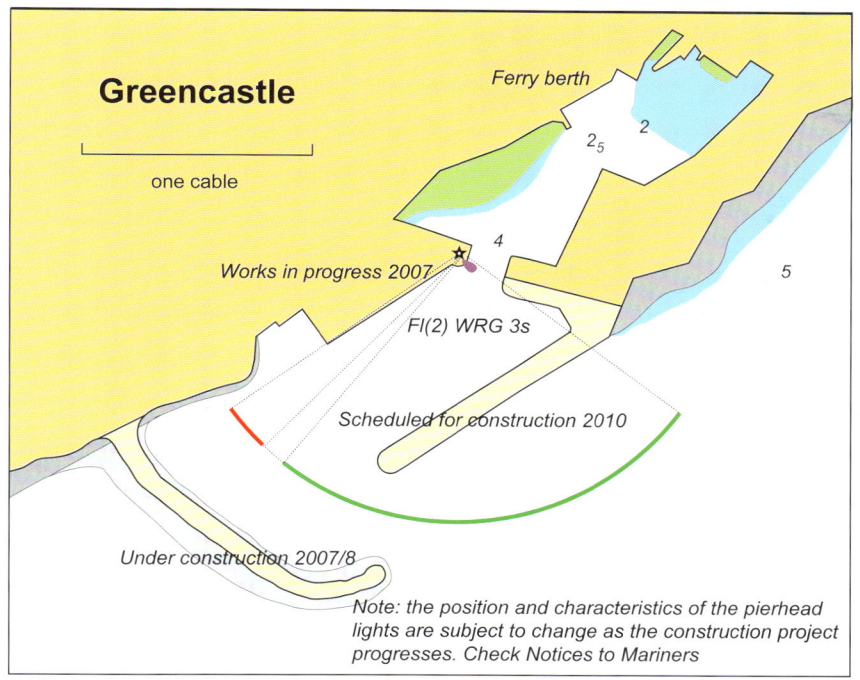

**Greencastle**

one cable

Ferry berth

2₅ 2

4

Works in progress 2007

*Fl(2) WRG 3s*

5

Scheduled for construction 2010

Under construction 2007/8

Note: the position and characteristics of the pierhead lights are subject to change as the construction project progresses. Check Notices to Mariners

## Directions

The shores to NE and SE of the harbour are clean. Approach from the main channel of Lough Foyle steering NE, keeping a sharp lookout for fishing vessels and the ferry.

## Harbour

Small yachts should berth or raft up in the E corner of the harbour. Larger vessels should contact the HM, preferably in advance, for instructions. HM phone 087 250 2231.

## Facilities

crowded harbour extends a warm welcome to yachts, and there are outline plans for improved facilities. Greencastle is the western terminal of the Magilligan car ferry and the base for the Foyle pilot boats.

Water, shore power, diesel by hose (phone 086 254 5099), shop, PO, pubs and restaurants, filling station. McDonald's boatyard, hull (wood and GRP) and mechanical repairs, phone 07493 81420. Rigging repairs, Dougal's 07493 82222 or 087 260 2018. Ferry to Magilligan Point.

The former anchorage S of Magilligan Point

*Greencastle from the E*

is no longer available due to ferry traffic and shifting of the sandbanks.

## Moville

55°11'N 7°02'·5W, *AC2511, SC5612·22*

Approach from the NE either S or close N of Moville light. The pier has 1·5m at its outer end and offers an alongside berth in settled weather or offshore winds, but the NW face is often occupied by small fishing craft and the SW and SE faces are swept by the ebb tide. There are visitors' moorings in the bay. Constant +0215 Galway, MHWS 2·3m, MHWN 1·8m, MLWN 0·8m, MLWS 0·3m. Shops, pubs, restaurants, banks, ATM.

## Carrickarory Pier

The pier 6 cables SW of Moville has 3m at its head but is heavily occupied by fishing vessels. There are visitors' moorings off the pier but they are in the full run of the tide.

## Lough Foyle

The channel SE of Moville has a maintained depth of 8m over a width of 0·4 cable and is marked by port and starboard hand pile beacons Fl R and Fl G. Do not stray outside the lines of the beacons since the depth reduces very rapidly on either side.

There are oil and chemical jetties at Maydown, N of Coolkeeragh power station, with its three conspicuous chimneys; and 1M further upstream at Lisahally on the SE side is the city's main commercial port, and the harbour office. At the S end of the dock complex is a pontoon.

## Culmore

55°02'·8N 7°15'·5W, *AC2510, SC5612·23*

The bay opposite Lisahally and W of Culmore Point is an attractive anchorage in 4 to 7m, mud. Shop and pub ashore.

## LONDONDERRY

55°00'·1N 7°19'·1W, *AC2510, SC5612·23*

The city straddles the river 4M SW of Lishally, the stretch between being wooded and scenic. The Foyle Bridge, with a clearance of 32m, spans the river 3M S of Lisahally, and Craigavon Bridge in the city centre represents the limit of navigation for masted yachts. Passing under the Foyle Bridge, leave Madam's Bank light to starboard and then stay close to the W bank,

*River Foyle, looking upstream; Culmore Point, centre, with Lisahally Docks beyond, Foyle Bridge and Londonderry in the distance*

*The pontoon at Queen's Quay, Londonderry*

leaving Clooney, St Columb's and Aberfoyle beacons to port.

## Mooring

At Queen's Quay on the W bank is a 200m pontoon parallel to the quayside and directly in front of the conspicuous City Council office building. On the way upriver, stop at the pontoon at Lisahally to register and collect a key for the security gate. The harbour office monitors VHF Ch 16 and 14, 24 hours. The pontoon at Queen's Quay gives access to all city centre facilities.

Anchorage is also available in mid-river between Queen's Quay and Craigavon Bridge. Constant +0305 Galway, MHWS 2·7m, MHWN 2·1m, MLWN 1·2m, MLWS 0·5m.

## Facilities

Diesel by tanker, filling stations. Water and shore power on the pontoon. Showers at City Hotel, 200m. Restaurants, pubs, supermarkets, laundry, PO, banks, ATMs, Internet access, doctors, regional hospital with full A&E facilities; mechanical, electrical and electronic repairs available. Train connections to Belfast, buses to Belfast and Dublin, car rental, taxis; regional airport 4M E on the Limavady road.

## River Foyle above Londonderry

In the city centre the river is spanned by Craigavon Bridge, with headroom 1·2m. For vessels which can pass under the bridge, the river is navigable for 16M to Strabane.

## LOUGH FOYLE TO MALIN HEAD
*AC2811*

The NE coast of the Inishowen peninsula is bounded by cliffs rising to 230m W of Glengad Head and enclosing four small bays, two of which – Culdaff Bay and Slievebane Bay – offer reasonable temporary anchorages. Inishtrahull, with its important lighthouse and its anchorage sheltered from the west, is Ireland's most northerly point. Six miles NE of Malin Head across a tideswept sound, the island was evacuated in 1928, and from then until 1987 was home only to the lighthousekeepers. The ruined school building still bears its carved nameplate "INISHTRHULL NATIONAL SCHOOL 1901" as witness to the need for its services. The gneisses of Inishtrahull are the oldest rocks in Ireland, dated at almost 1,800

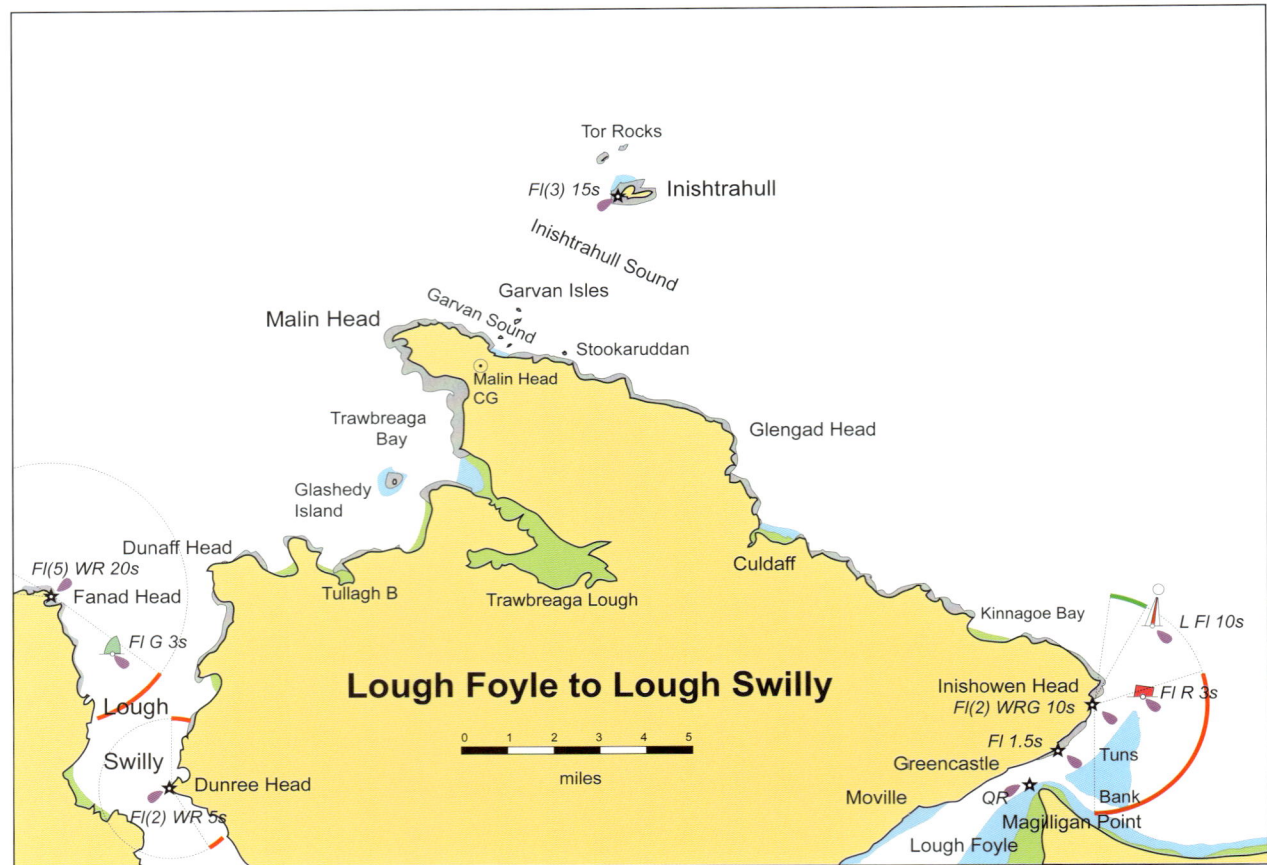

Tor Rocks

Fl(3) 15s   Inishtrahull

*Inishtrahull Sound*

Garvan Isles

Malin Head   *Garvan Sound*

Stookaruddan

Malin Head
CG

Trawbreaga
Bay

Glengad Head

Glashedy
Island

Dunaff Head   Culdaff

Fl(5) WR 20s

Fanad Head   Tullagh B   Trawbreaga Lough

Fl G 3s

Kinnagoe Bay   L Fl 10s

**Lough Foyle to Lough Swilly**

Inishowen Head   Fl R 3s
Fl(2) WRG 10s

Lough   0  1  2  3  4  5

Swilly   Fl 1.5s
         Greencastle   Tuns

miles

Dunree Head   Moville   QR   Bank

Fl(2) WR 5s   Magilligan Point

Lough Foyle

million years, and the island's springy turf and vibrant plant life stand in contrast to the scalped and spray-washed ground of Tory Island; but at least Tory still has its people. Close to the mainland shore opposite Inishtrahull are the Garvan Isles, a group of tiny islets and drying rocks. With its exposure to the W and NW and its strong tides, Inishtrahull Sound can raise the steepest and heaviest seas on the north coast. In favourable weather or in the absence of wind-over-tide conditions, however, the passage is straightforward.

**Tidal Streams** *(see diagrams on pp 156/7)*
The coastwise tides are strong and govern passage timing, and consideration must be given to the combined effects of wind and tide, which can raise steep and unpredictable seas. Off Glengad Head, a rip begins to form at HW Galway –0520, extends to the centre of Inishtrahull Sound at Galway –0420, and starts to subside at Galway –0320. It is particularly severe at springs and with NW winds; in these conditions the race extends 7 cables E of Glengad Head. At Galway –0220 the tide is slack inshore at the Head, and at Galway +0100 it runs strongly SE within 2 cables of the Head.

In Inishtrahull Sound and near Malin Head the tidal streams are complex and have not been comprehensively studied. The spring rate is 3 knots near Malin Head and 4 knots in Inishtrahull Sound. The main stream runs W for only 3 hours in Inishtrahull and Garvan Sounds, commencing about HW Galway –0530, but a W-going eddy starts in Garvan Sound on the second half of the E-going tide, about +0400 Galway. The stream in Garvan Sound runs very strongly just at the start of the E-going tide.

**Dangers**
**Tuns Bank**, sandbank drying in places, extending 3M NE from Magilligan Point
The **Garvan Isles**, a group of islets 2M E of Ireland's North Point, with drying and underwater rocks extending NW and SE. The largest of the islets, Green Island and Middle Island, are 20m high. **Lackgolana**, the 21m-high stack 2·5 cables offshore S of the Garvans, and **Rossnabartan**, the 3m-high islet 2·5 cables NW of Lackgolana, are important marks for pilotage of Garvan Sound. Neither of these is named on AC2811. An **unnamed rock** with 2·1m lies 1·5 cables NE of Rossnabartan.

*Bunagee Pier, Culdaff, from the SW*

**Blind Rock** (1·8m) 5 cables NW of Rossnabartan
**Doherty Rocks** (dry 1·2m), the NW outliers of the Garvans
**Tor Rocks**, a group of stacks and drying rocks 8 cables N of Inishtrahull
**Blind Rocks**, reef extending 3 cables from the N shore of Inishtrahull

### Lights and Marks

**Inishowen Head (Dunagree Point)**, white tower, black bands, Fl(2)WRG 10s 28m, W18M R14M G14M, G197°–211°, W211°–249°, R249°–000°. Shows white over the approach from the NE and the fairway buoy, red over the Tuns Bank and green to the N.
**Tuns** buoy, PHM Fl R 3s

**Foyle** buoy, safe water mark RWVS, L Fl 10s
**Inishtrahull**, white tower Fl(3) 15s 59m 19M, Racon (T) 24M, 060°–310°.

### Culdaff Bay

55°18'N 7°08'·4W, *AC2697*
Culdaff Bay is out of the main stream of the tide but on the W-going stream a counter-eddy runs SE in the bay. A berth of 2 cables avoids **Bo Rock** to the N and **Carratra More** to the SE. Anchor as convenient on the W side of the bay, SE of the piers. There are visitors' moorings. Somewhat subject to swell. The piers at Bunagee have 1·6m at their heads and the slip is suitable for trailer sailers. Shop, pubs, restaurants and filling station at Culdaff village, 1 km.

Constant +0105 Galway, MHWS 2·8m, MHWN 2·2m.

*Bunagee Pier*

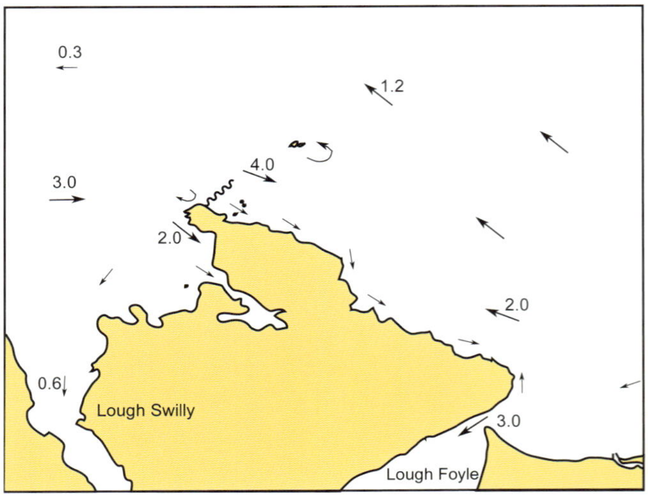

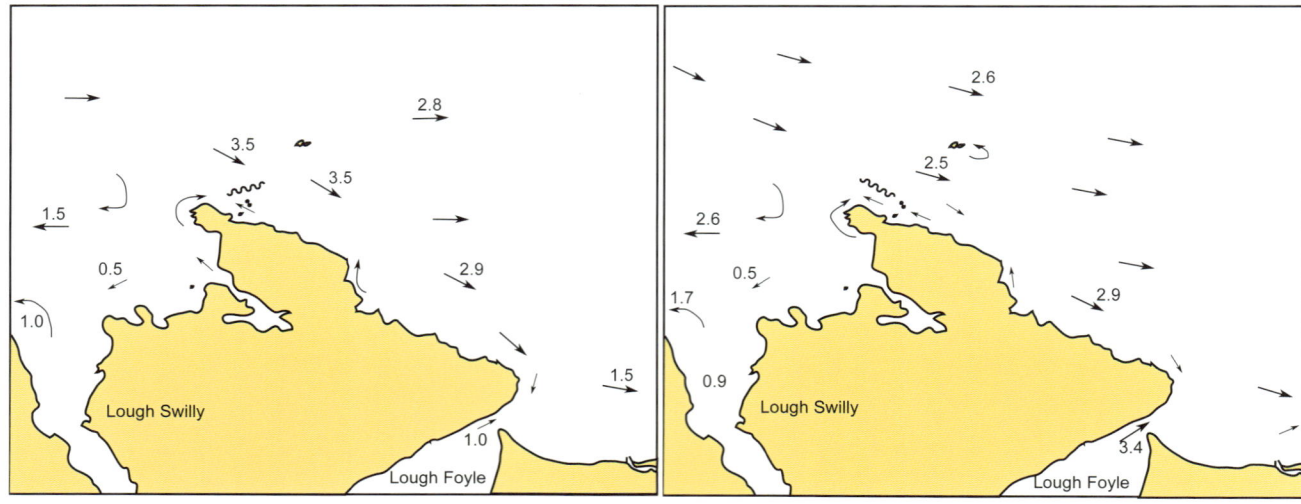

0.3

1.2

3.0

4.0

2.0

2.0

0.6

Lough Swilly

3.0

Lough Foyle

6 hours before HW Belfast
0.5 hours after HW Galway

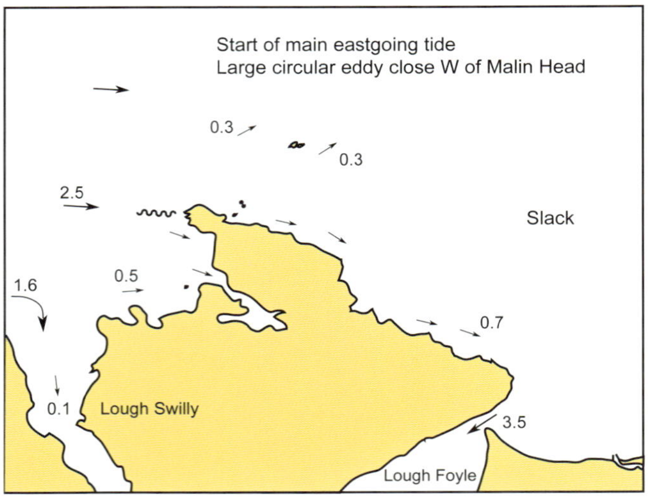

Start of main eastgoing tide
Large circular eddy close W of Malin Head

0.3    0.3

2.5

Slack

1.6    0.5

0.7

0.1    Lough Swilly

3.5

Lough Foyle

5 hours before HW Belfast
1.5 hours after HW Galway
approx HW Lough Swilly
0.5 hours before HW Portrush

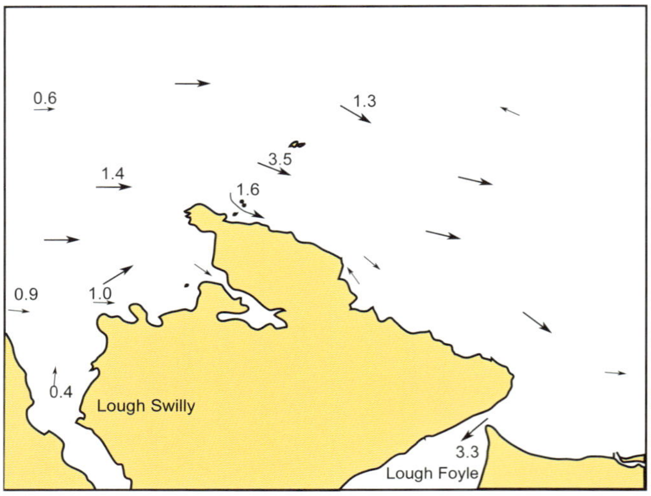

0.6

1.3

1.4    3.5

1.6

0.9    1.0

0.4    Lough Swilly

3.3

Lough Foyle

4 hours before HW Belfast
2.5 hours after HW Galway

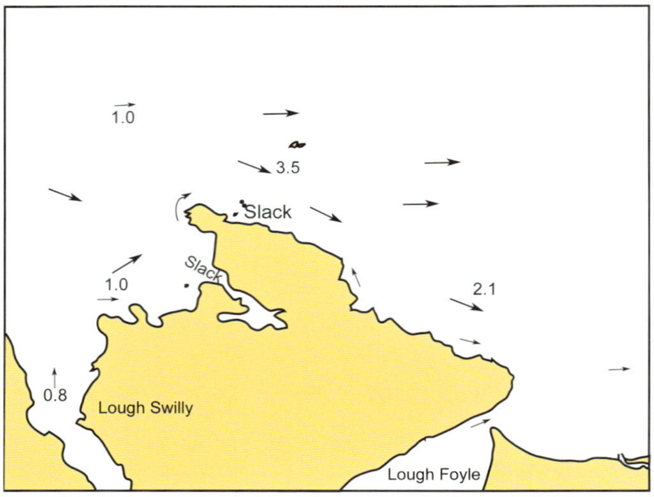

1.0

3.5

Slack

1.0    Slack

2.1

0.8    Lough Swilly

Lough Foyle

3 hours before HW Belfast
3.5 hours after HW Galway

2.8

3.5    3.5

1.5

0.5

1.0

2.9

Lough Swilly

1.5

1.0

Lough Foyle

2 hours before HW Belfast
4.5 hours after HW Galway

2.6

2.5

2.6

0.5

1.7

0.9    Lough Swilly

2.9

3.4

Lough Foyle

1 hour before HW Belfast
5.5 hours after HW Galway

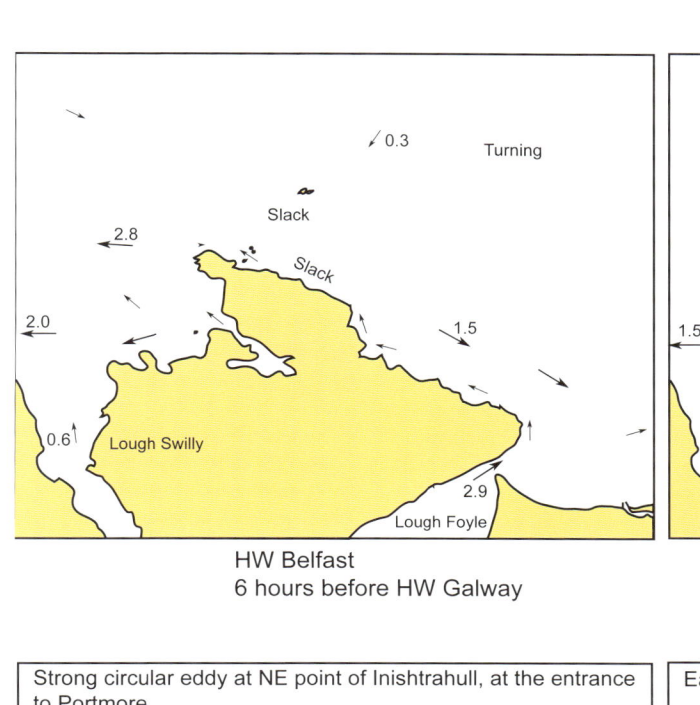

HW Belfast
6 hours before HW Galway

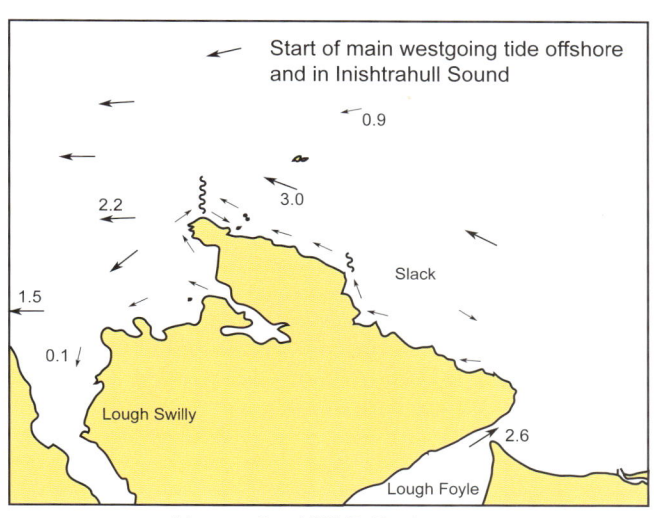

1 hour after HW Belfast
5 hours before HW Galway
approx LW Lough Swilly

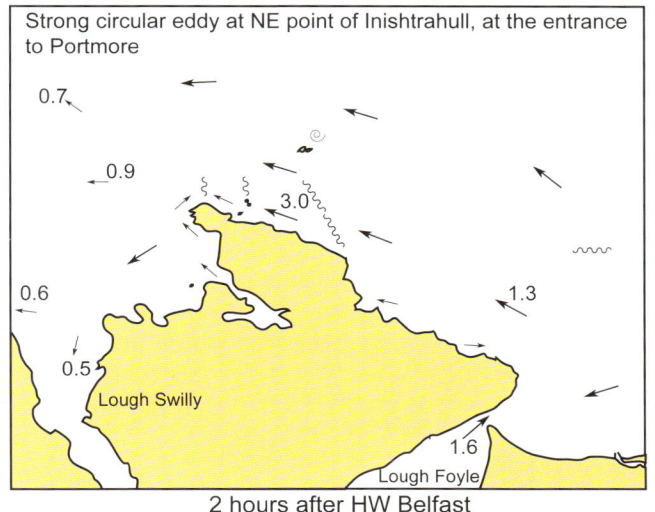

2 hours after HW Belfast
4 hours before HW Galway
approx LW Portrush

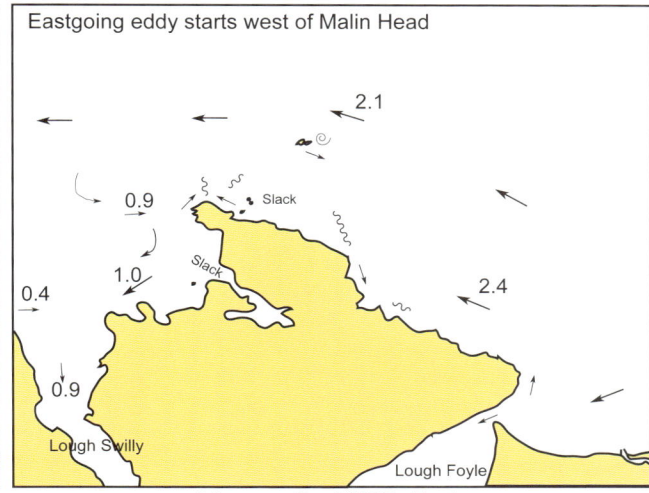

3 hours after HW Belfast
3 hours before HW Galway

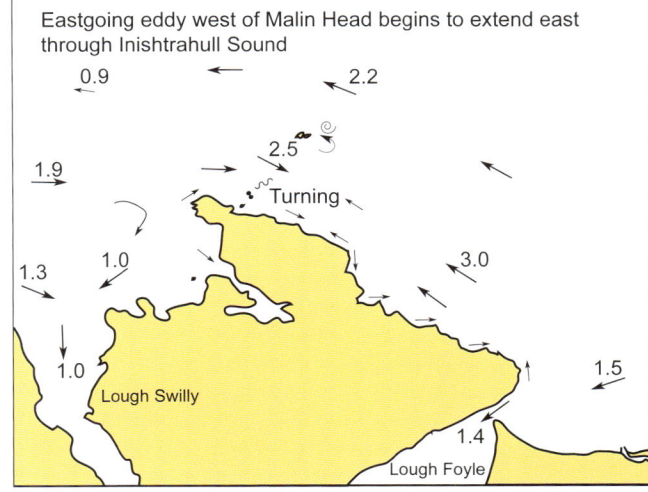

4 hours after HW Belfast
2 hours before HW Galway

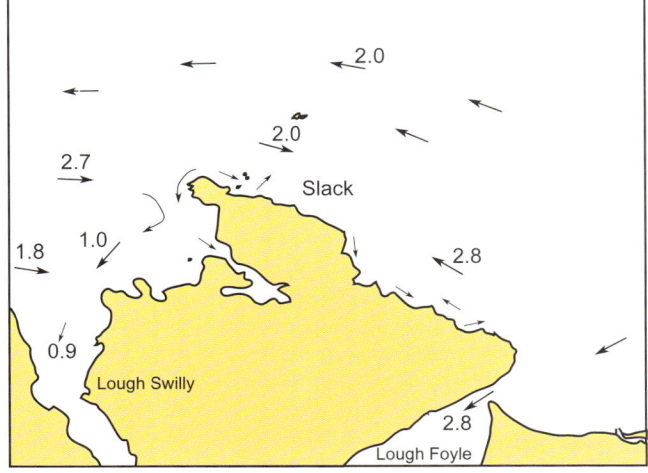

5 hours after HW Belfast
1 hour before HW Galway

Note: rates shown are for mean spring tides. Mean neap rates are approximately 55% of these.

*Portaleen; half the slip visible L of the pier*

## Portaleen
55°20'N 7°09'·5W, *AC2811*
This small pier and slip lies on the S side of
Portnalong Bay, 1M S of Glengad Head.
The pier has 1·2m at its head but is generally
unsuitable for yachts. The approach is between
the drying Mullandoo Rock to the N and a
sunken reef to the S, steering 240° with half of
the width of the slip visible left of the pier *(see
photograph)*. Temporary anchorage is available
in the bay, N of Mullandoo Rock, and there is
a dinghy passage W of the rock offering a short
cut to Portaleen pier.

## INISHTRAHULL SOUND
*AC2811*
Inishtrahull Sound must be treated with respect

if there is any sea running. The combination
of strong tidal streams and exposure to the W
makes it a more challenging prospect than either
Rathlin or Tory Sounds. With strong winds
against the tide (particularly the W-going tide)
the swell is high and very steep, and conditions
can change quickly, especially around the turn
of the tide. When heading W, sea conditions
often suddenly become more severe as the N
point of the Garvans is passed. If the passage
must be made in heavy weather, it is advisable
to stay well offshore, 3M N of the Tor Rocks.

## GARVAN SOUND
55°22'·5N 7°18'·5W, *AC2811, see Plan and
photographs*
This sound, between the Garvan Islands and
the shore, offers a useful short cut in moderate
weather, but the tidal streams are strong, and
reliable power is essential. **From the E,** pass
close outside the 70m stack Stookaruddan and
from there steer 275° for Lackgolana (Saddle
Rock), 21m high, and identify the low flat-
topped Rossnabartan beyond it. Leaving
Lackgolana at least half a cable to port, steer
to leave Rossnabartan a cable to port so as to
avoid the rock with 2m, 1·5 cables to the NE.
When Rossnabartan is abaft the beam steer

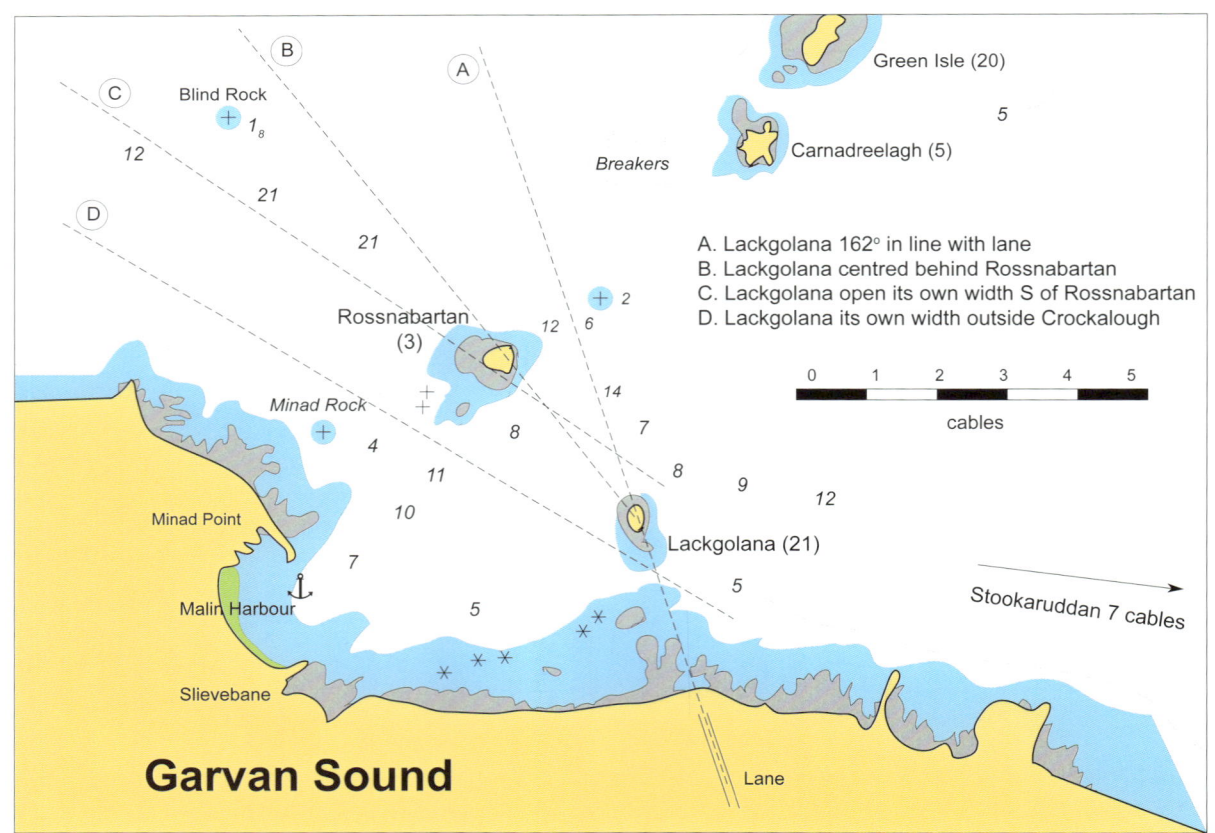

*Malin Head and the Garvan Isles; Lackgolana and Rossnabartan L centre, nearest to the mainland coast. Glashedy Island, in Trawbreaga Bay beyond Malin Head, upper L; Dunaff Head, Melmore Head and Horn Head in the distance*

*The approach to Garvan Sound from the SE; Lackgolana (L), Rossnabartan (R)*

*Lackgolana in line with the laneway between houses ashore leads between Rossnabartan and the 2m rock NE of it*

*Lackgolana centred behind Rossnabartan leads NE of Blind Rock*

*Lackgolana (R) open its own width S of Rossnabartan (centre) clears Blind Rock to the S. Crockalough (with its radar dome) is the highest summit on the skyline. Stookaruddan, L*

towards Ireland's North Point so as to pass well S of Blind Rock. **From the W,** steer 106° from a point a cable N of Ireland's North Point until Rossnabartan is identified, leave it a cable to starboard and Lackgolana half a cable to starboard. The plan and photographs show the transits for avoiding the dangers in the Sound. Lackgolana in line 162° with a conspicuous laneway between houses ashore leads between Rossnabartan and the 2m rock NE of it; Lackgolana centred behind Rossnabartan leads NE of Blind Rock; Lackgolana open its own width S of Rossnabartan leads S of Blind Rock; and Lackgolana in line with the summit of Crockalough (282m) leads between Rossnabartan and Minad Rock. Crockalough has a conspicuous radar dome on its summit.

*Malin Harbour from the W; Lackgolana, centre R, Rossnabartan, L*

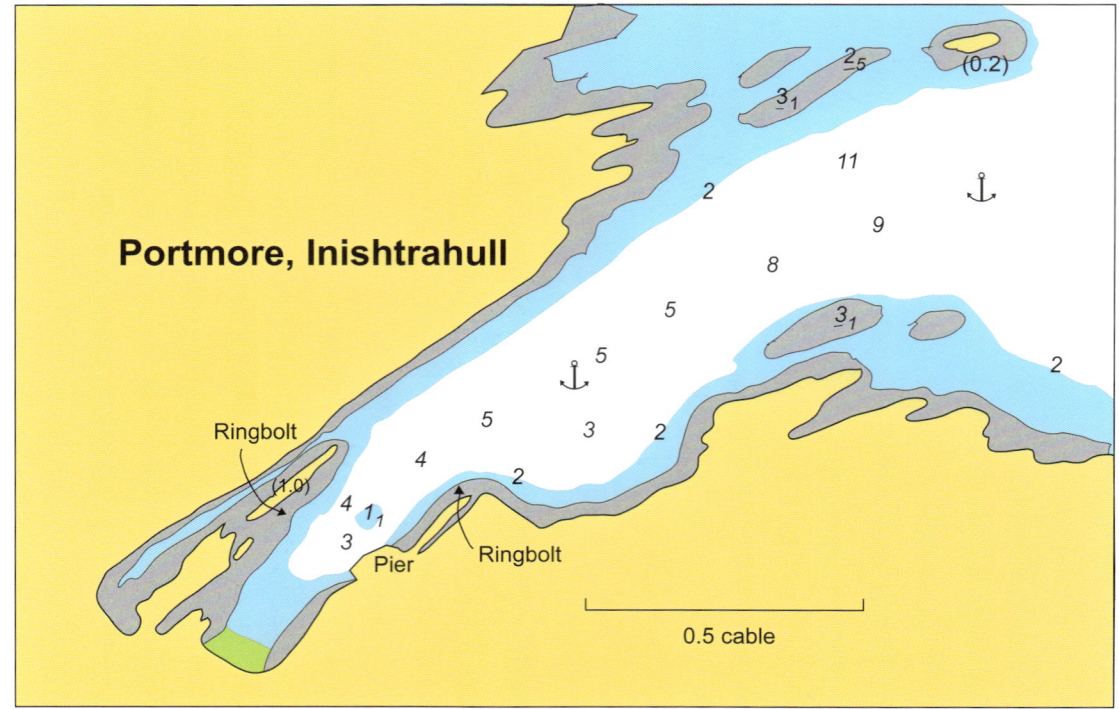

*Portmore, Inishtrahull, from the W; the signs of habitation, from more than 80 years ago, are clearly visible. The remains of the old lighthouse, upper R; the pier, lower R*

## Malin Harbour (Slievebane Bay)

55°22'·4N 7°19'·6W, *AC2811*

This bay, marked as "Portmore" on the charts (and not to be confused with Portmore, Inishtrahull) is entered between Lackgolana and Rossnabartan. The anchorage, with 3 to 5m, sand, is out of the tide but somewhat subject to swell. The pier *(see photograph)* extends SSE then S and has 2m at its head. Water on the pier, shop, small supermarket, pubs. Seafood available at the fishermen's co-op. Malin Head Coastguard MRSC and radio station is 1 km from the pier.

## INISHTRAHULL

55°25'·5N 7°14'W, *AC2811*

On the N side of Inishtrahull, rocks and reefs extend for 3 cables, but the channel between them and the Tor Rocks to the N has deep water over a width of 5 cables. The S and E shores of Inishtrahull are clean, and in suitable weather and tide may be approached to within half a cable. The main anchorage, Portmore, is a wide rocky gut on the NE side. The one-time drying rock within yards of the pier at Portmore, bane of generations of yachtsmen, has recently been cut down and now has 1.1m at LAT.

### Portmore *(see Plan)*

From the E, steer to pass a cable off the NE point of the island. The entrance to Portmore is flanked by two rocks, one to the N which never covers and one to the S which dries 3.1m and shows except at HWS. Steering in mid-channel

*Portmore anchorage near LW*

between these two, identify the lighthouse pier with its red-painted sheerlegs crane and head for it, steering 228°. The gut is clean on both sides and has 10m decreasing to 4m abreast the pier. Anchor either off the gut in deep water or in mid-channel SE of the N point of the gut in 5 to 8m. An alongside berth at the pier is feasible for a yacht under 10m, which can turn round in the limited space available, or for a larger vessel provided she can back out in a straight line. The pier has 3m alongside, but a rock with

1.1m, hazardous at low spring tides, lies 8m N of the NE corner of the pier. There are ring bolts in the rocks E and NW of the pier, as shown on the plan. On the cliff face in the approach is a painted anchor, black on a white background, but this is aimed at larger vessels.

## Portachurry

This narrow gut on the SW side of the island has a jetty with 1·5m and a slip. It is severely exposed to swell and not recommended.

Constant +0110 Galway, MHWS 3·3m, MHWN 2·5m, MLWN 1·6m, MLWS 0·4m.

## Malin Head

The headland itself is clean on its N side but should be given a berth of a cable in even the calmest of weather. Above-water and drying rocks extend W of the Head, and its W side should be given a berth of 3 cables.

## Trawbreaga Bay

55°21'N 7°25'W, *AC2811*
This wide bay S of Malin Head is usually subject to heavy swell and is fringed with rocks

*Inishtrahull from the SW; Portachurry, R centre, below the lighthouse*

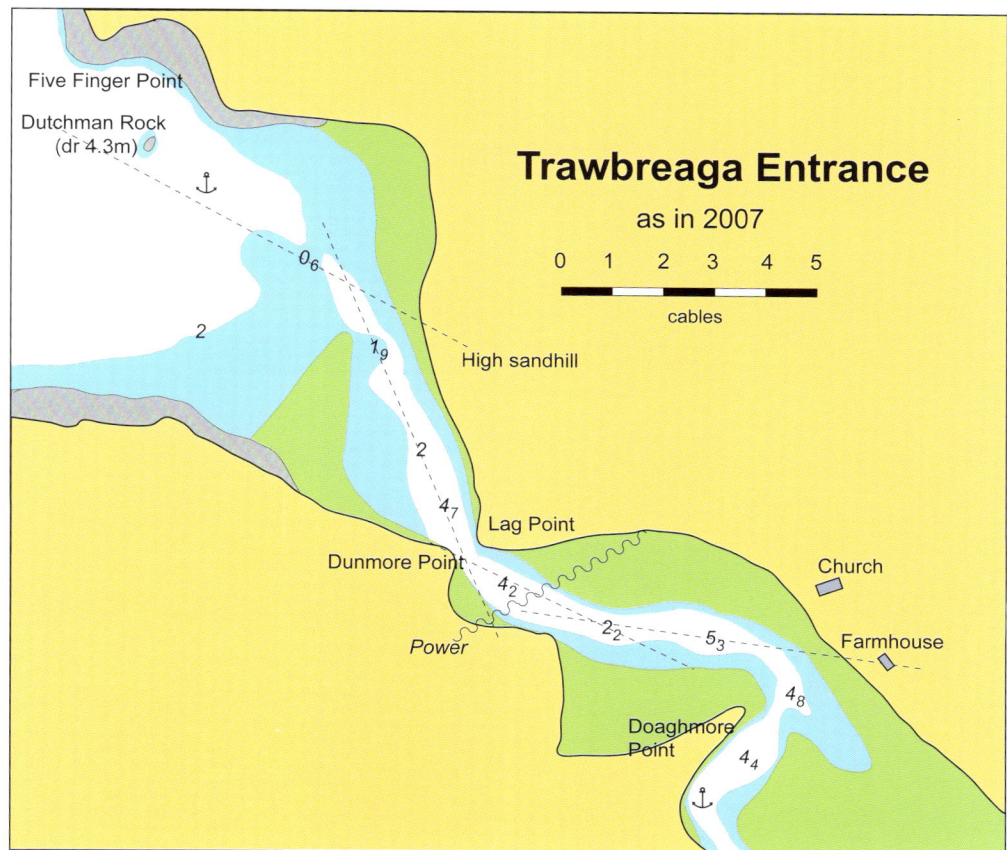

Five Finger Point

Dutchman Rock
(dr 4.3m)

**Trawbreaga Entrance**

as in 2007

0  1  2  3  4  5

cables

High sandhill

Lag Point

Dunmore Point

Church

*Power*

Farmhouse

Doaghmore
Point

and reefs. Glashedy Island, cliffbound and rectangular in outline, lies on the SW side of the bay. There is a clear passage inside it but the island must be given a good berth. In the SE corner of the bay is the entrance to Trawbreaga Lough, an extensive and mostly drying inlet. The bar at the entrance is hazardous and usually impassable due to swell, but in settled and swell-free conditions it is navigable, and the Lough is a beautiful and tranquil spot.

In settled conditions or offshore wind there is a feasible anchorage a cable SE of the Dutchman Rock, but this is unsafe if there is any chance of winds between SW and NW.

**Trawbreaga Lough**
55°19'·5N 7°21'W, *AC2697 and Plan*

**Caution**
AC2697 in this area is based on a survey of 1855-59 and does not accurately depict Trawbreaga Bar as it is today. Care is required in the use of GPS chartplotters in particular, and good traditional pilotage must be maintained, with continuous use of the echosounder. The bar should only be attempted in settled conditions with no swell, on a high and rising tide, and it must be borne in mind that a change in the weather or swell conditions may result in a yacht having to be left in Trawbreaga Lough for longer than expected. The following Directions are based on an ICC survey of 2007 but since

*Five Finger Point from the NW; Dutchman Rock, R. The conspicuous sandhills, beyond*

*Entrance to Trawbreaga Lough from the SE; Doaghmore Point, centre, with Lag Point beyond*

there is doubtless continual movement of the sandbars, the greatest caution is required and prior reconnaissance by dinghy is advisable. A submarine power cable crosses the channel close E of the First Narrows.

**Directions** *(see plan and photographs)*
From a position 1 cable S of the Dutchman Rock, steer 120° for the highest of the sandhills behind the beach. This leads over the bar in a least depth of 0·6m. The sand spit to the S of the bar, even in the calmest conditions, is usually marked by breakers or "blind breakers", waves which pile up into peaks but do not actually break. Once over the bar and in 2m or more of water, steer 160° for the First Narrows, between Dunmore Point and Lag Point. Beyond Lag Point, there are extensive shallows to the E; steer 116° from the narrows, keeping a continuous watch on the depth. Once past the next promontory on the S shore (3 cables SSE of Lag Point) make a turn to port and head for the farmhouse on the N

shore, E of the conspicuous white church. At the Second Narrows, NE of Doaghmore Point, the deepest water is one-third of the width from the NE shore, and the channel then runs S and lies very close to the SE shore of the Doaghmore Point promontory. The anchorage, in 4m, is in the bay 2 cables SSW of Doaghmore Point. No facilities ashore; the nearest shop, pub and restaurant are at Malin village, 3 km E on the N shore.

**Tullagh Bay and Rockstown Bay**
Although exposed to the N these bays E of Dunaff Head offer attractive temporary anchorage in settled weather. Anchor on the W side of Tullagh Bay, or as convenient in Rockstown Bay, in 3m, sand.

**LOUGH SWILLY**
55°17'N 7°35'W, *AC2697*
The deep and sheltered inlet of Lough Swilly is the principal sailing centre on the north coast.

*View E from a position SE of Lag Point; the church, L, and farmhouse R*

*Tullagh Bay, foreground, with Rockstown Bay beyond*

The Lough is rich in history. It was from here in 1607 that the great Ulster leaders O'Neill, Earl of Tyrone, and "Red Hugh" O'Donnell, Earl of Tyrconnell, departed for France, in the "Flight of the Earls", the last dramatic act of the great Anglo-Irish wars of Tudor times. The ancient Celtic ring fort of the Grianan of Aileach, a thousand years old even then, watched them go. Two hundred years later the Lough was to bristle with guns as six Martello towers were built to defend the port against the territorial ambitions of Napoleon. The guns were to be replaced more than once as the Lough remained a naval base, and one of the four Treaty Ports of 1921, until finally relinquished by the Royal Navy in 1937. Fort Dunree, until recently the principal military establishment on Lough Swilly, is now a museum.

In 1917 the White Star liner *Laurentic* sailed from Lough Swilly for New York. Twelve miles north of Fanad Head she was torpedoed and sunk, which might have been regarded as just one more tragedy of war had she not been carrying gold bullion worth €500 million at today's prices. The wreck of the *Laurentic* remains a magnet for divers, amateur and professional, to this day.

The lighthouse at Fanad Head, and the name of Saldanha Head, south of Portsalon, owe their existence to an earlier shipwreck, that of the frigate *Saldanha* nearby in 1812.

## Tidal Streams

Tidal streams in the Lough are significant in places, notably at Rathmullan and in Fahan Channel, where they can reach 2 knots or more at springs, changing at HW and LW by the shore and running in line with the deep channels.

## Dangers

**Swilly Rocks**, drying ledges 4 cables offshore 1·7M SSE of Fanad Head, comprising **Swilly More** (dries 1·5m) and **Swilly Beg** (dries 0·9m)

**Colpagh Rocks**, drying 4·1 and 2·9m, 2M SE of Dunree Head

**Carrickacullin** (dries 3·2m), 3 cables offshore 1M S of Buncrana Pier

**Kinnegar Spit** (0·4m), sandbank extending from the W shore 1·2M N of Rathmullan Pier

**Inch Flats**, drying sandbanks extending 1M N of Inch Island

A group of drying and above-water rocks lie close inshore within 1M NW of Macamish Point, but these are well out of the fairway, and the drying rocks almost always show. S of Rathmullan, on the W side, there are extensive drying sandbanks in the approaches to Ramelton, and the innermost part of the Lough, between Inch and Letterkenny, is bordered by wide drying banks of sand and mud.

## Lights and Marks

**Fanad Head**, white tower Fl (5) WR 20s 39m, W18M R14M, R 100°–110°, W110°–313°, R313°–345°, W345°–100°. Shows red over Limeburner and Swillymore Rocks, white elsewhere

**Swillymore** buoy, SHM Fl G 3s

**Dunree Head**, white tower Fl(2) WR 5s 46m, W12M R9M, R 320°–328°, W328°–183°, R183°–196°, shows red over Colpagh and White Strand Rocks and close inshore to the N, white elsewhere

**Lough Swilly**

**Colpagh** buoy, PHM Fl R 6s
**Saltpans** buoy, E Card Q(3) 10s
**White Strand** buoy, PHM Fl R 10s
**Buncrana Pier**, white tower Iso WR 4s 8m
W14M R11M, R shore–052°, W052°–139°,
R139°–shore, shows red over White Strand
Rocks to the NW and Inch Flats to the S, white
elsewhere
**Kinnegar** buoy, SHM Fl G 10s
**Inch Spit** buoy, PHM Fl R 3s
**Inch Flat** buoy, PHM Fl(2) R 6s
**Rathmullan Pier**, Fl G 3s 5M
The channel between Inch Spit buoy and
Fahan marina is marked by five unlit port-hand
buoys.

**Directions**
Entry to Lough Swilly is straightforward by
day or night in any weather. The Lough is
well buoyed and lit for 12M from Dunaff and
Fanad Heads to Rathmullan. There is usually a
confused sea close to Dunaff Head, caused by
the ever-present swell reflected off the cliffs,
but the headlands on each side of the entrance
are clean and steep-to, and in settled weather
Fanad Head may be approached closely. The
Swilly Rocks, 1·7M within the entrance, are
marked by a starboard-hand buoy, but there is
a deep channel W of them; keep the prominent
stack Stookamore (14m high), on the mainland
side, close aboard *(see photograph)*. The drying
rock Carrickacullin, between Buncrana and
Fahan, is the only other significant hazard in
the Lough. Yachts may safely pass the Saltpans
buoy on either hand. The outer part of the
Lough, especially N of Dunree Head, is subject
to swell, and in heavy weather between W and
N the swell may penetrate as far S as Macamish
and Buncrana. There is an extensive fish farm N
of Macamish Point.

*Stookamore from the S*

*Portsalon from the SE*

Portsalon, in the NW corner of Ballymastocker Bay on the W side, is the first convenient port of call in the Lough, but the most attractive anchorage is Macamish Bay, 4·5M further S; while Rathmullan has a handy pontoon attached to its deep-water pier. Fahan, on the E side opposite Rathmullan, has a 170-berth marina and is the main sailing centre in the Lough and the base of Lough Swilly YC. Several other bays in the outer part of the Lough offer temporary anchorages. Buncrana (3000) has no facilities for yachts, and its pier is exposed and has limited depth. The pretty village of Ramelton lies at the head of a shallow creek on the W side, and the upper part of the Lough, leading to the thriving town of Letterkenny (12500), is winding and unmarked between wide drying banks.

## Anchorages

- **Pincher Bay**, immediately S of Fanad Head, is a feasible temporary or passage anchorage in settled weather. Anchor in the centre of the bay in 3 to 7m, sand.

- **Lenan Bay**, on the E side 2·5M S of Dunaff Head, offers temporary anchorage in 4m, sand, and has a modern concrete pier with 1m at its head. Alongside berthing or drying out are seldom practicable due to the swell and surge, but small fishing craft are kept here on moorings.

- **Portsalon** (55°12'·3N 7°37'W) has a splendid sandy beach and a useful stone pier with 0·5m at its head. Anchor S of the pier in 2 to 5m, sand. There are visitors' moorings. A temporary alongside berth may be available with sufficient rise of tide. Pub/restaurant, showers available at the watersports shop.

- **Crummie Bay**, immediately N of Dunree Head, is also a pleasant temporary anchorage. The head of the bay dries out; anchor between the points of the entrance in 5m, sand.

- **Macamish Bay** (55°08'·5N 7°31'·3W, *see plan*), on the W side, is the most attractive anchorage in the Lough, and also has a

*Macamish Bay from the N*

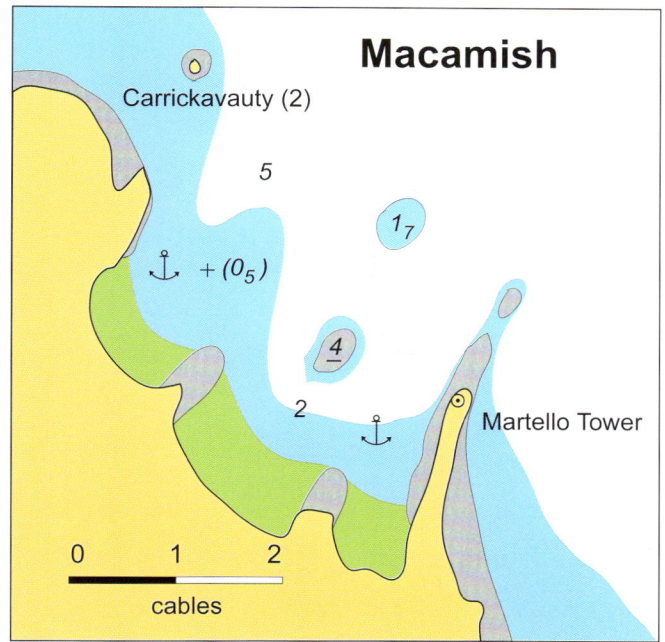

Macamish

Carrickavauty (2)

Martello Tower

fine beach. It is well sheltered from winds between SE and N and less subject to swell than the bays further N. Anchor either NW of the above-water rock in the centre of the bay or in the SE half, close SW of the Martello tower, in 2 to 4m, sand. The tower is a private residence, and the land adjoining the beach is a charming 9-hole golf course.

## Buncrana

55°07'·6N 7°28'·2W, *AC2697*

The pier at Buncrana almost dries at its head but has 3m halfway up its SE side for a limited width. It provides a convenient temporary berth for a short run ashore or loading stores. The town has supermarkets, shops, banks, ATMs, pubs, restaurants and doctors. RNLI all-weather lifeboat station.

*Buncrana Pier*

*Rathmullan from the SW; the pier and pontoon, lower R, Dunree Head, top L*

## RATHMULLAN

55°05'·7N 7°31'·6W, *AC2697*

Rathmullan has a piled concrete pier with deep water alongside, but the pier itself is not suitable for berthing a yacht. A pontoon extends 60m S from the side of the pier and is available for the use of visitors. Anchorage N of the pier is also feasible but the tide runs at 2 knots at springs and the sand bottom shelves away steeply.

Rathmullan has shop, pubs and restaurants and a ferry to Buncrana.

## Ramelton

55°03'·5N 7°33'·7W, *AC2697 and Plan*

This pretty village lies at the head of a winding channel, the inner part of which dries, but it is navigable by small shallow-draft yachts near HW. A survey in 2007 indicated little change from the Admiralty's observations of 1855. Steer 255° from the Letterkenny Channel to the bar, which has 1·7m and lies 4 cables N of Whale Head, and stay on this course, with continuous use of the echosounder, until 4 cables from the shore of Aughnish Island. The channel then turns WNW and passes 1·5 cables N of Aughnish, where it shallows to 1m, then running essentially as shown on AC2697 and drying

*Ramelton from the SW near LW; the boatyard, centre L*

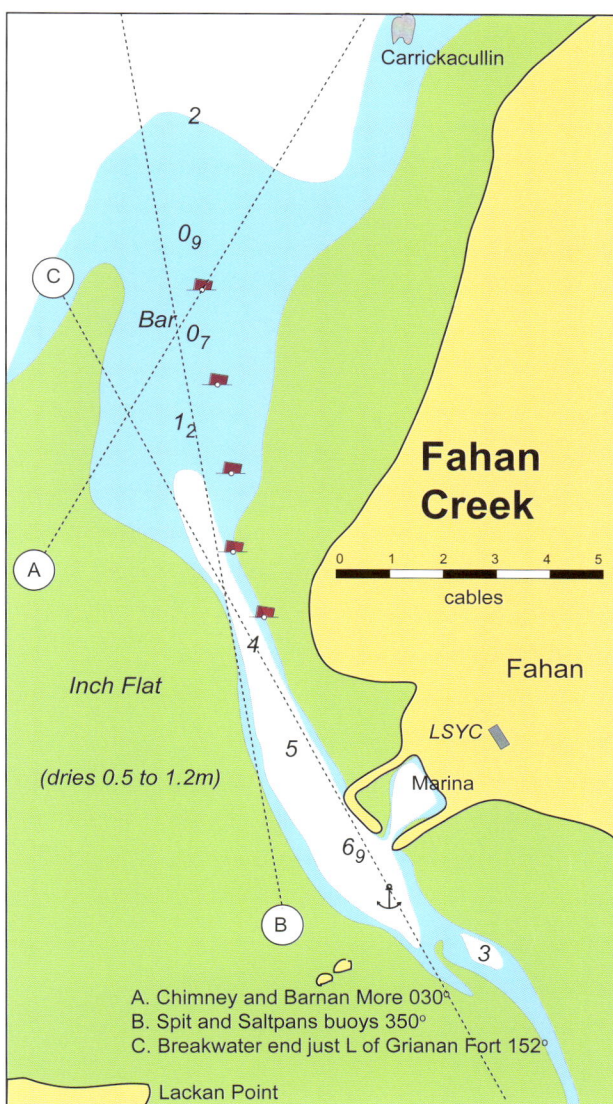

**Fahan Creek**

Carrickacullin

2

0₉

C

Bar
0₇

1₂

0 1 2 3 4 5
cables

Inch Flat

4

Fahan

5

LSYC

(dries 0.5 to 1.2m)

Marina

6₉

A

B

3

A. Chimney and Barnan More 030°
B. Spit and Saltpans buoys 350°
C. Breakwater end just L of Grianan Fort 152°

Lackan Point

out completely, N of Craig's Islands. There is a rock, drying 1·5m, on the S side of the channel 5 cables above Aughnish, at 55°03'·36N 7°36'·84W; at this point hold very close to the N shore, where there is a conspicuous boulder covered in yellow lichens. Ramelton Quay dries about 1·5m. Boatyard (Allan Stewart) 7 cables below the Quay. Shops, pubs, restaurants at Ramelton.

## FAHAN
55°06'·5N 7°29'·5W, *AC2697 and Plan*
Fahan Creek is accessible in daylight and at all states of the tide except low water springs. The drying rock Carrickacullin may be avoided by keeping the factory chimney at Buncrana in line with the prominent hill Barnan More 030° *(see photograph)*. This transit also leads to Fahan Bar. The bar has 0·7m, and the channel to the marina and anchorage is marked by five unlit port-hand buoys. The transit of Inch Spit and Saltpans buoys astern leads over the bar; then identify the first of the channel buoys and leave them close to port. At the fourth buoy the channel narrows to less than a cable and begins to deepen, reaching 6.9m at the marina breakwater. There is deep water for 3 cables beyond the marina entrance.

(Once over Fahan Bar, keeping the end of the marina breakwater just left of the Grianan of Aileach fort (on the hilltop behind) 152° also

*Buncrana factory chimney in line with Barnan More clears Carrickacullin (R)*

*Grianan of Aileach fort (on the hilltop) above Fahan marina breakwater*

*Fahan Marina entrance*

leads up the channel *(see photograph)*.)

Anchor in 5m in mid-channel S of the marina entrance. A tripping line is advised due to the presence of old mooring chains on the seabed. The tide runs at 2 kn springs and yachts will normally be tide-rode. Note that the channel off the breakwater is now somewhat wider and deeper than shown on AC2697, which is based on a survey carried out in 1984, before the marina was built.

Constant +0110 Galway, MHWS 4·3m, MHWN 3·2m, MLWN 1·9m, MLWS 0·5m.

## Marina

Entering the marina near LW, stay close to the SE breakwater to avoid a sandbar which has built up on the NW side of the entrance. The marina basin has 2m, but the SW half of the

*Fahan Creek at LW; marina, centre. Macamish Point, top L, with Dunree Head and Fanad Head beyond. Buncrana, top R*

basin has not been excavated. This is obvious at LW, but near HW take care to stay within the channel marked by red- and green-painted piles.

## Facilities

Water and shore power on the pontoons. Diesel by tanker, phone 07493 74149 or 07493 68702. Fahan Marine Services, mechanical, hull and rigging repairs, Volvo, Yanmar and Mercruiser specialists. Pub/restaurant. Filling station and shop 1 km SE on the Derry road. Lough Swilly YC clubhouse, adjacent to the marina, welcomes visitors, has bar and showers and is open at weekends and on some weekday evenings.

## Passage E from Lough Swilly round Malin Head

A yacht capable of 6 knots bound E from Lough Swilly will gain the most benefit from the tides if she rounds Dunaff Head at –0130 Galway (2·5 hours before HW in Lough Swilly). This means leaving Portsalon at local HW –0345 and Rathmullan or Fahan at local HW –0500. If conditions are favourable she will arrive off Malin Head just before the turn of the tide, and may carry the E-going stream as far as Ballycastle, Rathlin or Port Ellen. If heading for Coleraine or Portrush, leaving Lough Swilly 2 hours later will give a faster passage. If heading for Lough Foyle it is better to take the second half of the E-going tide and leave Portsalon at local HW –0030 or Fahan at local HW–0145; this will mean arriving at Inishowen Head as the outgoing stream in the Foyle is slackening.

*Fanad Head from the NE*

# Chapter 5

## Fanad Head to Bloody Foreland

*Horn Head from the SE; Bloody Foreland, Inishbofin, Inishdooey and Inishbeg top L, Tory Island top R.*

This spectacular coast is among the least-often-travelled by cruising yachts in Ireland; it includes Mulroy Bay, an extraordinary and convoluted inlet penetrating many miles inland, and the beautiful gulf of Sheep Haven. The broad ridge of Muckish (670m) and further west the quartzite cone of Errigal (853m) dominate the views from seaward.

Six miles north of Bloody Foreland lies Tory Island, for long Ireland's remotest community and only recently drawn from its isolation by the construction of a fine new harbour. It used to be commonplace for Tory's 130-or-so inhabitants to be cut off for weeks, even months, in winter as the island's old stone jetty was inundated by the swell, and the fishing boats were safely drawn up on the slip beyond. Tory Island is the home of the fearsome Celtic god Balor of the Evil Eye, whose powers were last invoked in 1883,

when the gunboat HMS *Wasp* was rounding the island on her way to Inishtrahull to enforce eviction orders. The *Wasp* unaccountably struck the rocks of Tory, and sank with heavy loss of life.

More recently, Tory has gained fame for its school of primitive painters, who were encouraged and promoted by the artist Derek Hill, a resident and long-time campaigner on behalf of the island's community. Tory's name comes from the prominent *tors* or rock stacks around the island; but *Tories* became a by-word for lawless freebooters, reflecting the 18th-century activities of some of the islanders – and hence came to be applied, originally as a derisive nickname, to one of the two main parties in the British parliament.

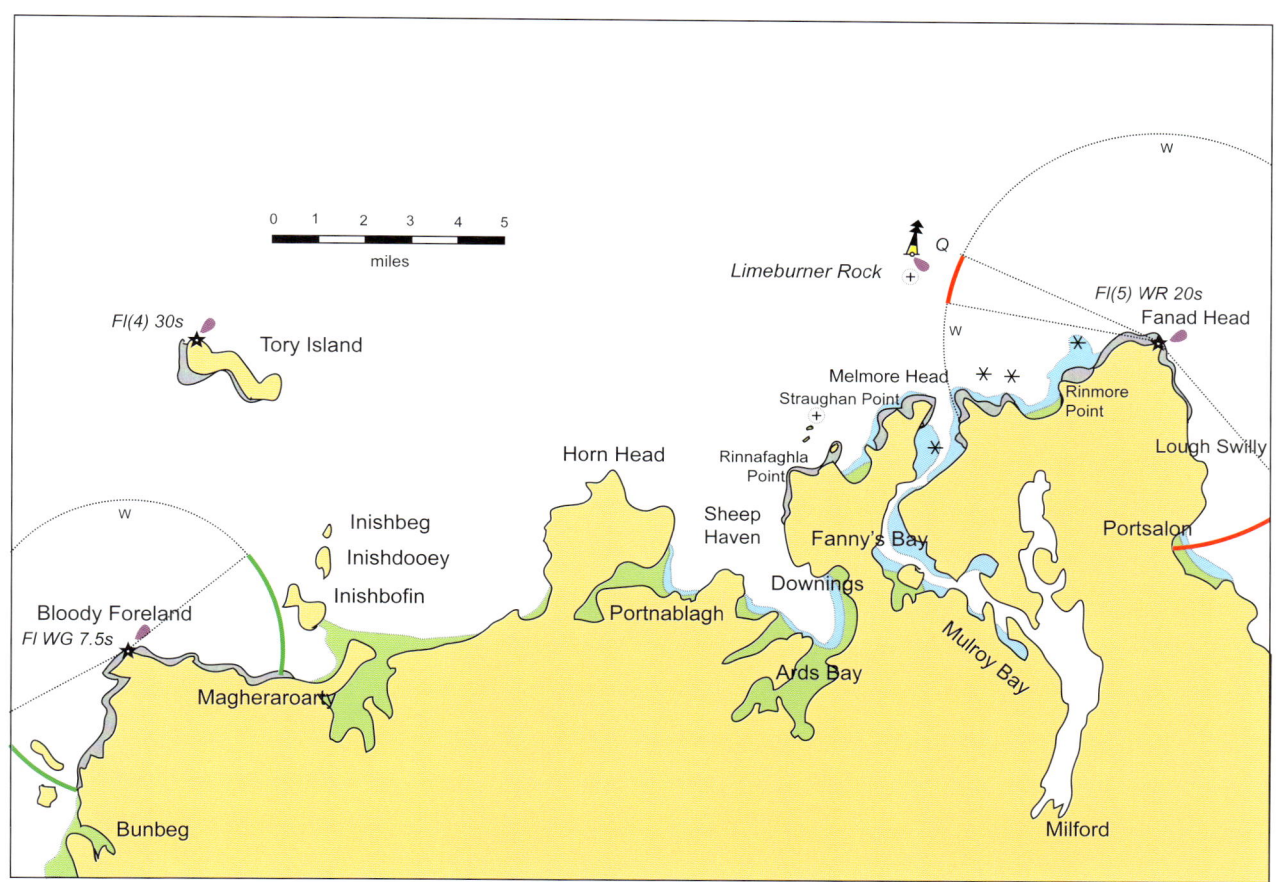

## Charts

AC2699 Horn Head to Fanad Head and AC2752 Bloody Foreland to Horn Head, on a scale of 1 to 30,000, provide excellent detail coverage (subject to the age of the survey data) and are essential. The 2007 edition of AC2699 reflects a welcome new survey of the entrance to Mulroy Bay, which hitherto had perhaps the most significantly outdated hydrographic data in Ireland.

## LOUGH SWILLY TO MULROY BAY
*AC2697, 2699*

The coast between Fanad Head and Mulroy Bay is fringed with reefs, and rocks and shoals extend up to 3 cables offshore. Mulroy Bay extends 10M inland from an open N-facing bay through three sets of narrows, then opening out into what amounts to an inland lake of seawater. The narrows attenuate the tide to such an extent that the rise and fall in the Broad Water at neaps is almost negligible. The bottom is extremely irregular, with many rocks and shoals, and the pilotage is tricky but not unduly challenging. With due care, the entrance is straightforward in all but heavy onshore weather or a high swell.

## Tidal Streams

Tidal streams on this section of the coast are relatively slight, seldom exceeding 1·5 knots, turning E at HW Galway –0220 and E at HW Galway +0400.

## Dangers

**Currin Rock** (dries 0·5m), 6 cables NE of Rinmore Point, with dangerous reefs between it and the shore to the SW, S and SE

**Frenchman's Rock** (dries 1·5m), 1·3M W of Rinmore Point

**Carrickcannon** (awash at LAT), 7 cables NE of Ballyhoorisky Point

**Flughog Rock** (dries 0·9m), 3 cables N of Ballyhoorisky Point

**Blind Rock**, 1·5m, 3 cables SW of Ballyhoorisky Point

**High Bar Rock** (dries 3·6m), and **Low Bar Rock** (dries 2·6m), in the entrance to Mulroy Bay 1·1M SSW of Ballyhoorisky Point

**Sessiagh Rocks**, drying 3·8 and 2·6m, 3 cables ENE of the High and Low Bar Rocks

**Dundooan Rocks**, drying reefs on the W side of the channel 0·5M SW of the First Narrows of

Mulroy Bay
**Limeburner Rock**, 2m, 2·5M N by W of Melmore Head

Within Mulroy Bay there are many dangerous reefs and shoals, some drying and some below-water; several but by no means all of these are marked. An exhaustive list would be very long but the principal hazards in the channel are **Leat Shoal** (0·6m), between the First and Second Narrows, **Seedagh Bank** (just dries), between the Second and Third Narrows, and **Scalpmore** (dries 1·8m), where the Third Narrows opens into the Broad Water; all of these are in mid-channel, and unmarked.

### Caution
Do not confuse the drying Frenchman's Rock, E of Mulroy Bay entrance, with the above-water rock of the same name W of Melmore Head.

### Lights and Marks
**Fanad Head**, white tower Fl (5) WR 20s 39m, W18M R14M, R 100°–110°, W110°–313°, R313°–345°, W345°–100°. Shows red sectors over Limeburner and Swillymore Rocks, white elsewhere

**Limeburner** buoy, N Card Q, AIS, 5 cables N by W of the rock

**Ballyhoorisky Point,** stone pillar beacon, unlit

**Ravedy Island**, white square tower, Fl 3s 9m 3M, 4 cables SSE of Melmore Head

**Dundooan Rocks**, green square tower, QG 4m 1M, immediately S of the First Narrows of Mulroy Bay

**Crannoge Point**, green square tower, Fl G 5s 5m 2M, 9 cables SSW of Dundooan Rocks beacon.

**Four buoys** also mark the channel up to the Second Narrows: (1) PHM Fl R 1·5s, 4 cables S of the High Bar Rock; (2) SHM Fl G marking the N end of the Ottier Runa bank at Fanny's Bay; (3) SHM Fl G at the turn of the channel ENE of Inishlaugh; and (4) PHM (unlit) ESE of Island Roy and WSW of the Second Narrows.

**Third Narrows,** unlit stone pillar on the rocks in mid channel W of Marks Point

Unlit, short, tapering stone beacons also mark many of the dangers in the Broad Water.

### Passage – Lough Swilly to Mulroy Bay
The peninsulas of Rosguill and Fanad make up a spectacular coastline; lower in aspect than the mighty cliffs of Horn Head to the west, or Dunaff Head to the east, but broken up by offshore reefs and sandy bays, exposed to the unceasing swell and breakers of this coast. The cliffs of Fanad Head are steep-to and may be approached to within a cable in settled weather, but a N'ly heading should be maintained for 3 cables beyond the lighthouse to avoid a spit with 1·5m, close NW of the Head. There is often a confused sea close NW of Fanad Head, particularly during the ebb in Lough Swilly. Give Magheranguna Point a berth of at least 3 cables and then keep the summit of Dunaff Head open N of Magheranguna Point to clear Currin Rock. This rock, and also Frenchman's Rock and Carrickcannon, are frequently marked by breakers. Frenchman's Rock, being the highest of the three, will break first; beware of confusing it then with the more dangerous Carrickcannon, further offshore. Croaghnamaddy (the highest summit on the Horn Head peninsula to the SW), in line with Melmore Head, leads N of Carrickcannon *(see photograph)*. All that remains of the ruined Melmore Tower (45m), on the summit of Melmore Head, is a chimney stack, and from a distance the tower presents the appearance of a standing stone.

In settled weather and with careful use of judiciously chosen GPS waypoints it is possible to pass inside Frenchman's Rock and Carrickcannon, and particular care is then needed to avoid Flughog Rock. This route

*Croaghnamaddy in line with Melmore Head leads N of Carrickcannon. Horn Head, R*

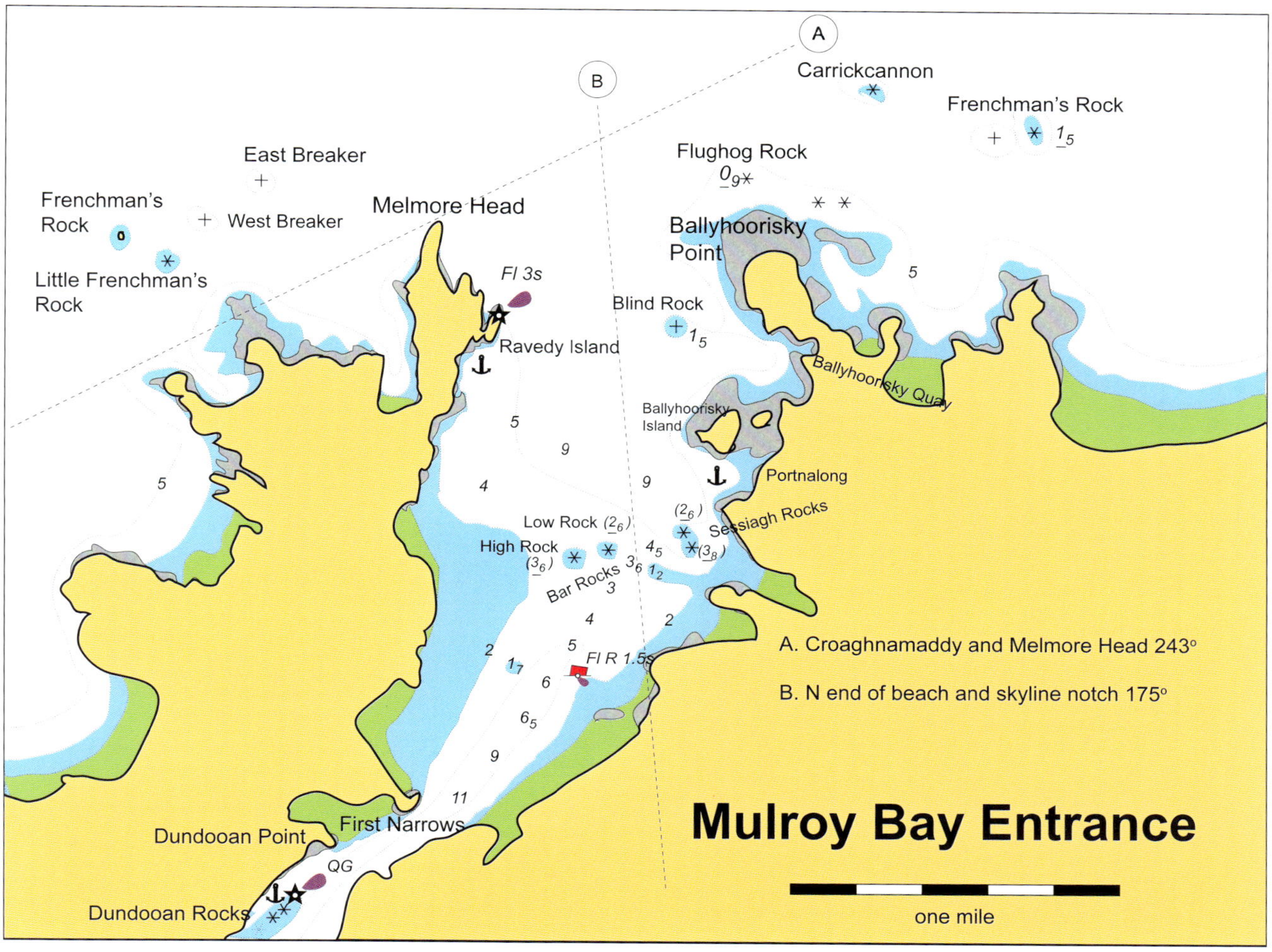

## Map: Mulroy Bay Entrance

Carrickcannon

Frenchman's Rock
+ * 1_5

East Breaker
+

Flughog Rock
0_9*

Frenchman's Rock
o    + West Breaker

Melmore Head

Ballyhoorisky Point

Little Frenchman's Rock
*

5

Fl 3s
☆

Blind Rock
+ 1_5

Ravedy Island
⚓

Ballyhoorisky Quay

5

Ballyhoorisky Island

9

5

4

9

⚓ Portnalong

Low Rock (2_6)

(2_6)

Sessiagh Rocks

High Rock (3_6)
*    *
Bar Rocks    4_5  *(3_8)
3_6  1_2
3

4    2

2  1_7
5
FlR 1.5s
6

A. Croaghnamaddy and Melmore Head 243°

B. N end of beach and skyline notch 175°

6_5

9

11

Dundooan Point    First Narrows

**Mulroy Bay Entrance**

QG

Dundooan Rocks ⚓☆
* *

one mile

is not recommended to the stranger on a first passage.

In any case give the long, low and rocky spit of Ballyhoorisky Point a berth of at least 4 cables. Beyond it, the dangerous Blind Rock often does not break, and can be avoided by holding a SW'ly course until midway between Ballyhoorisky Point and Ravedy Island, with its conspicuous beacon. The skyline to the S features a tiny notch, which is between the twin summits of Trusk More and Trusk Beg; keeping this notch in line with the NE end of the sandy beach 175° *(see photograph)* leads clear of all dangers in the outer bay until past the Bar Rocks.

**Outer Bay – Anchorages**

- **Ravedy Roads,** on the W side of the entrance, is a convenient passage anchorage in winds from S to NW. Anchor in 2·5m, sand, 0·75 cable S of Ravedy Island beacon. This anchorage is surprisingly free from swell. Note that Melmore Spit, shown on the old edition of AC2699 just S of this location, no longer exists.

- **Portnalong,** S of Ballyhoorisky Island on the E side of the entrance, is better in winds between NE and S but is more subject to swell than Ravedy Roads. Anchor in 3 to 4m with the S point of the island in line with its summit.

*Notch between Trusk More and Trusk Beg above the NE end of the beach (centre L)*

*Mulroy Bay from the NE; Ballyhoorisky Point, foreground, with Flughog Rock, breaking; Ballyhoorisky Quay in the lower L corner of the bay beyond the point. High and Low Bar Rocks, centre L, with the First Narrows beyond. Melmore Head R, Sheep Haven and Horn Head upper R*

- The refurbished **Ballyhoorisky Quay** lies on the S side of a narrow rocky inlet N of Ballyhooriskey Island, and has 3m in the approach and 1·5 to 2·2m alongside. The reef forming the breakwater on the S side is marked by a short stone pillar beacon. The gut is about 30m wide. A temporary alongside berth may be available for small yachts but local fishing boats take priority.

## MULROY BAY ENTRANCE

55°15'·6N 7°46'·1W, *AC2699 (but see caution below) and Plan*

A stranger should only enter in daylight. The Bar has 2·8m, and may break in strong onshore winds, particularly near LW.

**Caution**

Editions of AC2699 prior to 2007 are based on a survey carried out in 1856 and show the entrance channel lying W of the Bar Rocks, with a long drying sandbar extending N from the SE shore. These charts carry a note to the effect that the channel is now reported to lie E of the Bar Rocks. It has indeed lain E of the Bar Rocks since at least 1930, and for this reason GPS chartplotters in particular should be used with great caution in this area. It is essential to maintain good traditional pilotage, with continuous use of the echosounder. However the channel is more than a cable wide, the banks W and SW of the Bar Rocks have 2 to 3m of water, and the sandbar to the S has gone. There is 4m of water

*Bar Rocks from the N at half tide; the first port-hand buoy, extreme L*

close W of the High Rock and deep water in mid-channel between it and the Low Rock, but a stranger is cautioned against attempting these passages.

The 2007 edition of AC2699, reflecting some new survey work in 2006, is completely up-to-date in respect of the entrance and the channel to the Third Narrows, and is still remarkably accurate in the Broad Water, where the survey data is still very old.

**Tides**

The tidal stream reaches 5 knots at springs in the First Narrows, and for that reason as well as the many shoals, it is preferable to enter Mulroy Bay on a rising tide if proceeding through the Narrows. Arrival off the Bar one to two hours before HW is ideal. At the Second and Third Narrows the stream may reach 8 knots with rapids forming; these channels are best negotiated at or near slack water. Each set of Narrows reduces the tidal range and delays the time of high and low water inside it, as follows:

Outer Bay – const +0100 Galway, MHWS 3·9m, MHWN 2·9m
Between First and Second Narrows – const (est) +0140 Galway, MHWS 2·9m, MHWN 2·2m
Between Second and Third Narrows – const (est) +0215 Galway, MHWS 2·0m, MHWN 1·6m
Broad Water – const +0315 Galway, MHWS 1·4m, MHWN 1·1m

This has several interesting results, not least of which is the fact that with good timing, slack water can be carried all the way from the outer bay to the Broad Water; conversely, leaving the Broad Water at slack in the Third Narrows will mean arriving at the First Narrows three hours or more into the tide. Heading out, it may be preferable to negotiate the Third Narrows against the slackening flood tide so as to arrive at the Bar while there is still a good depth of water.

A further result is that in the outer bay, the ebb stream at the Bar continues for an hour or more after LW by the shore, and conversely.

No official data is available on the heights of LW in Mulroy Bay but MLWS is probably 0·5m at the bar and between 0·5m and 0·7m in the Broad Water.

**Directions – First Narrows**

From a position midway between Ballyhoorisky Point and Ravedy Island, steer 175° to pass between the Low Bar Rock and the Sessiagh Rocks (which show except at HWS) keeping to the W of mid-channel to avoid a patch with 1·2m, ESE of the Low Bar Rock. From this po-

*Fanny's Bay from the S*

*The Second Narrows from the S; note the fish farms in Millstone Bay (R) and Glinsk Bay (upper L). A bridge is under construction (2007) across the Second Narrows.*

sition the opening of the First Narrows is hard to discern, and the head of the bay appears closed. Head for the port-hand buoy, steering 205°, and leave it close to port, when the Narrows will open up. South of the buoy, the deep water runs very close to the beach on the SE side. Keep the SE shore close aboard until through the First Narrows and past Dundooan Rocks, then stay close to the W side to avoid **Church Bank** and **Ottiergarve**, drying sandbanks to the E.

A submarine power cable runs NW-SE across the First Narrows from just N of Dundooan Point.

## Anchorages

- **Dundooan Rocks** – the inlet to the W of the rocks is out of the main stream of the tide although subject to eddies. Anchor in 3 to 5m, sand.
- **Fanny's Bay** 55°12'N 7°48'·6W, *AC2699 and Plan* This delightful and perfectly shel-

tered anchorage is a convenient stop on the coastwise passage and only a short walk from the village of Downings over the hill. Give Rannaroe Point at the entrance a berth of a cable and anchor as convenient clear of the moorings, in the middle of the bay in 2 to 4m, mud. The inner part of the bay to the NW is shallow. Land at the disused boatyard slipway. Shops, restaurants, pubs at Downings, 1 km W.

## Inner part of Mulroy Bay – Fanny's Bay to Broad Water
*AC2699 and Plan*

From Fanny's Bay, steer to pass a cable N of Inishlaugh (12m high), leaving the green buoy close to starboard, and hold this course until 1·5 cables from the E shore with the depth increasing to between 8 and 12m and the next starboard-hand buoy close aboard. Then turn S and steer to pass a cable E of Island Roy, to

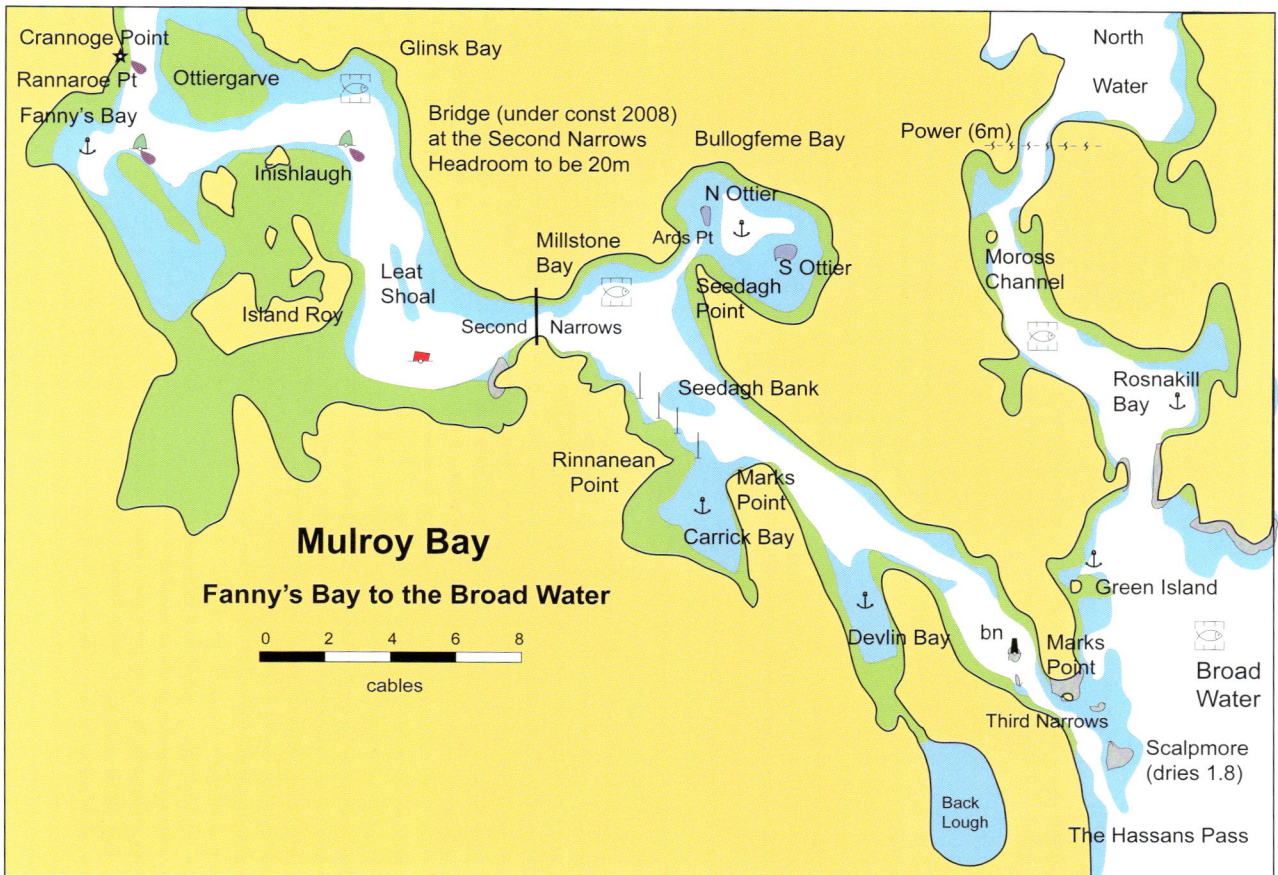

avoid Leat Shoal to the E. When the Second Narrows bear due E, turn E round the port-hand buoy and take the Narrows in mid-channel. The channel widens into Millstone Bay at this point. Hold the course until a cable off the E shore and keep the E shore close aboard from here to the Third Narrows. This passes E of Seedagh Bank and the rocks NW of Marks Point at the Third Narrows. Leave the stone beacon on these rocks to starboard and take the Third Narrows in mid-channel, then keep the SW shore close aboard to avoid Scalpmore, which dries 1·8m and almost always shows, and stay within 50m of the W shore until well into Pan Bay. The shallowest point in the whole passage is at the Hassans Pass, 2 cables S of Scalpmore, where the depth is barely 2m and the channel less than half a cable wide.

There are fish farms in Glinsk Bay and Millstone Bay. Note that there are two headlands named Marks Point, one to the E of Carrick Bay and the other forming the E side of the Third Narrows.

**Anchorages**

- **Bullogfeme Bay** – this completely sheltered pool, 4 cables across, opens off the channel just E of the Second Narrows. There are two drying rocks in the pool – North and South Otters – but they are easily avoided.

*Bullogfeme Bay; view SW out through the entrance. Seedagh Point, L, Ards Point,R, and Muckish Mountain. The crane is part of the bridge works at the Second Narrows*

*Third Narrows (R centre) from the SE; Scalpmore bottom R, Devlin Bay upper L with the Back Lough L, Carrick Bay beyond to the L. Bullogfeme Bay upper centre, Green Island and the North Water upper R*

Approach the entrance between Ards Point and Seedagh Point steering 020° and hold mid-channel until the pool opens up. There is 4m in the entrance and a least depth of 2m on the bar N of Seedagh Point. Once in, the steep tree-clad Ards Point under the peak of Muckish *(see photograph)* leads clear S of the North Ottier. Anchor in 3 to 7m in the middle of the bay.

• **Carrick Bay** is on the S side, S of the Seedagh Bank and 7 cables above the Second Narrows. The shore between Rinnanean Point, the W extremity of the bay, and the ruined pier 3 cables NW, is marked by four poles with yellow cross topmarks. Heading SE, leaving these poles 50m to starboard leads clear S of Seedagh Bank and into Carrick Bay in least depth 1·6m. From the main channel N of Seedagh Bank, enter the bay steering 200° with the conspicuous shed just hidden behind Marks Point, then in mid channel when the bay opens up. The bay has 1·5m in the centre.

• **Devlin Bay** is on the S side 7 cables below the Third Narrows. Anchor as convenient in the middle of the bay in 2 to 2·5m. A narrow tidal channel, which is not navigable, leads

*Fish farm in Millstone Bay*

*Typical Mulroy Bay stone beacon*

from the head of the bay to a lagoon called the Back Lough.

## Broad Water – Third Narrows to Milford Quay

The N part of the Broad Water is wide and deep but has many large fish farms and mussel rafts, while the S part is narrow and requires even more careful pilotage, but has fewer in the way of man-made obstructions. From Pan Bay, keep the W shore close aboard. The main channel then runs:

- close E of the stone beacon on Cranford Rock, then
- 50m E of Otter Island (the tiny islet 2·5 cables S of Park Point, unnamed on AC2699, then
- 0·5 cable W of Greencastle Islet, capped with grass, and Gowan Black Rocks, marked with a stone beacon, and thence halfway to Ranny Point on the E shore, then
- 0·5 cable W of the stone beacon on Ranny Rock, then
- 205° for Inishyweel, the conifer-clad islet 7 cables SSW *(see photograph)* When Long

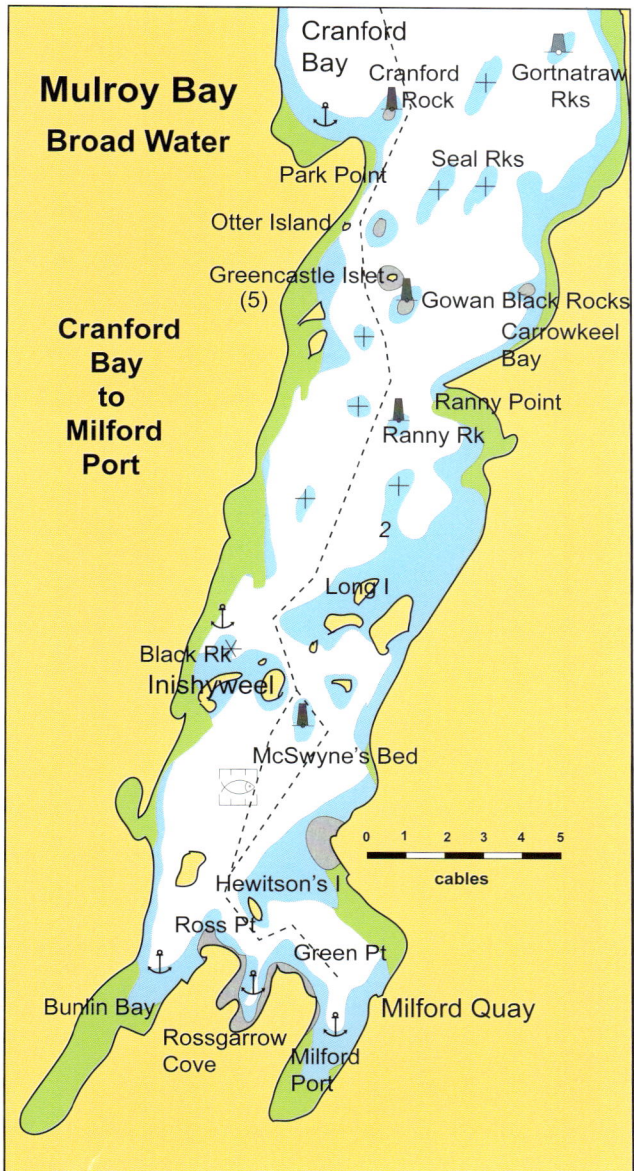

*Inishyweel from the N*

Island is abeam, turn SW to clear the spit to the S.

When the derelict flour mill at Milford Quay comes in line with the E side of Inishyweel, steer to pass close NE of that islet. Leave Mc-Swyne's Bed, marked by a stone beacon, on either hand, and steer to leave the low grassy Hewitson's Island to port. (There is 8m in mid-channel between Inishyweel and McSwyne's

Bed.) Hold mid-channel between Hewitson's Island and Ross Point to the S, give Green Point a berth of 2 cables and head for Milford Quay. Note that there are no longer beacons on Ranny Point or Ross Point, on the rock (drying 1·5m) 1·5 cables N by W of Green Castle islet, or on Seal Rocks, 2 cables E by S of Cranford Rock.

There are mussel rafts E and SE of Cranford Rock, close NW of Seal Rocks, and S of Mc-

*Broad Water from the S; Milford Port, foreground, with Milford Quay centre R. Rossgarrow Cove centre L with Hewitson's Island above. Inishyweel upper L centre*

Swyne's Bed.

**Anchorages**

- **Cranford Bay** – the NW corner of the bay is occupied by moorings for fish farm tenders and support vessels but the S part offers good anchorage sheltered from SE to NW. Anchor in 2 to 7m, sand.
- **NW of Inishyweel** – the bay inside Black Rock has a concrete pier with 1·5m at its head, and offers anchorage in 3m.
- **Bunlin Bay,** the SW arm at the bottom of the Broad Water. Approach from close E of Cratlagh Island and anchor in 3m, mud, W of Ross Point and no further in than the house and jetty on the W side.
- **Milford Port** – anchor in 3m, mud, W of the quay. The quay itself is derelict and un-

suitable for berthing.
- **Rossgarrow Cove** – the tiny inlet between Bunlin Bay and Milford Port offers charming anchorage for a small yacht. The bottom is however irregular with boulders and care must be taken on entry.

**Facilities**

Shops, pubs and banks at Milford, 2 km from Milford Port, Bunlin Bay or Rossgarrow.

Constant (Milford Quay) +0315 Galway, MHWS 1·4m, MHWN 1·1m.

**W and N sides of the Broad Water**

Heading N from Ranny Rock beacon, Carrowkeel Bay is difficult of access since the beacons on the rock 2 cables WNW of Pan Point, and on

*The derelict fliour mill at Milford Quay; McSwyne's Bed and its beacon in the foreground*

Seal Rocks 2 cables N, no longer exist, and passage around Seal Rocks is obstructed by a large mussel raft. The beacon on Gortnatraw Rocks, 4 cables ENE of Cranford Rock, is short and may cover at HW. Once N of Cranford Rock, however, Carlan Island (2m high) is a good mark, and the only significant hazard on the W side is the unmarked Campbell's Bed (0·3m). There are no mussel rafts N of Scalpmore, and there are fish farms, which are easily avoided, only E of Green Island and in Moross Channel. This channel leads to the North Water but **there is no access for masted vessels** since the channel is crossed at Ross Point by a **high voltage power cable with only 6m clearance** and at Moross Castle by a low telephone cable as well.

### Anchorages

- **Keadew Bay,** in the NE corner of the Broad Water, has anchorage in 4m but is open to the S and SW.
- **Green Island**, on the W side 5 cables N of The Hassans, is a lovely spot. Anchor in 2m, mud, NE of the island.
- **Rosnakill Bay**, just N of Rosnakill Strait at the entrance to Moross Channel, offers charming and tranquil anchorage in the SE corner of the bay in 3·5m, mud.

### Passage E from Mulroy Bay

Leaving Mulroy Bay between the Bar and Sessiagh Rocks, head for the middle of the entrance, steering slightly west of north, until the coast to the E is well open of Ballyhoorisky Point. This avoids the dangerous Blind Rock, which may not break in the absence of a heavy swell. Reefs extend 3 cables N of Ballyhoorisky Point, and the drying rock Carrickcannon is 7 cables to the NE. Croaghnamaddy (the highest summit of the Horn Head peninsula) open of Melmore Head leads N of Carrickcannon.

Frenchman's Rock, 5 cables E by S from Carrickcannon, is well inside the direct line to Fanad Head, but 2M further E care must be taken to avoid the Currin Rock and the mass of rocks and reefs inside it. Keep Magheranguna Point broad on the bow until Fanad Head opens up.

### Direct passage W from Lough Swilly

A yacht bound W for Tory Sound should leave Ballyhoorisky Point and Melmore Head a mile to port. At night, once clear W of Currin Rock, stay in the white sector of Fanad Head light to avoid the Limeburner Rock. The rock, 5 cables S by E of its N Cardinal buoy, breaks in a heavy swell, and is then a most spectacular sight.

### MULROY BAY TO SHEEP HAVEN

The passage from Melmore Head to Downings is straightforward, but on the N-facing coast, a prudent distance from dangers must take account of the swell in addition to the hydrography.

### Dangers

**Limeburner Rock**, 2m, 2·5M N by W of Melmore Head

An area of rocks extending 0·5M N of Straughan Point and 1M W of Melmore Head, with **Frenchman's Rock**, 1m high, defining its W limit and **East Breaker**, 4·3m, its N limit. **Little Frenchman's Rock**, drying 2·4m, is 2 cables SE of Frenchman's Rock. (These are not to be confused with the other Frenchman's Rock, NE of Ballyhoorisky Point)

**Guill Breaker**, 0·6m, 1M NE of Rinnafaghla Point, with drying rocks and a 2·4m shoal extending 3 cables SW from it.

**Black Rock**, 6m high, 2 cables offshore 1·2M S of Rinnafaghla Point, and drying rocks within a cable N of it.

**North Wherryman Rock** (dries 1·5m) and

*Frenchman's Rock (R) and Little Frenchman's Rock (L) from the NE; Muckish Mountain on the skyline*

**South Wherryman Rock** (dries 2m), 1 cable offshore 6 cables NW of Rinnaskeagh at the entrance to Downings.

**Lights and marks**

**Limeburner** buoy, N Card Q, AIS, 5 cables N by W of the rock

**Downings Pier**, Fl R 3s 5m 2M

**Portnablagh**, leading lights 125°, Oc 6s 2M, black columns, white bands, front 7m rear 12m

**Bar Rock**, unlit green conical beacon, on a dry-ing rock close NE of Horse Park Point, Ards Bay.

**Yellow Rock**, derelict pole beacon S of Bar Rock

**Directions – Mulroy to Sheep Haven**

From Melmore Head, steer N of W until the above-water Frenchman's Rock is clearly identified, then steer to leave it a cable to port. Identify Carrickguill (12m high) and its smaller

*Downings Bay and pier from the SE; Pollcormick, centre L. Wherryman Rocks, breaking, upper L*

*Black Rock open of Coolbunbocan Cliff 338° leads W of the Wherryman Rocks*

companions, 6 cables NE of Rinnafaghla Point, Give the point and these stacks a berth of 3 cables and steer to pass a cable W of Rinnafaghla Point. The coast S of here is clean but beware Black Rock (6m high) and a dangerous rock 0·5 cable NW of it which dries 1·2m. The North and South Wherryman Rocks may be avoided by staying 2 cables offshore in the approach to Downings; Black Rock open of Coolbunbocan Cliff 338° leads W of the Wherryman Rocks.

**Tranarossan Bay**
55°14'·2N 7°49'·6W, *AC2699*
This is a pleasant temporary anchorage in offshore winds. Anchor either in 8m, E of Carnabantry, or in not less than 5m off Rosses Strand. In settled conditions it is safe to pass inside Frenchman's Rock and between Carrickguill and Carnabollion, but keep a sharp lookout for lobster pots.

**SHEEP HAVEN**
*AC2699*
**Downings**
55°11'·3N 7°50'·3W
Downings ("Downies" on the chart) is a bustling holiday village with a good anchorage and a useful pier. Constant +0045 Galway, MHWS 4·0m, MHWN 3·0m. The pier has 4m on its outer face but shallows rapidly, and the bay also shallows abruptly, with less water than charted. Anchor S of the pier. There are visitors' moorings. Diesel available by hose on the pier. Shop, pubs, restaurants.

**Pollcormick**
55°11'·3N 7°50'·8W
This bay immediately W of Downings pier offers good anchorage in peaceful surroundings. It is sheltered from W to SE.

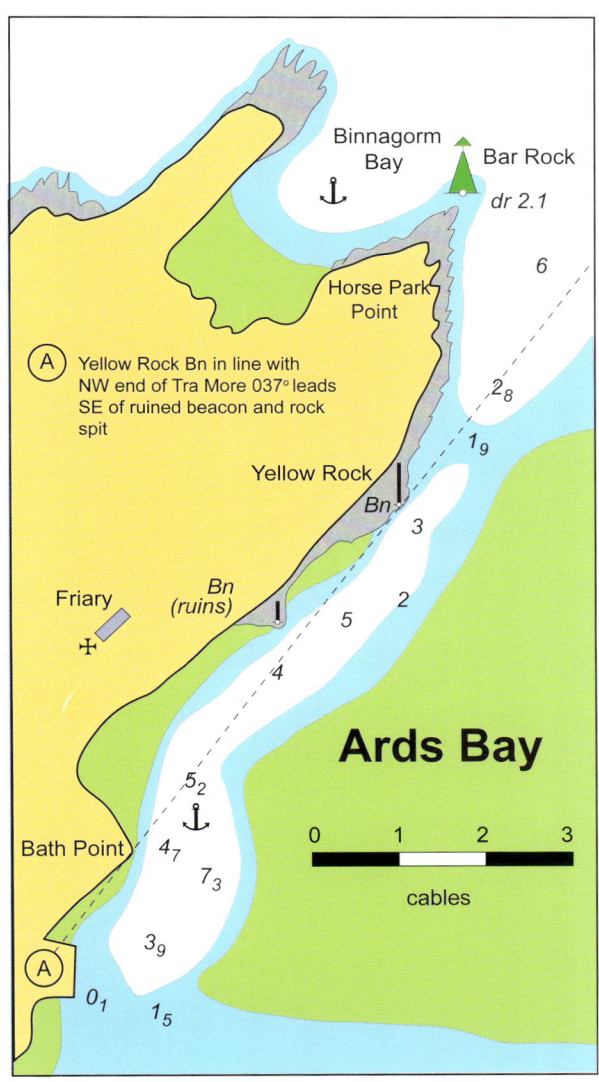

*Ards Bay; view N from Yellow Rock beacon; Bar Rock beacon, L, and Downings beyond. Tra More is out of the picture to the R*

*Ards Bay from the NE; Yellow Rock R, Bath Point and the anchorage centre R*

## Ards Bay

55°10'N 7°51'W, *see Plan*

This is the most sheltered anchorage in Sheep Haven and is a beautiful and tranquil spot. The Bar Rock beacon at the entrance is conspicuous, and Yellow Rock (3 cables to the S, dries 4m) seldom covers and is marked by a derelict but clearly visible pole beacon. Keep both marks close to starboard on entering, and once past the Yellow Rock beacon bring it into transit with the NW end of the sandy beach of Tra More astern. This clears a boulder spit 2 cables S of Yellow Rock, on which the remains of a beacon cover at half flood. The bar, which is just N of Yellow Rock, has 1.9m, and the channel has 3.5 to 7m. The bay close NW of Bath Point dries out, and the deep channel extends only just S of Bath Point. The channel then shallows and runs E, not SE as shown on AC2699. Anchor N of Bath Point, with the friary chapel just coming into view behind the trees. A yacht will normally lie tide-rode in the channel. Coffee shop at the friary, but no other facilities ashore.

## Binnagorm Bay

54°10'N 7°51'·3W

This pretty anchorage, known locally as Monks' Bay, lies between Binnagorm Point and Ards Point. Good shelter in SE to SW winds. Anchor in 3 to 5m, sand.

*Ards Bay anchorage; the friary buildings, L, Bath Point in the foreground*

*Marble Hill Bay from the S*

## Marble Hill

55°10'·7N 7°53'·3W

Marble Hill has a fine sandy beach and offers an attractive temporary anchorage, although exposed to the N and more subject to swell than Downings. Anchor in 2 to 4m in the NW corner of the bay.

## Portnablagh

55°10'·7N 7°55'·8W, *see Plan*

The pier at Portnablagh (Portnablahy on the chart) has 0·2m at its head but offers an attractive temporary berth above half tide in settled or offshore weather. The inner side of the breakwater has a shelf which dries 2·6m and cov-

*Portnablagh leading line (centre); the pole beacons, L and R, and the pier head, L*

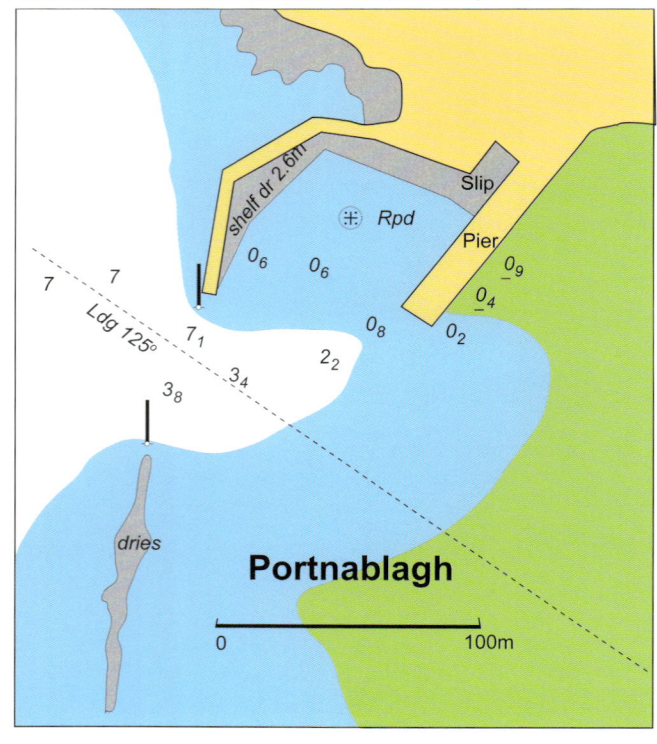

*Portnablagh from the W; the slip has been built since the picture was taken*

ers at HW, and it has 0·6m alongside. Square concrete beacons in line lead 125° through the gap between the breakwater end and the reef; the deepest water in the entrance is on the N side, where there is 7·1m, but it shallows quickly once inside. The bay to the SW, with small craft moorings, dries out. There is reported to be a rock in the middle of the basin between the breakwater and the pier. Slip suitable for trailer sailers. Portnablagh is a thriving holiday village but there are no facilities closer than Dunfanaghy, 4 km W.

## HORN HEAD TO BLOODY FORELAND

The mainland coast here is remarkable for its fine sandy beaches and dunes, and many new houses have been built, most of them second homes. Ballyness Harbour, a drying inlet leading to the village of Falcarragh, has a dangerous bar and is inaccessible to a stranger, but the new pier at Magheraroarty, the mainland terminal of the Tory ferries, offers a temporary berth. The island of Inishbofin, joined to the mainland by a drying sandspit, has a few seasonal residents; Inishdooey and Inishbeg are uninhabited.

## Dangers
**Ummera Rocks,** drying, 2 cables offshore 5 cables SW of Horn Head

**Carricknaherwy,** 1m high, 7 cables offshore 1·3M SW of Templebreaga Head, and rocks within 4 cables of the shore to the NE, E and SE of it.

**Bo Rocks,** drying 0·6m, in the entrance to Keelasbeg Sound 2 cables SW of Inishbeg

**Toberglassan Rock,** 1·5m, in Keelasmore Sound

**Reefs** extending 3 cables W and SW from Tory Island, culminating in **Rinnamoreeny**, awash at LAT

## Lights and Marks
**Ballyness Harbour**, leading lights Iso 4s 1M, front 25m rear 26m

**Inishbofin Pier,** Fl 8s 3m 3M

**Tory Island**, black tower with white band, Fl(4) 30s 40m 27M

**Camusmore Bay** leading lights 001° Iso 2s 7M, yellow triangles, red stripe

**Camusmore Bay Pierhead,** red pole beacon Fl R 3s 2M

**Bloody Foreland**, white tower Fl WG 7·5s 14m W6M G4M, W062°–232°, G 232°–062°, shows green over the coast and Inishsirrer to the SW and Inishbeg to the NE, white out to sea and over Tory Island.

## Directions
Making W from Horn Head towards Keelasmore Sound or Tory Island, a berth of 2 cables clears Ummera Rocks and all dangers close W of Horn Head. Carricknaherwy never covers, and the bare sandhills beyond Ballyness Bar are conspicuous. The shore here should not be approached closer than 5 cables since it shallows suddenly and the sandbars shift. Ballyness Bar is now W of its charted position, and although there are leading marks, this is no place for a

*Inishbofin Roads and Tory Sound from the S. Magheraroarty Pier, lower R; Inishbofin, centre, with Keelasmore Sound, Inishdooey and Inishbeg beyond, and Tory, top L*

*Magheraroarty Pier from the SW; Horn Head beyond*

stranger. Although the bar between Inishbofin and the shore is well covered at HW, crossing it is dangerous and should not be considered. Keelasmore Sound, between Inishbofin and Inishdooey, offers the most straightforward passage; steer to pass 2 cables S of Inishdooey and then a cable N of Tonamoylemore, at the NW end of Inishbofin. Keelasbeg Sound, between Inishdooey and Inishbeg, is trickier; from the E, leave Inishbeg a cable to starboard and then steer SW to avoid Bo Rocks in mid-channel to the W and Blind Rock to the SE.

Between Magheraroarty Pier and Bloody Foreland a berth of 4 cables clears all dangers.

## Toberglassan Bay
55°10'·9N 8°10'·3W, *AC2752*
This bay on the NE side of Inishbofin is sheltered from SE to NW and offers safe and attrac-

tive anchorage in moderate weather. Toberglassan Rock, off the centre of the bay, is a hazard towards LW; the transits marked on AC2752 are now difficult to discern due to new building on the mainland. Anchor in 2 to 4m, clean sand.

## Magheraroarty Pier
55°09'·1N 8°10'·2W, *AC2752*
The pier is 300m long and L-shaped, and has 2·5m at its outer end, shallowing to 1·6m at the second set of steps. The area around the pier, and the approach channel, were recently (2007) dredged to 3m but the whole area is exposed to heavy weather from the NW and a single winter storm can significantly affect the depths; so care is required, with continuous use of the echosounder. The approach channel leads 181° towards the E side of the pier head, with the ruined schoolhouse on Inishbofin (the W-most

*Inishbofin seen from Magheraroarty Pier; the ruined schoolhouse is the L'most building*

*Tory Island; approach to Camusmore Bay harbour from the S*

*Tory Island from the E; Port Doon, lower L, West Town and Camusmore Bay harbour, centre*

building on the island, *see photograph*) directly astern. The Tory Island ferryboats use the berth immediately inside the pierhead. Temporary anchorage in suitable weather is available 3 to 5 cables NE of the pier in 3 to 5m, sand. Shop, PO and pubs at Meenlaragh, 1 km W.

### Inishbofin Roadstead
Anchor SW of the spit and S of the village, clear of local moorings.

### TORY ISLAND
*AC2752 and Plan*
The crossing from Horn Head, Keelasmore Sound or Magheraroarty is straightforward in fine weather, but with strong winds between SW and NW there can be a very high swell in Tory Sound. The principal harbour is in Camusmore Bay. Approaching from the E, give the coast of the island a berth of 2 cables and approach the harbour along the leading line 001°, erring nothing to the W.

### Camusmore Bay Harbour
55°15'·6N 8°13'·5W, *see Plan*
The harbour has 3m in the entrance and along-

side the outer half of the pier. The ferry berth is signposted and should be left clear, although it is normally available overnight since the ferry spends the night at Bunbeg on the mainland. The harbour entrance may become hazardous in strong to gale force SW to W winds with a heavy swell.

### Facilities
Water on the pier. Hotel with restaurant and bar, shop, PO. Ferries to Magheraroarty and Bunbeg.

### Anchorages
- Anchorage is available in 5 to 7m, a cable S of the harbour entrance at Camusmore Bay and clear of the leading line. Very subject to swell.
- Port Doon, at the E end of the island, is sheltered from SW to NNW. Anchor in the mouth of the bay in 6m, sand. In swell-free conditions it is possible to lie alongside the pier, which has at least 1.5m over an irregular rocky bottom.
- Portnaglass, on the N side 5 cables E of the lighthouse, is sheltered from SE through W

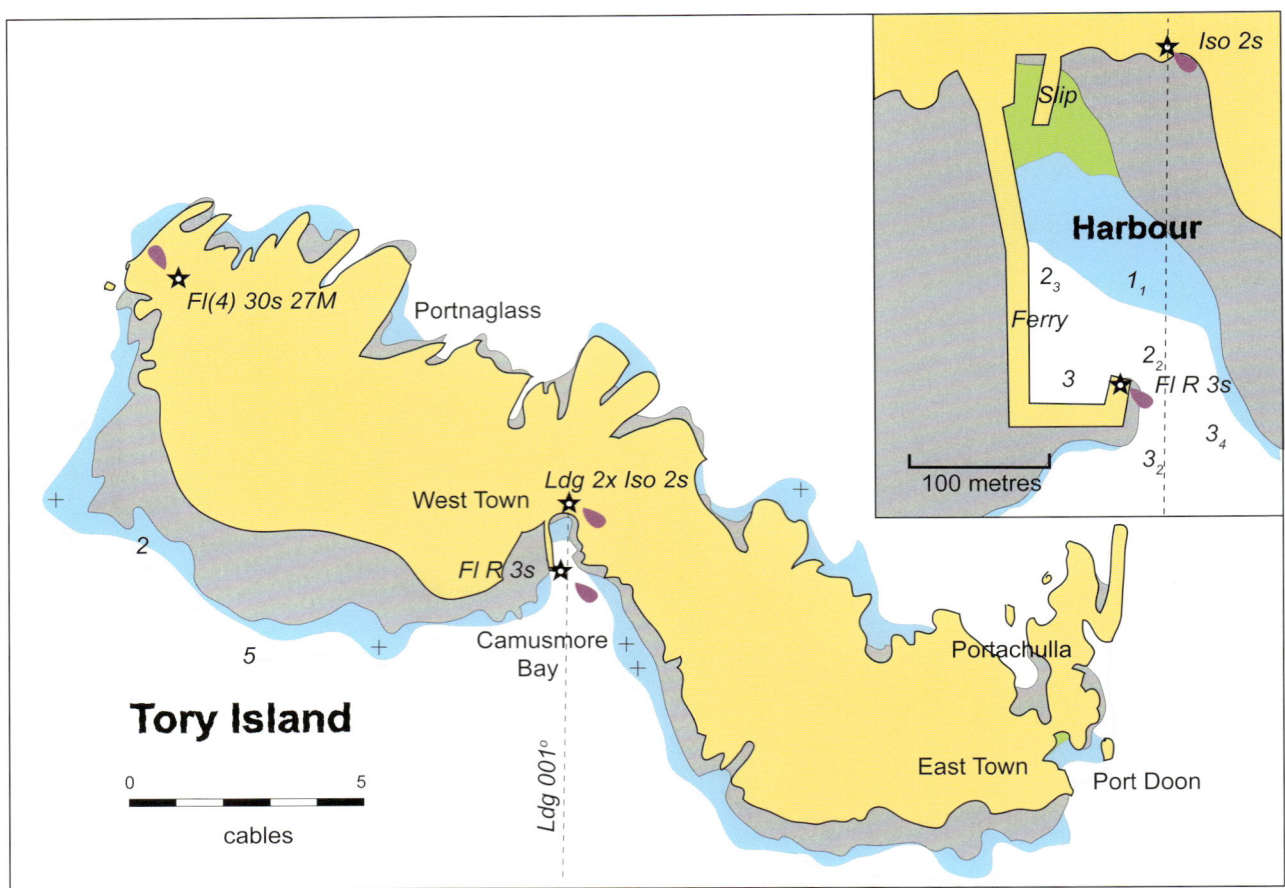

*Iso 2s*

*Slip*

**Harbour**

$2_3$     $1_1$

*Ferry*

$2_{2_1}$

*Fl R 3s*

3

$3_4$

$3_{2_1}$

100 metres

*Fl(4) 30s 27M*     Portnaglass

*Ldg 2x Iso 2s*

West Town

*Fl R 3s*

Camusmore
Bay

2

5

**Tory Island**

0          5

cables

*Ldg 001°*

Portachulla

East Town

Port Doon

*West Town and Camusmore Bay harbour, Tory Island, from the S*

*Camusmore Bay harbour; Errigal (853m) on the mainland to the S*

to NW. Anchor in 10m or more. There is a jetty where lighthouse supplies used to be landed.

Portachulla, opposite Port Doon on the N side, looks like a possible anchorage on the chart but is not suitable.

**Bloody Foreland**

Bloody Foreland Hill, 315 m high, slopes down gradually to the low point of the headland from which reefs extend for 1 cable. Swell is apt to run high off the point, so it should be given a berth of at least 5 cables.

*Port Doon*

# Chapter 6

## Crossing to Great Britain and the Isle of Man

*Loch Drumbuie, near Tobermory, Argyll*

The waters between Ireland and its neighbouring islands can be challenging, but with good passage planning the hazards of weather, tide and traffic are minimised, and the crossing can be made by a well-found yacht in any reasonable weather.

### SCOTLAND

Yachts crossing to Scotland have, in general, one of three areas in view.

Portpatrick, 19M from Donaghadee and the closest Scottish port to Belfast Lough, is a popular day trip or weekend destination for yachts based on the Irish side of the North Channel.

Further north, the Firth of Clyde, east of the Kintyre peninsula, is one of the finest stretches of sheltered recreational seawater in Europe. The Firth is the principal sailing area in Scotland and the venue for the Clyde Cruising Club's annual Scottish Series races.

North and west of Kintyre, the west coast of Scotland, 300 miles in length with a plethora of islands and sea lochs, is a cruising ground to rival Ireland; and the south coast of Islay, the southernmost island, is only 20 miles from Rathlin. The west coast of Scotland is the venue for West Highland racing week, and for the popular annual Classic Malts Cruise. The west coast is connected to the Firth of Clyde by the Crinan Canal, a delightful and scenic waterway used by thousands of yachts each year.

All of the waters between Ireland and Scotland have very strong tidal streams, and in planning a crossing, the tide is a primary consideration. Strong winds blowing against the tides can raise steep and dangerous seas, especially near the salient points; Malin Head, the Rhinns of Islay, the Mull of Oa and the Mull of Kintyre are particularly exposed. The North Channel is more prone to days of poor visibility than the waters to north, south and west – at the Mull of Kintyre, the mist rolling in from the sea has been appropriately immortalised in song – but further out to sea, it is likely to be clear.

Yachts crossing to Scotland should carry an

up-to-date set of the relevant Sailing Directions such as the excellent series published by the Clyde Cruising Club. The information below is intended only to assist in passage planning, and assumes a mean speed through the water of 6 knots.

*The Mull of Kintyre, 12M from Fair Head*

## Scottish Lights

The major lights in the approach from Ireland are on the Mull of Galloway, Corsewall Point, Ailsa Craig, Turnberry Head, Pladda, Davaar, Sanda, the Mull of Kintyre, Orsay, Dubh Artach, Skerryvore and Barra Head. Note that Killantringan Head light, south of Portpatrick, has been permanently discontinued.

## Portpatrick

Portpatrick has a small sheltered harbour. The approach is however shallow and may be hazardous in onshore winds. The crossing from Donaghadee or Belfast Lough (18M) is across the tide, and provided appropriate allowance is made, this is one of the few crossings to Scotland where the tidal stream need not govern the hour of departure; the weather, daylight and the height of tide at Portpatrick are more important.

## Firth of Clyde

The North Channel tides are not felt north and east of a line from Corsewall Point to Rhu Stafnish. Tidal streams in the Firth of Clyde are generally insignificant. Loch Ryan, although within the Firth's tidal regime, is a long way from other ports in the Firth. Troon and Ardrossan are easily accessible and have sheltered harbours and full-service marinas. Girvan, further south, has an awkward bar at the harbour entrance. Lamlash, on the Isle of Arran, 58M from Bangor, has a fine, natural, accessible, big-ship harbour sheltered by Holy Island; it is a charming village with visitors' moorings in the bay. On the east coast of the Kintyre peninsula and 46M from Bangor, Campbeltown (6000) stands at the head of an excellent natural harbour, has all the facilities of a mid-sized fishing port and is the first all-weather harbour east and north of the Mull of Kintyre. There is a feasible temporary anchorage at Southend, and Sanda Island has a bay with good anchorage, a visitor mooring and a welcoming pub. The splendid harbour of Tarbert, on Loch Fyne 28M north of Campbeltown, is the venue for the annual Scottish Series races. The eastern entrance to the Crinan Canal is at Ardrishaig, 10M north of Tarbert. North of Little Cumbrae Island, the upper Firth has yet more scenery, marinas at Largs, Inverkip, Rhu and the Holy Loch, and easy access to the historic and beautiful cities of Glasgow and Edinburgh.

Leaving the Belfast area for the Firth of Clyde, it is best to take the north-going tide, which runs for six hours after HW at Belfast. From Carnlough or Glenarm, departure time doesn't matter provided due allowance is made for the tide, whether N- or S-going. From Ballycastle or Rathlin, departure between LW Belfast and HW Belfast –0400 ensures a fast passage and carrying the E-going tide beyond Rhu Stafnish. From Portrush or Coleraine, the optimum departure time is at HW Belfast +0500, stemming the last of the W-going tide along the north Antrim coast but carrying the flood through Rathlin Sound and as far as Rhu Stafnish.

## West Coast of Scotland

The nearest harbour is Port Ellen, on the island of Islay, 20M N of Rathlin, 30M from Portrush and 40M from Glenarm. Port Ellen has a modest marina and is accessible day or night at any state of the tide, but the south coast of Islay in general is rock-strewn, tide-swept and hazardous, and the stranger is best advised to approach in daylight. The shortest crossing, from Rathlin, is

Barra
Castlebay
Barra Head

Coll
Tiree
Skerryvore

Loch Drumbuie
Tobermory
Mull
Oban

Iona
Dubh Artach
Colonsay

Crinan
canal
Holy
Loch
Rhu
Glasgow

Jura
Tarbert
Islay
Craighouse
Rhinns of Islay
Gigha
Port Ellen
Orsay
Mull of Oa

Inverkip
Largs
FIRTH
Little Cumbrae
Ardrossan
Arran
Troon
Lamlash
O F
CLYDE

Inishtrahull
Malin Head
Tory

Rathlin
Portrush
Coleraine
Ballycastle

Campbeltown
Mull of
Kintyre
Rhu
Stafnish
Sanda
Pladda
Ailsa Craig
Turnberry Head
Girvan

Corsewall Pt
Loch Ryan
Portpatrick

Lough
Swilly

Carnlough
Glenarm
Larne
Black Head

Maidens

Mew Is
Bangor
Portavogie

Strangford
Lough

Mull of Galloway

Point of Ayre
Peel
Man
Douglas
Port St Mary
Calf of Man

Ardglass
St John's Point

South Rock

Carlingford
Haulbowline

Crossings to
**Scotland**
and the
**Isle of Man**

0    10    20    30    40    50
miles

Rockabill
Malahide
Howth

best made on the NW-going ebb tide. The main stream runs past the two SW points of Islay, the Mull of Oa and the Rhinns, and off both headlands it raises steep and at times dangerous overfalls. Portnahaven, on the Rhinns, is a feasible but tricky anchorage, and is not for the fainthearted. Lagavulin (55°37'·9N, 6°07'·5W, east of Port Ellen), is the starting point for the annual Classic Malts Cruise, and Iomallach Rock (2m high, 55°37'·3N, 6°04'·7W), SE of Lagavulin, is the key to pilotage of the S coast of the island. From Belfast Lough, it is best to set off before HW, and once N of Rathlin seven or eight hours later to steer NE of the rhumb line to stay out of the strengthening flood stream. From Portrush or Coleraine, take the E-going tide to Port Ellen; from Rathlin, the W-going gives a marginally better lift.

The NW-going tide in the North Channel divides, and a branch runs N, between Islay and Jura and the mainland of Scotland. Leaving Belfast before HW gives a N-going tide as far as Ardminish in Gigha or Craighouse in Jura (both of which have good sheltered anchorages) or Port Askaig in the Sound of Islay. The stream strengthens farther N in the Sound of Jura, and to reach Crinan it is necessary either to stem the tide or lie over until it turns.

Eastbound for Scotland from W of Malin Head, a yacht should plan to be off the entrance to Lough Swilly at –0130 Galway. This will give the best chance of carrying the tide to Port Ellen or Rathlin, but in the absence of a lie-over an onward voyage up the Sound of Jura or round the Mull of Kintyre will inevitably involve stemming a strong tide.

Fast power craft may of course disregard the foregoing recommended departure times, and should calculate their own based on their cruising speed.

Tidal streams W of Malin Head are slacker, and a passage from north Donegal to Iona (75M), Coll (89M), Tobermory (104M) or Castlebay (102M) is relatively free of tidal considerations. The west coast of Islay should be given a wide berth, particularly in heavy weather.

## THE ISLE OF MAN

The shortest crossing is 30M from Strangford entrance to Peel. From Belfast Lough or points north, and heading for Douglas or Port St Mary, the preferred route is south-about the island; the waters around the Point of Ayre, at the NE end, are shallow, with fast tides and few good landmarks. Calf Sound, N of the Calf of Man, has strong tides but is navigable in daylight and settled weather. *Isle of Man Sailing Directions* (Hunter Publications) are recommended.

### Manx Lights

The major lights are on the Point of Ayre and the Calf of Man.

### Harbours

Peel has a flap gate which retains water in the inner harbour and allows access two hours either side of HW; there are also visitors' moorings in the bay. Port St Mary, perhaps the most popular landfall for yachts coming from Ireland, also has visitors' moorings; its bay is sheltered in winds between S and NE. Douglas offers limited berthing in the outer harbour, and 70 pontoon berths in the inner harbour, behind a flap gate open approximately 2 hours either side of HW.

## WALES

Holyhead is 94M from Belfast Lough, 69M from Strangford entrance, 65M from Carlingford entrance, 53M from Howth, Dun Laoghaire or Wicklow. Pwllheli is 65M from Wicklow or 80M from Dublin Bay. Milford Haven is 85M from Wicklow, 60M from Rosslare.

*Castlebay, Isle of Barra, 95M north of Malin Head*

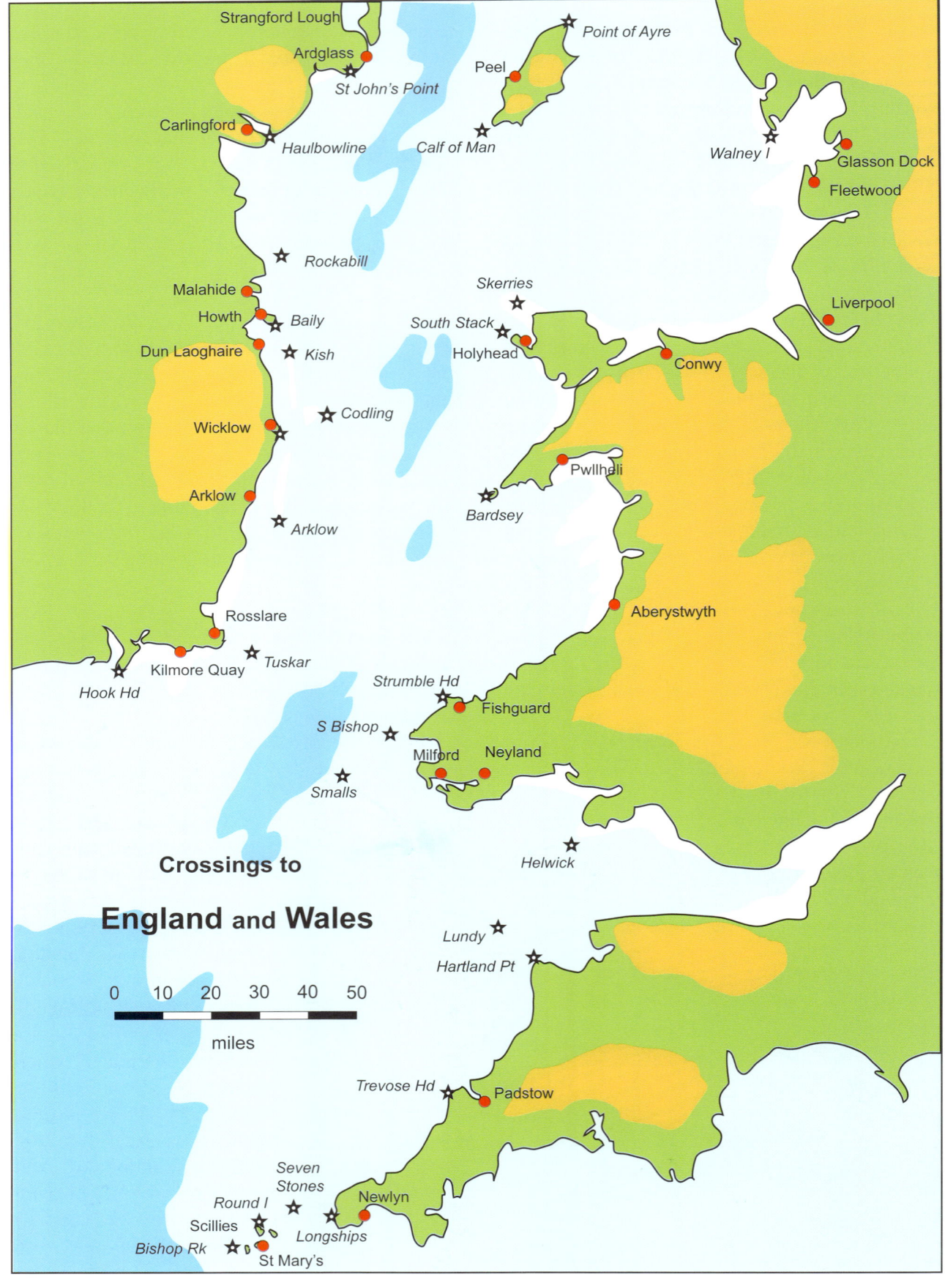

Strangford Lough

Ardglass

St John's Point

Point of Ayre

Peel

Carlingford

Haulbowline

Calf of Man

Walney I

Glasson Dock

Fleetwood

Rockabill

Skerries

Liverpool

Malahide

Howth

Baily

South Stack

Holyhead

Conwy

Dun Laoghaire

Kish

Codling

Pwllheli

Wicklow

Arklow

Arklow

Bardsey

Aberystwyth

Rosslare

Kilmore Quay

Tuskar

Hook Hd

Strumble Hd

Fishguard

S Bishop

Milford

Neyland

Smalls

Helwick

**Crossings to**

**England and Wales**

Lundy

Hartland Pt

0  10  20  30  40  50

miles

Trevose Hd

Padstow

Seven
Stones

Round I

Newlyn

Scillies

Longships

Bishop Rk

St Mary's

Tidal streams run at 5 knots around Holyhead and between Anglesey and the Skerries, and at 6 knots in Bardsey Sound. Off the Pembrokeshire coast, the streams reach 3 to 4 knots among the islands, and 6 knots in Ramsey Sound.

*Cruising Anglesey and North Wales* (NW Venturers YC) and Imray's *Lundy and Irish Sea Pilot* cover the coast in detail.

### Welsh Lights
The major lights around the Lleyn peninsula and Anglesey are on the Skerries, the South Stack, Point Lynas and Bardsey Island. On the Pembrokeshire coast the major lights are on Strumble Head, the South Bishop, the Smalls, Skokholm and St Ann's Head.

### North Wales
The main destinations are Holyhead, Conwy and Pwllheli, all of which have full-service marinas; those at Holyhead and Pwllheli have all-tide access, while Conwy and Deganwy Quay marinas, in the Conwy River, are accessible above half tide.

### South Wales
The ferry port of Fishguard is sheltered in winds between SE and W, but the major harbour on this coast is Milford Haven, which extends 8M from St Ann's Head to the marina at Neyland.

Neyland has all-tide access, and Milford Dock marina is accessible above half tide. Anchorage is available at Dale Roads and other bays close within the entrance to the inlet.

### CORNWALL
The passage from Kilmore Quay or Rosslare to Lundy is 90M, to Padstow 116M, to St Mary's 138M and to Newlyn 146M.

### Lights
The major lights are on Lundy Island, Hartland Point, Trevose Head, Pendeen Head and the Longships; while around the Scillies are Round Island, the Bishop Rock, the Seven Stones and the Wolf Rock.

### Harbours
Padstow is the only good harbour on the N coast of Cornwall; it lies 3M up the River Camel across a shallow bar, and has a wet dock with a flap gate which opens around HW. Newquay and St Ives are sandy bays offering anchorage in offshore weather, but completely exposed to the N and NW.

In the Scillies, the approaches to St Mary's from the N are well buoyed and lit, but New Grimsby Sound, W of Tresco, and Old Grimsby Sound, E of Tresco, are attractive anchorages, easily accessible in daylight, and have visitors' moorings. St Mary's also has moorings but they are slightly too close together for comfort, and the bay is exposed to the NW. Tean Sound, between Bryher and St Martin's, is a fine anchorage but demands careful pilotage.

Newlyn has all-tide access by day or night and a fine sheltered harbour where yachts are welcome. As one of England's largest fishing ports it has excellent repair facilities, and for the yacht skipper arriving from Ireland in need of technical services, it is far and away the best choice of landfall. There are no marinas on this coast.

*Newlyn Harbour, Cornwall, 146M from Kilmore Quay or Rosslare*

# Appendix 1

## CHARTS AND ADMIRALTY PUBLICATIONS

Admiralty (UK Hydrographic Office) Charts:

| No | Title | Plans | Scale 1: | Pub date |
|----|-------|-------|----------|----------|
| 1123 | Western Approaches to St George's Channel and Bristol Channel | | 500,000 | 12-99 |
| 1121 | Irish Sea with St George's Channel and North Channel | | 500,000 | 11-00 |
| 2049 | Old Head of Kinsale to Tuskar Rock | | 150,000 | 2-95 |
| 2740 | Saltee Islands | | 25,000 | 8-76 |
| 1772 | Rosslare Europort, Wexford Harbour and Approaches | | various | 7-05 |
| 1787 | Carnsore Point to Wicklow Head | | 100,000 | 11-91 |
| 1468 | Arklow to Skerries Islands | | 100,000 | 6-99 |
| 633 | Plans on the East Coast of Ireland | Arklow, Wicklow, Malahide, Rogerstown, Skerries, Killough, Ardglass | various | 9-05 |
| 1415 | Dublin Bay | Howth | various | 8-02 |
| 1447 | Dublin and Dun Laoghaire | | various | 8-02 |
| 44 | Nose of Howth to Ballyquintin Point | | 100,000 | 2-01 |
| 1431 | Drogheda and Dundalk | | various | 1-01 |
| 2800 | Carlingford Lough | Kilkeel | various | 10-04 |
| 2093 | Southern Approaches to the North Channel | | 100,000 | 3-01 |
| 2156 | Strangford Lough | Portavogie | various | 6-88 |
| 2159 | Strangford Narrows | Strangford | various | 12-83 |
| 1753 | Approaches to Belfast Lough | Donaghadee Sound, Bangor | various | 3-04 |
| 1752 | Approaches to Belfast | | various | 3-04 |
| 2198 | North Channel, Southern Part | Portpatrick | 75,000 | 8-04 |
| 1237 | Larne Harbour | | 10,000 | 1-04 |
| 2199 | North Channel, Northern Part | | 75,000 | 11-04 |
| 2798 | Lough Foyle to Sanda | | 75,000 | 5-05 |
| 2494 | Plans on the North Coast of Ireland | Ballycastle, Rathlin Sound, Portrush, River Bann | various | 12-04 |
| 2511 | Lough Foyle and Approaches | | various | 6-05 |
| 2510 | Approaches to Londonderry | | various | 6-05 |
| 2811 | Sheep Haven to Lough Foyle | | 75,000 | 7-05 |
| 2697 | Lough Swilly | Culdaff Bay | 37,500 | 3-05 |
| 2699 | Horn Head to Fanad Head, Mulroy Bay | | 30,000 | 10-07 |
| 2752 | Bloody Foreland to Horn Head, Tory Island | | 30,000 | 12-75 |

The above are all available in electronic format via the Admiralty Raster Chart Service (ARCS). Up-to-date information on chart availability, both paper and electronic, is obtainable on www.ukho. gov.uk.

## Standard Caution on Accuracy
The following Note appears on charts 44, 1468, 1787 and 2752.

"Owing to the age and quality of some of the source information, the charted detail may not be positioned accurately with respect to the horizontal datum, and therefore positions obtained from Global Navigation Satellite Systems such as GPS should not be relied upon when using this chart.

"Mariners are advised to use other methods to determine their position, particularly when navigating close to the shore or in the vicinity of dangers."

## Admiralty Small Craft Folios
These Folios comprise charts in a 600 by 420mm format displaying all the coastal detail from the relevant individual charts (with one exception, AC1431, Drogheda and Dundalk) and also selected areas from the smaller-scale charts. SC5621 Carlingford Lough to Waterford (published Sept 2006) has 19 charts and SC5612 Carlingford Lough to Lough Foyle (published December 2007) has 24. GPS positions may be plotted directly on these charts; there is no offset in horizontal datum.

## Other Admiralty Publications
Irish Coast Pilot, NP40, 16th edition 2003
Published annually:
Admiralty Tide Tables, NP201 Volume 1 UK & Ireland
Admiralty List of Lights, NP74
Admiralty List of Radio Signals, NP281 Maritime Radio Stations
Admiralty List of Radio Signals, NP282 Aids to Navigation
Admiralty List of Radio Signals, NP283 Maritime Safety Information Services

## Agents for Admiralty Charts and Publications
• Windmill Leisure and Marine Ltd, 18A The Crescent, Monkstown, Co.Dublin, 01 460 0345, www.windmillleisure.com
• Todd Chart Agency Ltd, Navigation House, 85 High Street, Bangor BT20 5BD, Northern Ireland, 028 9146 6640, fax 028 9147 1070, admiralty@toddchart.co.uk; www.toddchart.com

## Imray Charts
C61 St George's Channel, 1:270,000; with plans of Wexford, Arklow, Wicklow, Dublin Bay
C62 Irish Sea, 1:280,000; with plans of Malahide, Skerries, Carlingford Entrance, Kilkeel, Ardglass, Strangford Entrance
C69 Belfast Lough to Strangford Lough, 1:90,000, with plans of Ardglass, Strangford Entrance, Strangford, Portaferry, Donaghadee Sound, Bangor, Carrickfergus, Larne, Carnlough
C64 Belfast Lough to Lough Foyle and Crinan, 1:160,000, with plans of Belfast Lough, Bangor, Carrickfergus, Larne, Portrush, Lough Foyle
C53 Donegal Bay to Rathlin Island, 1:191,200, with plans of Portrush, Lough Swilly, Mulroy Bay, Sheep Haven.

206

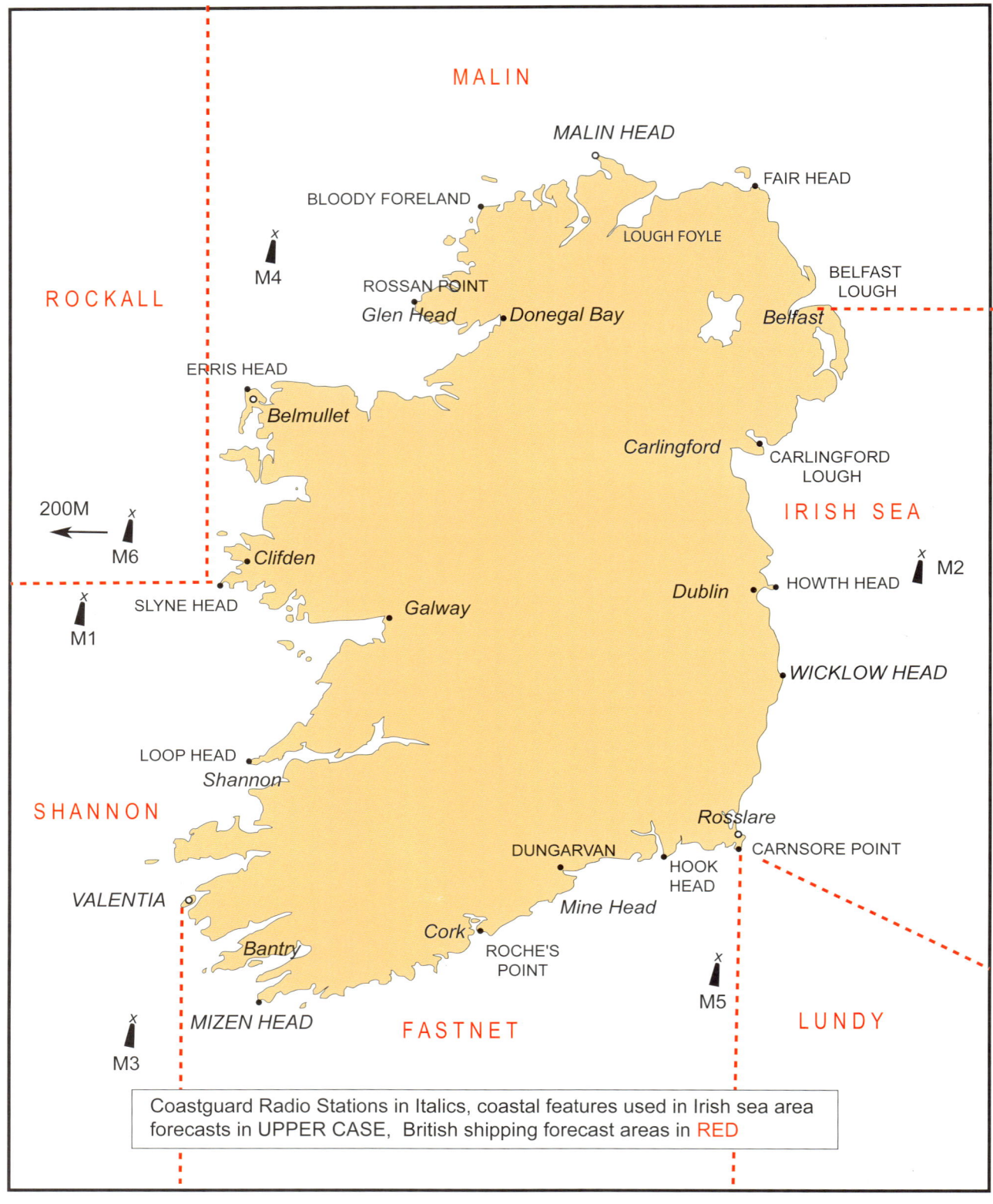

MALIN

MALIN HEAD

FAIR HEAD

BLOODY FORELAND

LOUGH FOYLE

ROCKALL

BELFAST LOUGH

ROSSAN POINT

M4

Glen Head · Donegal Bay

Belfast

ERRIS HEAD

Belmullet

Carlingford

CARLINGFORD LOUGH

200M

IRISH SEA

M6

M2

Clifden

Dublin

HOWTH HEAD

SLYNE HEAD

Galway

M1

WICKLOW HEAD

LOOP HEAD

Shannon

SHANNON

Rosslare

CARNSORE POINT

VALENTIA

DUNGARVAN

HOOK HEAD

Bantry

Cork

Mine Head

ROCHE'S POINT

M5

MIZEN HEAD

FASTNET

LUNDY

M3

Coastguard Radio Stations in Italics, coastal features used in Irish sea area forecasts in UPPER CASE, British shipping forecast areas in RED

# Appendix 3

## TABLES OF DISTANCES

*Nautical miles*

| | Glenarm | Carrickfergus | Bangor | Donaghadee | White Rock | Portaferry | Ardglass | Carlingford | Port Oriel | Malahide | Howth | Dun Laoghaire | Wicklow | Arklow | Rosslare |
|---|---|---|---|---|---|---|---|---|---|---|---|---|---|---|---|
| Kilmore Quay | 187 | 172 | 168 | 162 | 154 | 146 | 136 | 117 | 98 | 87 | 85 | 82 | 61 | 48 | 15 |
| Rosslare | 175 | 160 | 156 | 150 | 142 | 134 | 124 | 105 | 86 | 75 | 73 | 67 | 46 | 33 | |
| Arklow | 147 | 132 | 128 | 122 | 114 | 106 | 96 | 82 | 63 | 40 | 38 | 34 | 13 | | |
| Wicklow | 136 | 121 | 117 | 111 | 103 | 95 | 85 | 71 | 52 | 28 | 26 | 21 | | | |
| Dun Laoghaire | 116 | 101 | 97 | 91 | 83 | 75 | 65 | 51 | 32 | 12 | 7 | | | | |
| Howth | 109 | 94 | 90 | 84 | 76 | 68 | 58 | 44 | 25 | 5 | | | | | |
| Malahide | 103 | 89 | 85 | 79 | 71 | 63 | 53 | 39 | 20 | | | | | | |
| Port Oriel | 87 | 72 | 68 | 62 | 54 | 46 | 36 | 19 | | | | | | | |
| Carlingford | 78 | 63 | 59 | 53 | 45 | 37 | 27 | | | | | | | | |
| Ardglass | 51 | 36 | 32 | 26 | 18 | 10 | | | | | | | | | |
| Portaferry | 51 | 36 | 32 | 26 | 8 | | | | | | | | | | |
| White Rock | 59 | 44 | 40 | 34 | | | | | | | | | | | |
| Donaghadee | 25 | 10 | 6 | | | | | | | | | | | | |
| Bangor | 22 | 5 | | | | | | | | | | | | | |
| Carrickfergus | 23 | | | | | | | | | | | | | | |

| | Bloody Foreland | Tory Island | Downings | Fanny's Bay | Fahan | Portsalon | Inishtrahull | Londonderry | Greencastle | Coleraine | Portrush | Ballycastle | Glenarm |
|---|---|---|---|---|---|---|---|---|---|---|---|---|---|
| Bangor | 117 | 113 | 106 | 103 | 104 | 97 | 79 | 87 | 70 | 66 | 58 | 42 | 22 |
| Glenarm | 95 | 91 | 84 | 81 | 82 | 75 | 57 | 65 | 48 | 44 | 36 | 20 | |
| Ballycastle | 75 | 71 | 64 | 61 | 62 | 55 | 37 | 45 | 28 | 24 | 16 | | |
| Portrush | 61 | 57 | 50 | 47 | 48 | 41 | 25 | 28 | 11 | 9 | | | |
| Coleraine | 62 | 58 | 51 | 48 | 49 | 40 | 26 | 29 | 12 | | | | |
| Greencastle | 56 | 51 | 44 | 41 | 42 | 35 | 19 | 17 | | | | | |
| Londonderry | 73 | 68 | 61 | 58 | 59 | 52 | 36 | | | | | | |
| Inishtrahull | 41 | 36 | 29 | 26 | 27 | 20 | | | | | | | |
| Portsalon | 29 | 25 | 18 | 14 | 9 | | | | | | | | |
| Fahan | 37 | 33 | 26 | 22 | | | | | | | | | |
| Fanny's Bay | 22 | 19 | 12 | | | | | | | | | | |
| Downings | 17 | 14 | | | | | | | | | | | |
| Tory Island | 6 | | | | | | | | | | | | |

208

# Appendix 4

## ABBREVIATIONS

| | | | | | |
|---|---|---|---|---|---|
| AC | Admiralty Chart | kHz | kilohertz | Q | quick-flashing |
| AIS | Automatic Identification Systems | kn | knots | | |
| Alt | alternate | L (in captions) | left | R | red |
| | | LAT | Lowest astronomical Tide | R (in captions) | right |
| Bn | beacon | Ldg | leading | RoRo | roll-on, roll-off |
| | | L Fl | long flash | RWVS | red & white vertical stripes |
| Card | cardinal | lt | light | | |
| CG | Coastguard | LW | low water | S | south |
| Ch | channel | LWM | low-water mark | s | second(s) |
| col | column | LWN | low water neaps | SC | sailing club |
| | | LWS | low water springs | SHM | starboard-hand mark |
| Dir | directional | | | | |
| | | m | metres | t | tonne |
| E | east | M | miles | TSS | Traffic Separation Scheme |
| | | MF | medium frequency | twr | tower |
| F (wind) | Beaufort force | MHWN | mean high water neaps | | |
| F (light) | fixed | MHWS | mean high water springs | unintens | unintensified |
| Fl | flashing | MHz | megahertz | | |
| | | ML | mean level | vert | vertical |
| G | green | Mo | Morse | VHF | very high frequency |
| | | | | VQ | very quick flashing |
| h | hour(s) | N | north | | |
| HM | Harbour Master | | | W | west |
| hor | horizontal | obsc | obscured | W | white |
| HW | high water | Oc | occulting | | |
| HWM | high-water mark | Or | orange | Y | yellow |
| HWN | high water neaps | | | YC | yacht club |
| HWS | high water springs | PHM | port-hand mark | | |
| | | PO | post office | | |
| Iso | Isophase | | | | |

# Appendix 5

## IRISH LANGUAGE GLOSSARY

The following table lists some of the placename elements found in the area of this book, with their Irish Gaelic word origins and English translations. Also included are some of the Irish words commonly met with on signs, particularly in Gaeltacht areas.

| English rendering | Gaelic | English translation | Examples of derived placenames / expressions |
|---|---|---|---|
| | abhaile | homewards | Slan abhaile! - Safe home! |
| | aerfort | airport | |
| agh, agha | achadh | field | |
| ail-, alt- | ailt | ravine | |
| | aimsir | weather, season | |
| aird-, ard- | ard (noun) | height, top, highest point | Ardmore - the high headland |
| | aire | notice, attention | Pobal ar Aire - Neighbourhood Watch Area |
| anna- | atha | ford | Annalong - ford of the ships |
| anna, annagh | eanach | marsh | |
| ard- | ard (adjective) | high, (of a person) chief | |
| bal-, bally- | baile | town, townland | |
| bal- , bel- , val- | beal | mouth, entrance | Belfast - river-mouth of the sandbank |
| -ban, -bane, -van,-vane, bawn | ban | white, fair | |
| ban, ben | bean (pl mna) | woman | Mna - Ladies |
| beg | beag | small | |
| bo | bo | cow | Inishbofin - white cow island |
| brack, breck | breac | speckled, dappled | |
| bradden | bradan | salmon | Portbradden - salmon port |
| | bruscar | litter | |
| bullig- | bolg | bulge, blister; hence underwater rock, breaker | Murlough - murbholg, sea-swell |
| bun- | bun | base, bottom, (of a river) mouth | Buncrana - mouth of the Crana River |
| bwee, boy (suffix) | buidhe | yellow | |
| cairn, carn | carn | heap, mound, cairn | Carne - place of cairns |
| camus | camas | bay, cove | Camusmore - big bay |
| can-, ken-, kin- | ceann | head | |
| carrick, carraig | carraig | rock | Carrickfergus - Fergus's rock |
| | ceol | song, music | ceol agus craic - songs and laughter |
| cush | cois | foot | Cushendall - foot of the river Dall |
| | comhairle | council | |
| cool, cul, cole | cul | back, corner | Coleraine - ferny corner |
| coon | cuan | haven, harbour | |

| | | | |
|---|---|---|---|
| corran, corraun | corran | crescent | |
| | craic | fun, jokes, laughter | ceol agus craic - songs and laughter |
| | deas | south | |
| | deoch | drink | |
| derg | dearg | red | |
| derry, darry | doire | oakwood | Derry |
| dillisk | duileasc | dulse, edible seaweed | |
| donagh- | domhnach | church | Donaghadee - church of the rampart |
| doo, duff, duv | dubh | black | Pollduff - black pool |
| dooey | dubhthaigh | sandhill | Inishdooey - island of the sandhill |
| droghed- | droichead | bridge | Drogheda - bridge of the ford |
| drum-, drom- | druim | ridge | Dundrum - fort of the ridge |
| dun, doon | dun | fort | Dun Laoghaire - Leary's fort |
| -een | -in | little (diminutive suffix) | |
| fahan | fathain | burial-place | Fahan |
| | failte | welcome | Bord Failte - the Irish Tourist Board |
| fer, var | fear (pl fir) | man | Fir - Gents |
| gall | gall | stranger | Donegal - fort of the stranger |
| gar- | gearr | short | |
| garve, garriff | garbh | rough, rugged | Garvan Islands |
| glas, glass | glas | green | Ardglass - green height |
| glinsk | glinn uisce | clear water | Glinsk Bay (Mulroy Bay) |
| gore, gower | gobhar | goat | |
| gorm | gorm | blue | |
| gwee, -gee | gaoth | wind | Bunagee - river-mouth of the wind |
| | iar | west | |
| illan, illaun, illane | oilean | island | |
| inish, innis, ennis | inis | island | Inishmore - big island |
| | iur | yew-tree | Newry |
| keel, kill, kyle, quoile | caol | strait, narrows | Kilkeel - church of the narrows; Quoile River |
| keeragh, cooragh | caorach | sheep | |
| kil- | cill | church, monk's cell | Kilmore - big church |
| knock-, crock-, croagh | cnoc | hill | |
| lack- lackan | leaca | stony slope | |
| leck, lick | leac | slab, flat rock | |
| lee, lea | liath | grey | |
| long | long | ship | LE=Long Eireann - Irish Ship, a Naval Service vessel |
| mac, mic, vic-, vick- | mac, mhic- | son of | |
| magher, maghera | machair | grassy plain | |
| mara | mara | of the sea | |
| more, vore | mor, mhor | big | |

| muck | muc | pig | Isle of Muck; Muckish Mountain |
| mullagh, mala- | mullach | summit | Malahide - Ide's summit |
| mul-, mullaun | mullan | hillock | |
| oir | oir | east | |
| owen-, own- avon-, | abhainn | river | |
| pool | poll | pool | Poolbeg - little pool |
| port | port | port, harbour | Portavogie - port of the bog |
| portan, partan, bartan | portan | crab | Rossnabartan - crab promontory |
| rath | rath | earth fort | Rathmullan - fort of the mill |
| reen, ring, rin | rinn | point, promontory | |
| | rogha | choice | rogha bia - choice of food, menu |
| ron | ron | seal | |
| roo, row, roe | rua | red | |
| ross | ros | promontory | Rosslare - middle promontory |
| shan-, shen- | sean | old | |
| skellig | sceilg | steep rock, crag | |
| skerries | sceiri | reef islands | Skerries |
| | slan, slainte | health | slan abhaile - safe home. Slainte! - Cheers! |
| slieve | sliabh | mountain | |
| stack, stag, stook | stac | pinnacle rock | Stookaruddan, Stookamore |
| tear-, tyre- | tir | land | |
| ti- | teach, ti | house | |
| tober | tobar | well | Toberglassan - well of the little stream |
| tor, tur | tor | clump, tower | Tory Island |
| tra, traw | tra | beach, shore | Portballintrae - port of the homestead of the beach |

# Appendix 6

## CUSTOMS AND IMMIGRATION REQUIREMENTS

*We are obliged for the following to HM Revenue & Customs and the Revenue Service of Ireland*

### Both jurisdictions

Yachts arriving from other countries of the European Union are normally required to report to Customs only if they have on board persons who do not have right of residence in the EU. This requirement is, however, waived in the case of voyages between the United Kingdom (including Northern Ireland and the Isle of Man) and the Republic of Ireland or *vice versa,* since there are normally no immigration formalities between the two jurisdictions. Yachts arriving from countries outside the European Union must report to Customs on arrival in either Northern Ireland or the Republic of Ireland. Yachts with goods to declare, or carrying restricted items such as firearms, must also report in both jurisdictions and when crossing between them.

### Reporting procedure - Northern Ireland

The report should be made by telephone to the National Customs Yachtline, 0845 723 1110. The full requirements for Northern Ireland are contained in Customs Notice No.8, available on www.hmrc.gov.uk.

### Reporting procedure - Republic of Ireland

The report should be made by telephone to the nearest customs office to the port of arrival: there are offices at Rosslare 05391 61310, Arklow 0402 20450, Wicklow 0404 67222, Dublin 01 877 6200, Dundalk 04293 53700 and Letterkenny 07491 69400. In the event of difficulty the report may be made at the nearest Garda station or by telephoning 1800 295 295. Harbourmasters can also provide advice. Yachts required to report should fly flag Q until clearance is obtained. Yachts being permanently imported from outside the State are also required to notify Customs within 3 days of arrival. For further information see www.revenue.ie.

### General advice

Under international law, the Customs authorities of a state have the right to examine any yacht within the territorial waters of the state, and in exceptional circumstances (such as suspicion of illegal goods on board) in international waters as well.

Yachts owned by EU residents should carry proof of VAT-paid status at all times.

# Index